Wisconsin Studies in Classics

General Editors
Barbara Hughes Fowler and Warren G. Moon

The Archaeology of the Olympics

The Olympics and Other Festivals in Antiquity

Edited by Wendy J. Raschke

The University of Wisconsin Press

Published 1988

The University of Wisconsin Press
114 North Murray Street
Madison, Wisconsin 53715

The University of Wisconsin Press, Ltd.
1 Gower Street
London WC1E 6HA, England

First printing

Printed in the United States of America

For LC CIP information see the colophon

ISBN 0-299-11330-2 cloth, 0-299-11334-5 paper

Dis Manibus

J.F.   A.M.

Contents

Illustrations

Editor's Note

Abbreviations used in this volume are in accordance with those prescribed by the *American Journal of Archaeology* in "Notes for Contributors and Abbreviations," *AJA* 90.4 (October 1986), 384–94, and the *Oxford Classical Dictionary,* eds. N. G. L. Hammond and H. H. Scullard, 2d ed. (Oxford, 1970) for classical authors and works. The University of Wisconsin Press uses Webster's Third International Dictionary and prefers American spelling throughout. Ancient Greek names which have become established in English usage are employed in the familiar form: e.g., Homer, not Homeros; Pindar, not Pindaros. Where there is a recognized Latin equivalent, the Latin form is given: e.g., Bacchus, not Bakchos; Plato, not Platon. Less common Greek names are rendered by standard Greek transliteration. For technical terms, where a Greek word is in current use as a scholarly archaeological term, it is not italicized, e.g., kouros, stele, temenos. Where there exists a standard (often Latinized) form of transliteration in English usage, this form is employed, e.g., discus. A selected glossary of specialized terms has been provided. Modern Greek bibliographical sources cited in the notes are transliterated, Greek script being employed only for quotations from ancient sources cited in the original language. If, following a passage quoted from an ancient author in translation, no translator is credited, it is to be presumed that the translation is that of the author of the chapter.

Preface

The chapters in this volume are a revised version of papers delivered at an international symposium on "The Archaeology of the Olympics" held at the University of California, Los Angeles, on April 5 and 6, 1984, and designed as an academic precursor to the Olympic Games held in Los Angeles in the summer of that year. It is my pleasure here to express sincere appreciation for help and support for that symposium from a wide variety of sources, without which this volume would never have come to be. First and foremost to Ernestine Elster and Theresa Menard—friends, colleagues, and comembers with me on the committee for the symposium; their inspiration, vision, and business acumen were directly responsible for the success of the symposium and for the physical and mental well-being of its participants. The Institute of Archaeology at UCLA sponsored the venture and its then director, James Sackett, took time out from a busy schedule to open the proceedings. Financial support was similarly made available by the Olympic Academic Programs Committee, the Office of Instructional Development, the Fellows of the Institute of Archaeology, the Archaeology Graduate Program, the Friends of Archaeology, and the Department of Classics, all at UCLA. In addition, we are indebted to the Southern California Chapter of the American Institute of Archaeology and to a number of private donors: Marilyn Beaudry, Helen and Edwin Cooper, Sandy Elster, Helle and George Girey, Arlene and Leon Harris, Peter Menard, and Sam Young. We are also deeply grateful to those who so generously made available their homes to host and house the speakers during their visit.

The staff of the University of Wisconsin Press have been a delight to work with and I would like here to express special gratitude to Barbara Hanrahan, whose enthusiasm, sensitivity, and good sense guided the early progress of this volume. Jane Barry had the demanding task of copyediting the manuscript. Her keen eye and exacting standards have been greatly appreciated. Mary Reyes and Tammy Walker typed various drafts of the manuscript, working always with great efficiency, understanding, and grace in the warmth of a California summer. To those named, and to the many other unnamed colleagues, friends, and supporters who have contributed in various ways to this volume, my warmest thanks.

The Archaeology of the Olympics

Wendy J. Raschke

Introduction

It is not, it would appear, without irony that in 1864, just two years before the establishment of the first Amateur Athletic Club in London and in the same period when the young "gentlemen" of Oxford and Cambridge were beginning to compete in track and field events for the first time, Fustel de Coulanges in his study of the ancient city wrote of the Greeks and Romans that "what we have received from them leads us to believe that we resemble them. . . . Hence spring many errors. We rarely fail to deceive ourselves regarding these ancient nations when we see them through the opinions and facts of our own time. . . . Having imperfectly observed the institutions of the ancient city, men have dreamed of reviving them among us."

Coubertin was the first to envisage the revival in modern times of the ancient Greek Olympic Games. Unfortunately, in spite of his classical training, what he created was an event which existed only to serve an athletic purpose, lacking many of the associations and contexts which made the ancient Panhellenic games meaningful. In the world of Homer and of the Etruscans, athletic contests appear in funerary contexts: the funeral games of Patroclus or the Tomba delle Olimpiadi at Tarquinia. For the Greek hero they were, however, no simple funerary rite; rather they were an important aspect of the warrior's life, an exemplification of his *arete* (prowess), which was consistently being put to the test in battle in time of war, and in the field of sport in a nonbelligerent situation. Thus, for the early hero athletics were in a sense the peacetime counterpart of war. War for the ancient Greeks frequently was an internecine struggle for supremacy. Games, too, are competitive: they respond to a need for the assertion of pre-eminence (and it is appropriate here to remember that for a Greek of the historical period there was only one winner and a first prize): αἰὲν ἀριστεύειν καὶ ὑπείροχον ἔμμεναι ἄλλων ("always to be the bravest and stand out above the others"), as Homer expresses it.

"And yet the ancient games served the most significant cause of bringing the Greeks together under the aegis of a sacred truce and unified, if briefly, diverse groups from a common Greek-speaking heritage"—thus many a modern commentator, and this has become a standard view which contemporary journalists use against ourselves, recommending that we return to the customs of the Ancient Greeks and to apolitical Olympics. A closer inspection of the ancient evidence soon reveals, however, quite another picture—of the political use and abuse of the Games and of boycotts in antiquity even as now. The idealized impression grew not from what *was* in antiquity, but from what the Greeks themselves wished could be (Raubitschek). Such misconceptions of the ancient Olympic Games occur with disturbing regularity in modern writing; they are the products of nineteenth- and twentieth-century individuals who see the ancients "through the opinions and facts of our own time."

Likewise the persistent theory of the "amateurism" of the ancient athletes, a notion upon which the ethos of the modern Olympic movement was originally grounded, has no demonstrable basis in fact. Of course, some parallels might be adduced: the predominance of the aristocratic athlete was as evident in the early period of the ancient Greek games (if the Homeric picture is admissible as historical evidence) as it was in the evolving athletic clubs of mid-nineteenth-century Europe and America. But the rejection of all elements of professionalism, of monetary prizes or of athletes who had ever acquired them, is an idealistic and extreme concept developed by the modern movement which has no counterpart in the festivals of Greek antiquity. Not only did the Homeric heroes compete for prizes of monetary value, but it quickly became true that the victors in the Panhellenic games could expect to profit materially from their successes in the field through the generosity of their native cities and their sponsors. Moreover, although the Panhellenic festivals themselves were *agones stephanitai* (that is, they offered rewards only of crowns of laurel, celery, or bay leaves), concurrently other "chrematitic" games held in other locations offered direct pecuniary rewards. Clearly the Pythian, Isthmian, and Nemean Games followed the tradition of Olympia, but there remains the question why it was that the Olympic Games chose not to award value prizes, a question which cannot be readily answered by retreat to the obvious notions of tradition, sacrosanctity, or amateurism. In any case, it was the theoretical premise of the Olympic Games, which was taken up by the authors of the modern athletic movement—and they in their zeal overlooked the realities of the Greek situation—that the Greeks both admitted of "professional" athletes in the Panhellenic games and felt that subsequent material rewards were by no means inappropriate (Young).

The material benefits of archaeological excavation have contributed and continue to contribute greatly to our understanding of ancient history, athletic and otherwise. Not only does archaeology provide detailed information about the locales of the games; it also offers confirmation and elucidation of literary information on questions sociological, architectural, and artistic. The investigation of the site of Olympia, begun by the Germans in the late nineteenth century under Curtius and subsequently assumed by such leading authorities as Dörpfeld, Kunze, and Schleif, has been until recently under the tutelage of Mallwitz. His report on the most recent discoveries on the site have led him to question *inter alia* the traditionally accepted date of the first Olympiad (776 B.C.). Lee takes up this inquiry as part of his discussion of the format of the program of events in the Olympic Games of the Archaic period. That the early program incorporated most of the events of the Classical games was a supposition advanced by older scholarship, specifically the work of Gardiner and Herrmann, on the basis of Pindar, and it is now cast in a new light by a more cautious and scientific handling of the evidence. The Olympic Games, like the Pythian, Isthmian, and Nemean, provided for a variety of "track and field" events, including boxing and wrestling and equestrian competition. The provincial games of the Hellenistic period embraced some of the traditional events, but of particular interest in the games of Thessaly was the *taurotheria,* which appears to have consisted in bull-roping by a competitor on horseback, not unlike the activities of the American rodeo. Parallels between the *taurotheria* and Mycenaean bull-roping have attracted the attention of more than one leading scholar, but the Mycenaean event was conducted on foot, not on horseback (Gallis). The introduction of animals with its increased spectator appeal, however, points forward to the spectacles of the Roman Imperial period.

Knowledge of the second established Panhellenic sanctuary, Delphi, has similarly benefited inestimably from the contributions of archaeology. Delphi was, of course, the site of the Pythian Games held in honor of Apollo. Though there is some evidence of a small settlement in the area in Mycenaean times, there is no reason to imagine a sanctuary or an oracle in place before the eighth century B.C. The seat of the Oracle lay in the Temple of Apollo, and a number of different Temples of Apollo were erected at various stages of Delphi's history, the latest in the fourth century B.C. Apparently here, as is so far merely suggested for the other major Panhellenic sites, there are good grounds to believe that cult preceded games, the latter being created as Panhellenic games, an extension of the celebrations of Apollo, in 586 (Fontenrose). A number of elements, all belonging to the Greek concept of *mousike,* are common in greater or lesser degree to all the Panhellenic festivals: sport, drama, music and singing, dancing—all of which, incidentally, Huizinga envisages as belonging to the "play" aspect of culture. At Olympia the sports element predominates and the other factors—poets, choruses, and so forth—are largely reduced to the level of background entertainment, though it is worth observing that the notion of *rhythmos* present in *mousike* comes to the forefront during the track and field events, often depicted as performed to the accompaniment of the *diaulos* (double flute). At Delphi, home of Apollo and Dionysus, there is, not surprisingly, far greater emphasis on musical competition, this being the original nature of the contests prior to the introduction of athletic events in 586. Indeed, the contest of flute-players who played the Pythian nome, a re-enactment of Apollo's contest with Python, might be judged to be closer to the drama. Certainly performances of a dramatic character were planned for by the second century, when the stone theater was built.

Remains of a gymnasium (fourth century) and a stadium (originally fifth century, extant remains second century A.D.) have long been established. The hippodrome is believed to have been situated in the plain of Krisa. As at Olympia, the temenos at Delphi was the location of numerous dedications, sculptural and epigraphical, made by victors in the Games and in other, often bellicose, activities; many of them have survived to provide the modern scholar with valuable information.

It was Richard Chandler who in his travels in 1766 was first to rediscover Olympia; similarly in the same year he came to Nemea, but it was not until 1884 that the site received the attention of the archaeologists, in this case the French, whose progress was very limited and resulted only in the publication of some inscriptions. The site was subsequently plundered during the creation of the nearby town of Herakleia. American interest was initiated in 1924, when the French ceded rights to the site to the American School of Classical Studies at Athens, but the subsequent fifty years of investigation saw uneven progress. In 1974 the University of California at Berkeley assumed the responsibility, and the work of the last ten years has enabled us to form a more complete image of the site and of the Nemean Games, once of equal importance to those at Olympia, Delphi, and Isthmia. There are indications of chronological parallels with the other three sites in its development, of celebrations centered on both Zeus and a hero cult with its accompanying mythology, and also of possible violent destruction of this Panhellenic sanctuary in the later fifth century (Miller); this underlines earlier discussion of the failure of the Greeks to act out in practice their theories of Panhellenism and the sacred truce at the major festival sites.

Archaeology, then, offers continuing illumination in our search for the truth, but even the exact science of modern excavational technique has its limitations. The earth yields up only so much, and there remain questions which beg solutions. Not least of these is the early form and development of that assertedly "very Hellenic" phenomenon, the Greek gymnasium. No extant gymnasium can be dated prior to the fourth century, though literary evidence indicates the presence of such buildings already in the sixth century, and they were clearly a prerequisite for athletic training. Some general idea of their form can be derived from literary references. Moreover, there is an extremely narrow and ill-defined line between the gymnasium and the palaestra in our sources, a line which only finds clarification in the Delos excavations, where palaestra and gymnasium exist side by side. Nevertheless, the evidence which can be summoned points to a vaguely Vitruvian-style building already visible in the sixth and fifth centuries (Glass).

An area of practical interest which has received little attention in the histories of ancient athletics and even less from the excavators of the Panhellenic sites is that of nutrition. In the absence of evidence from the soil of Olympia, J. Renfrew has brought together some evidence for the type of diet upon which not only the athletes but also the spectators at the games might have been expected to support themselves. It seems likely that many of those traveling to the festival would bring supplies of food with them, but is clear that there would still be pressure on local resources. The evidence of the provision of an increasing number of wells in the vicinity of the places of the contest at Olympia offers indication of the growing numbers of those attending (Mallwitz; Lee). Provision of water and food was always a problem at Olympia, and the discomfort experienced has been vividly preserved for us in a well-known passage of Epictetus (*Discourses* 1.6.26–27). Eventually, in the Roman period, a convenient water source, the Nymphaeum, was established on the northern side of the Altis.

One characteristically but certainly not exclusively Greek aspect of the games of the Greek historical period was their intimate association with a religious festival, a concept alien to those accustomed to strictly secular sports activities. An amusing reminder of this presents itself in the form of an inscription in the stadium wall at Delphi, which forbids taking away from the stadium the wine intended for religious libations there (Fontenrose). Each of the Panhellenic festivals took place in the vicinity of a sacred temenos, a nonurban center whose *raison d'être* was purely religious, and it was in or into this context that the athletic contest was born. The question of whether the games preceded or were a product of cult has already been alluded to and is a fascinating one. Ideally the coexistence of cult and athletic performance might be traced back to the Bronze Age Aegean; there exists all too suggestive evidence in the frescoes: the shrine fresco at Knossos with its assembled spectators and religious architecture identifiable as the Central Court of the palace, the "Theatral Area" in the northern part of the palace complex, the bull-leaping activities of the young men (and women?) witnessed in the "Toreador" fresco, and the all-pervasive symbolism of the bull. Thera, moreover, whose cultural ties with Crete have recently been further emphasized by the discovery of "horns of consecration" at Akrotiri, is even more provocative, offering vivid evidence of the sport of boxing in one of the frescoes. In the subsequent Mycenaean period can be added representations of chariots—though we are not at liberty to judge them as contestants in races. With Nilsson in hand, then, we might embrace readily the common roots in Minoan-Mycenaean civilization of both Greek religion and Greek athletic activity. What we lack, however, is any indication either that they were interrelated or that such games were the focus of Panhellenic gatherings, as they were in the later periods (C. Renfrew).

Ill-defined as the Homeric evidence is, it must represent, at the latest, the activity of the eighth century, and it can be asserted that such relatively advanced athleticism as can be observed in the funeral games of Patroclus is unlikely to have developed suddenly and may readily be projected back to the Mycenaean period, particularly in consideration of the evidence of contemporary Hittite documents. The Hittite information is especially seductive because there are present elements both of religious ritual (rites of spring; ritual mock combat) and of the developed Panhellenic games, particularly the notion that "winning is everything," for the loser in the Hittite archery contest is subjected to penal humiliation (Puhvel).

Mock combat belongs to the form of ritual which might be defined as a test of fitness. Such rituals commonly in ancient usage attend specific stages of development in the maturing child, male and female, and are particularly associated with puberty, adulthood, and marriage. In the context of Olympia, an immediate example suggests itself in the mythical race of Pelops and Oinomaos; but initiatory rites of endurance of a more general nature are visible in Spartan society in the flogging of young men at the altar of Artemis Orthia upon reaching manhood. The race in myth and history becomes quite a standard form of initiatory ritual, observable first at Sparta and subsequently at Brauron and Olympia. "Athletic" nudity is frequently a feature of such cultic performances, particularly those which serve as prenuptial rites, and may be reflected in the minor arts of Sparta of the sixth and fifth centuries (Scanlon).

The notion of a struggle or contest as the means to an end, whether that end be a prize or a change of status, is one born not merely of men, but of gods: an abundance of myths portray the gods rising to their ultimate positions by means of struggles, competitions, races, or physical tests; the labors of Herakles and the struggle of Apollo with Python, preserved in the Pythian nome, are two obvious examples. Thus, athletic contests are in a sense a re-enactment by man of the activities of the gods. The Greek gods have human aspects—they get drunk, make love, experience jealousies—and thus it is easier for man to identify with them and to imagine himself becoming like them, even in their expectation of immortality. Man in his turn also tries to attain his goal, a goal which in the case of the athletes of the Panhellenic games may in effect be his share of immortality; and since he is participating in a festival in honor of the god, he might reasonably hope to have the god's favor in this endeavor.

A share of immortality was not, of course, the prescribed reward for any of the events of the Panhellenic games, but it was in many cases an actual benefit, effectively secured by the exaggerated reputation and subsequent heroization of the successful athlete. Not only would the Olympic victor be celebrated and financially rewarded in his home city, but a statue (or statues) would often be erected for him at home and/or in the Altis, and such statues were not infrequently reverenced and accredited with semidivine powers. It is perhaps something of this hope for immortality which motivates the athlete to follow in the footsteps of the gods and heroes. Thus, it is understandable that such figures as Herakles and Pelops are the object of admiration and reverence among athletes, and it is appropriate that these heroes are the focus of public and religious attention in the sanctuary of the Altis, not only in the Pelopeion, but as the subjects of the artistic decoration of the fifth-century Temple of Zeus. Herakles, an apposite bridge between the human and the divine, since he shares in both, above all exemplifies the successful struggle to the ultimate attainment of immortality, his "labors" being extremely physical in nature, and the poses which he assumes in the metopes of the temple easily recall those of the athletes depicted in contemporary sculpture and vase-painting (Raschke).

Pelops, too, has immortalized himself, likewise successfully going through a test of his *arete* to win his prize, Hippodameia. That he achieves his end by treachery has been a matter of some concern to modern scholars, whose twentieth-century standards demand that the rules be kept, but more sensitive scholarship has demonstrated that archaic culture thought differently and that many were the heroes of myth who won their contests by means of trickery or external assistance. The desire for immortality strikes a chord in most humans, ill-prepared to envisage nothing beyond this life. A Classical Greek dwelling in a politically democratic environment could take responsibility for his own future and seek his share of eternity through individual victory in the games. As the political tides shifted and democracy gave way to monarchy and empire, some modifications in the forms and experiences of the games were inevitable. Yet a number of characteristic factors persist.

On the Italian mainland Olympic-style events were popular already at the height of the Etruscan civilization, as the tombs of the fifth and fourth centuries B.C. reveal. However, hand in hand with the athletic motifs goes indication of apprehension concerning death and a sense that victory in the games can provide, in effect, victory over death. Thus is introduced a religious dimension comparable to one aspect of the Greek games. There are, too, elements of Etruscan imagery, such as the underworld-related figures of Charun and Phersu, which foreshadow the later Roman games. The apparent morbidity of the later Etruscan tomb paintings has been attributed to the Etruscan response to the rise of Rome. The culture of the fully developed Roman Empire would not and could not admit of games in the Greek mode with their opportunity for individual accomplishment and advancement; under Rome all eyes would ultimately be focused upon the emperor, and the individual's only hope for immortality was through the vicarious experience of the spectator sports arranged through the offices of the supreme ruler (Harmon).

It becomes clear, then, that while some parallels may be drawn between the modern Olympic Games and the ancient festivals at the Panhellenic sites of Olympia, Delphi, Isthmia, and Nemea, misconceptions sparked by nineteenth- and twentieth-century experience frequently color our vision of athletic competition in antiquity. Is is of prime importance that such misimpressions be corrected by a conscious and continual effort to move away from past, capricious use of source materials and toward a more critical scientific appraisal; this not simply in the interests of exactitude, but to enhance appreciation of the complex richness of our Graeco-Roman heritage and its sociopolitical and artistic values as they are conveyed through the phenomenon of ancient athletics. Thus, a symposium of the kind which the present collection of essays represents is of the utmost significance, and the promulgation of new research on both the Olympic and other Panhellenic and provincial games will, it is anticipated, be of benefit to the scholar and to the interested layman.

Part One

Bronze Age Antecedents

Colin Renfrew

The Minoan-Mycenaean Origins of the Panhellenic Games

1

The Early Origins of Greek Athletics

We have four principal sources of information about early athletics and early contests in the Greek world. We are thinking, of course, initially about the prehistoric period, the world of Minoan Crete and Mycenaean Greece which came to an end at 1100 B.C. or shortly after, with the onset of the Greek Dark Ages. After that our knowledge of athletics comes very much from the finds at Olympia and Delphi themselves, both the buildings there, notably the stadia, and the various objects dedicated to the deity. As we shall see, the written evidence for events following the Greek Dark Ages does not take us earlier than the traditional foundation date of 776 B.C., although the classical writers do make references to contests in the Golden Age prior to the Dark Ages of Greece.

Our first source is materials deriving from the sixteenth and fifteenth centuries B.C., when the Cretan palaces were flourishing, and Minoan art illustrates a whole series of scenes of life including a number of sporting scenes. This was the period when the Mycenaean civilization was developing, and there are relevant depictions from the mainland also.

Our second source of information comes from the period after the collapse of the Minoan palaces (in about 1450 B.C.) up to the ultimate demise of Mycenaean civilization in the eleventh century B.C. As we shall see, the evidence relating to sport in this period is much scantier than in the preceding one.

The third source of information is a more contentious one. The Homeric epics certainly document that athletic contests were held in Homeric times. This undoubtedly means that they were well known to Homer, who is generally thought to have lived in the eighth century B.C. Whether or not the descriptions given in Homer can be taken as depicting events in the Mycenaean period of three or more centuries earlier is a matter for endless debate. The point is again discussed below.

The fourth course is yet further open to dispute. Various writers from the fifth century onward, discussing the origins of the Olympic Games, regarded the foundation of 776 B.C. as a reinauguration rather than an inception. To various heroes such as Herakles and Pelops is accorded the honor of having instituted the Games for the first time in what we would regard as the Mycenaean period. These claims have to be taken seriously, but we must remember that the earliest evidence for them comes at least five hundred years after the alleged events in question.

The Minoans obviously practiced a number of sports. The principal evidence comes from depictions, of which the most notable are the relief decorations on the rhyton from Hagia Triada.[1] This is one of a series of vessels made in chlorite schist, some of them from ritual contexts, depicting a number of scenes of Minoan life. The rhyton in question has a number of registers on which we see boxers wearing gloves,[2] wrestlers, and perhaps indications of bull-leaping.[3] The depiction of boxers is particularly important because it implies that this is not merely a scene of battle but an agonistic contest with special equipment and (one may presume) rules, so that it is here appropriate to speak of organized sports. The reliefs from the Hagia Triada rhyton indicate that *pyx* (boxing) and *pale* (wrestling) were practiced in Minoan Crete prior to the year 1450 B.C. This impression is certainly supported by one of the splendid frescoes from the site of Akrotiri on Thera, where we see two boys boxing,[4] each with a glove on the right hand but not on the left. This may imply a different set of rules from those employed in Greek times, but there can be no doubt about the early origins of this form of sport. The frescoes at Akrotiri predate the volcanic eruption there, which probably took place somewhere around 1500 B.C. While discussing Thera, it is appropriate to note that nudity was already a feature of Aegean art, as the splendid fresco of the fisherman indicates.[5]

The other well-documented Minoan "sport," bull-leaping, is represented in a number of depictions. Once again, the Hagia Triada rhyton represents this hazardous enterprise, and its association there with the undoubted sports of boxing and wrestling perhaps serves to support the notion that this exercise involving bulls and men is indeed to be placed within the category of sport. A famous fresco on Knossos[6] shows athletes in front of the bull and undertaking a somersault over its back as well as landing safely behind it. These and other indications from sealstones have generally been taken to indicate a sport, perhaps taking place within a religious context.[7] The location for these enterprises has been much discussed, and some writers have suggested that the bull sport may have taken place within the central court of the Minoan palaces.[8] Others have suggested that the "theatral area" sometimes seen nearby, and at Knossos lying to the north of the palace,[9] may have been the site of sporting undertakings. These arguments are not altogether persuasive, but the difficulty in locating the Minoan bull sport does not detract from the secure evidence that bull-leaping took place. Curiously, there seems no memory of such a practice in Homeric times, and indeed the bull is much less often depicted in Mycenaean Greece. It is of very great interest that the sport of bull-wrestling was practiced in the games at Larisa in Thessaly, as Gallis shows in Chapter 13 in this volume. But this was a local custom for which no Mycenaean origin needs to be adduced. Certainly the bull played no role in the great stephanitic games of Greece. That so significant a sport should have found no real memory in Greek times is perhaps an indication that the sports and pastimes of Minoan Crete found no true successor in the games of Greece; if that argument were followed, the boxing of the Greeks would have an origin independent of that of Minoan Crete.

When we turn to the Mycenaean world, we find a much more martial atmosphere, with a much more evident linkage between sport and combat. The lion-hunt scenes depicted on the daggers from the shaft-graves of Mycenae[10] (dating from around 1600 B.C.) certainly indicate the princely pastime of the hunt. And the Warrior Vase from Mycenae,[11] dating from relatively late in the Mycenaean period, and long after the decline of the Minoan palaces, shows soldiers in full armor. It calls to mind depictions on Greek vases of the sixth century B.C. of the *hoplites* race. But there is no real suggestion here that a race is involved, and the resemblance is in reality a superficial one.

The existence of the chariot is first clearly indicated in Mycenaean times by the famous relief on the stele from the shaft-graves,[12] dating from around 1600 B.C. There we see horse, chariot, and charioteer. This does not in itself clearly document chariot races, but a number of writers have drawn attention to the association between chariots and burials in Mycenaean art (an association seen again in the Hagia Triada sarcophagus,[13] which, although from Crete, dates from the Mycenaean period there). In the light of the Homeric description of the funeral games of Patroclus, to be discussed below, the suggestion is indeed a plausible one that these depictions of chariots in Mycenaean funerary contexts refer to chariot races held at funeral games. Yet the suggestion cannot at present be documented more convincingly.

The archaeological evidence from the Minoan and Mycenaean worlds is thus indicative of the sports of boxing and bull-leaping with the suggestion that other martial games, including chariot racing, may well have been held in the Mycenaean world. The symbolic significance of the chariot is underlined by the number of terracotta figurines which, although lacking wheels, are generally, and I believe rightly, taken to represent chariots. One of these was recovered from my own excavation at the Mycenaean Sanctuary of Phylakopi on Melos.[14]

The Homeric Evidence

It is appropriate now to turn to our third source of information potentially bearing on Mycenaean times, namely Homer. While there are other fleeting references, two magnificent passages give us a very clear picture of princely sport in Homeric times. The first of these comes from Books 23 and 24 of the *Iliad,* in the description of the funeral games of Patroclus, organized by Achilles. There, the chariot race is described in graphic detail, and five charioteers are named. They were from the leaders of the Greek forces fighting at Troy. The first prize, a slave woman and a bronze tripod, went to Diomedes. The second prize was a mare carrying a foal; the third, a new cauldron; the fourth, two gold talents; and the fifth, a two-handled bowl. Although Homer's description of the chariot race is too long to quote in full, his description of the contest which followed, the boxing, gives something of the flavor of the games:

> Next he set out the prizes for the painful boxing. He led out and tethered in the field a mule, six years old, hardworking, and unbroken, and for the loser he set out a two-handled goblet. He then stood up and spoke to the Argives: 'I invite two men, the best among you, to box for these prizes. All you Achaians bear witness that he to whom Apollo gives endurance will take away to his tent this hardworking mule. The one who is beaten will take the two-handled goblet.' He spoke, and immediately a huge and powerful man, Epeios son of Panopeus, well skilled in boxing rose up, seized the mule, and said: 'Let the one who wants the two-handled goblet come near, for I say that none of you will beat me at boxing and take the mule; I am the greatest. Isn't it enough that I am deficient on the battlefield? A man can't be number one in everything. But I know what's going to happen here to any opponent of mine. I'll tear him limb-from-limb and smash his bones together. Let his friends huddle nearby to carry him out after my fists have beaten him to a pulp.' So he spoke, and they all kept their mouths shut. At last one Euryalos stood up. Diomedes was his second, and encouraged him, and wanted the victory for him. First he pulled the boxing belt on around his waist, and then gave him the *himantes* carefully cut from the hide of an ox. The two men, belted up, stepped into the middle of the assembly, squared off, and put up their hands. Then they fell upon each other with their heavy hands mixing it up. There was a gnashing of teeth, and sweat poured off their limbs. Then Epeios rushed in and hit him on the jaw as he peered through his guard, and his knees buckled. As in the water rippled by the north wind a fish jumps in the seaweed of the shallows, and disappears again into the dark water, so Euryalos left the ground from the blow. But greathearted Epeios held him upright in his hands. Euryalos' friends gathered around him and led him through the assembly

with his feet dragging as he spat up thick blood and rolled his head over on one side. They led him completely dazed, and they had to return for the two-handled goblet.[15]

The list of prizes for these games is informative and is worth examining in detail. As we have seen, the boxing contest has a mule of six years as the first prize and a two-handled goblet for second prize. The wrestling match had a tripod worth twelve oxen for first prize and a slave woman worth four oxen for second prize. The foot race had a silver mixing-bowl for first prize, a large fat ox for second prize, and half a talent of gold for third prize. The jousting, or combat with armor and spears, had as its prize the armor of the deceased warrior Sarpedon. The contest for throwing the weight had as its prize the weight itself, which was a substantial piece of iron. The archery contest had as first prize ten double axes of iron and, as second prize, ten single axes of iron. The javelin had as first prize a cauldron worth one axe and, for second prize, a spear.

In all of this we have the problem of deciding whether Homer is describing games in his own time or in the Mycenaean period, the period of the War of Troy, as many commentators have suggested. The latter remains a possibility, but I myself incline to the former explanation, and this view is certainly supported by the list of prizes. The emphasis on cauldrons is altogether an appropriate one for the eighth or seventh century B.C. The cauldron, for instance, is one of the most notable of the objects regularly dedicated during this period to Olympia.[16] But the cauldron on tripod legs was not a prominent feature among the bronze vessels of the Mycenaean period. Secondly, the award of a large lump of iron as the prize for the weight-throwing contest and the prizes for the archery of ten double axes and ten single axes of iron suggest a fully flourishing iron age once again appropriate to the time of Homer but not at all so to the Mycenaean period, in which iron objects, although known, were exceedingly rare and very small in size. But even if we accept the minimal view that the Homeric account reflects sporting practice in the eighth rather than the twelfth century B.C., the wide range of sports already recognized then is impressive when compared with the victor list for the Olympic Games given by Hippias. There, the chariot race does not make its appearance until the year 680 B.C.

The second major Homeric description comes in Book 8 of the *Odyssey*. Odysseus is entertained in the land of the Phaeacians, and after the meal King Alkinoos proposes a series of athletic contests by way of entertainment. These involve running, wrestling, the long jump, discus, and boxing. The story goes on with Odysseus being challenged to show his mettle and responding with a phenomenally long throw of the discus.

The Homeric evidence thus shows that a whole series of sporting contests was known and practiced in Homeric times at least. They included most of those which were held in the early Olympic Games, including the chariot race. We see them in two main contexts: first of all in funeral games celebrating the dead hero Patroclus, and, second, simply as an agreeable after-dinner entertainment, as sheer sport. Their occurrence in a religious context is indicated by the *Homeric Hymn to Delian Apollo,* probably written at about the same time as the epic poems, suggestive of athletic sports, as well as singing and dancing, in honor of Apollo at his sanctuary on Delos. Interestingly enough, the games at Delos never attained the same significance as the four major stephanitic games, although a stadium was later constructed there and the pilgrimage to Delos was one of the great religious festivals of the Greek world. It is perfectly possible to take the Homeric evidence as suggesting the existence of such sports at the time of the War of Troy, and hence in the Mycenaean period. But there is always the danger of projecting the evidence from one period back into a remoter past, and it is probably wiser to avoid this line of reasoning unless it is clearly supported by unequivocal archaeological evidence.

Later Greek Mythology

A number of legends surrounding the original foundation of the Olympic Games have been taken by various commentators to give evidence of the practice of sport in Mycenaean times, and specifically at Olympia itself. The geographer Strabo and the scholar Eusebius are among the later commentators, but the earliest statement of this kind comes from the *Olympian Odes* of Pindar, written in the fifth century B.C. In the first *Olympian Ode,* Pindar tells of the chariot race between Pelops and Oinomaos, the Lord of Pisa, which Pelops won, and of his wife, that hero's daughter Hippodameia. Pelops was supposedly buried at Olympia, and his tomb, the Pelopion, was one of the principal landmarks in the sanctuary there. In his second *Olympian Ode,* Pindar reports that Herakles was the founder of the Olympic Games, and the geographer Pausanias later reported other mythical foundations. The race between Pelops and Oinomaos was, of course, commemorated in the firth-century sculptures of the east pediment of the Temple of Zeus, while the foundation by Herakles was perhaps recalled in the choice of the labors of Herakles for the metopes of the temple at about the same time, but Raschke, in her illuminating chapter in this volume (Chapter 4), has stressed how the choice of mythological subject for such sculptures could be determined as much by political convenience as by historical veracity. I am inclined, therefore, to share Mallwitz's skepticism concerning these purported early foundations of the Olympic Games, for which, as he points out, we have no evidence at Olympia (see Chapter 6).

The Social Role of the Games: Peer-Polity Interaction

It is a common feature of many early state societies that they show a characteristic configuration.[17] The territorial organization is cellular and modular: that is to say, politically we see a number of relatively small units for each of which an organizing center may be recognized. It is modular in that these units are of approximately the same size. For many early societies, including the Mycenaean, the area of the territorial units is of the order of 1,500 square kilometers, with a distance of about 40 kilometers between the central places.[18] The city states of the early Greek world were very much smaller in territorial extent and very much more numerous than the Mycenaean polities, but the pattern otherwise holds, although on a smaller scale. When such configurations are seen, it may generally be stated: "Basic social groups do not exist in isolation, but affiliate into larger groups, meeting together at periodic intervals. The highest units of the social hierarchy (i.e. the polities) sometimes enter some kind of affiliation without losing any element of their autonomy. This may have been the case in the early Greek city leagues."[19] This, I believe, makes an important general point which is certainly of considerable relevance to the Panhellenic festivals.[20]

Certainly, it is pertinent to ask what were the unifying elements, in the Mycenaean world, which served to relate and in a sense unify the separate Mycenaean polities, and which distinguished those from the barbarian polities which surrounded them. There is, of course, abundant evidence for Mycenaean trade, and the unifying influence of Mycenaean religion will be further considered below. But is is pertinent to ask whether we have any evidence at all for Pan-Mycenaean collaboration.

Evidence for Mycenaean festivals of a Panhellenic nature is, quite simply, nonexistent. There is certainly no suggestion that Olympia or Delphi was the home of a Panhellenic festival in Mycenaean times. It cannot even plausibly be suggested that either site served as an important sanctuary in Mycenaean times: the evidence from each site constitutes no more than a few Mycenaean figurines, and there is nothing comparable to the evidence now available from the well-defined Mycenaean sanctuaries at Mycenae, Tiryns, or Phylakopi. Indeed, the evidence for continuity at any of the sites which later were the locations of important games is vanishingly small. Only at Delos do we have indications of some continuity from Mycenaean to Classical times of its sacred nature, indicated perhaps by the Artemision deposit.[21] There is absolutely no evidence, then, for meetings of a Panhellenic nature, let alone athletic contests in Mycenaean times. The best evidence we have for communal endeavour during that period is indeed given to us by the *Iliad* itself, when Agamemnon of Mycenae leads the host of Hellas, including King Nestor of Pylos, King

Menelaos of Sparta, and so on, to the War at Troy. This event, if it took place, was indeed a Pan-Mycenaean endeavor, and it is not unexpected that such transient unity should be seen only in time of war. But it should be remembered that the historicity of the Homeric account of the War of Troy has often been doubted, and we have no clear archaeological evidence for any Panhellenic endeavors until well into the Classical period.

But if the generalization set at the head of this section holds no clear relevance for Mycenaean times, it is certainly crucial to our understanding of the wide role of the Olympic Games and the other periodic games in the development of early Greek society. The vast number of offerings, from Geometric times onward, found at Olympia testifies to the great geographical extent of its influence, as indeed do the victors' lists, which indicate competitors from much of Greece and Magna Graecia from quite early days. The significance in this respect of the various treasuries at Olympia and Delphi[22] has already been indicated, and the whole range of dedicatory statues and other monuments, such as the Sphinx of the Naxians at Delphi,[23] in addition to many reported by Classical writers but no longer extant, emphasizes this point.

When we recall that the competitors came to Olympia under the protection of the Olympic truce, and when we note that the Panhellenic games, together with the other religious festivals such as that at Delos, were virtually the only time that the Greeks from different city states met together in a common endeavor, the significance of the games is scarcely to be exaggerated. Of course, trade between Greek cities was of great importance likewise, but Greek cities traded also and extensively outside the Greek world. Participation in the Panhellenic games was restricted to Greeks. This was perhaps the most significant occasion when the Greekness of the Greeks was insisted upon and emphasized. The point is further discussed below.

The Panhellenic Games and the Origin of the Greek Religion

In discussing the origin of the Panhellenic sanctuaries, it is not appropriate to assume that the Greek religion, as we see it fully fledged in the fifth century B.C., was already in existence in that form in the earlier days of the eighth or seventh centuries. Although evidence for religious continuity is lacking at the sanctuaries themselves (with the possible exception of Delos, indicated above), there are now several indications to support the conclusion, reached long ago by Nilsson,[24] that the religion of the Ancient Greeks had its roots in those of the Minoan and Mycenaean worlds. Indeed, with the abandonment of the notion that the Greeks entered Greece during the Dark Ages and with the discovery, through the decipherment of the Linear B script, that the Greek language was already spoken in Greece during Mycenaean times, we see more clearly that this must be so. There is simply nowhere else for the Greek religion to have formed than in Greece itself. Yet when we compare what we know of the religion of the Minoans, or indeed of the Mycenaeans, we see that it differs significantly from that of Greece in the fifth century B.C. Between the two must have come a whole series of transformations. I have argued elsewhere[25] that the Dark Ages (so called) should not be seen as a great chasm separating the Mycenaean world from a very different Greek world in the Proto-Geometric and Geometric periods. On the contrary, many of the significant transformations took place in the late Mycenaean period and others, I would argue, in early Greek times following the Dark Ages.

In support of this notion of substantial continuity in religious practice across the Dark Ages, it may be appropriate to cite the discovery at Phylakopi in Melos of a number of male terracotta figurines.[26] Hitherto, the religious figuration in the Mycenaean period had been predominantly female, and this of course contrasts strikingly with the position in the eighth and seventh centuries B.C., when, at sites like Delphi and Olympia, many of the votive offerings are male. The two bronze figurines in "smiting god" form found in the Mycenaean sanctuary at Phylakopi[27] are of a form long recognized as ancestral to that of the smiting Zeus, and it can now be argued, partly on the basis of evidence from Crete, that there was a measure of continuity in the manufacture and use of such figures from Mycenaean times through into the Geometric period. The point here is not to assert that there was any significant continuity at Olympia or the other Panhellenic sites, which would be difficult in view of the absence of significant Mycenaean finds there. It is rather to emphasize that the roots of the religious practices seen at these great sanctuaries do indeed extend back to the Mycenaean period and that the cult practices seen at Olympia and elsewhere were not an entirely novel formation but the result of a series of transformations operating upon the religious practices seen elsewhere during the Mycenaean period. Once again, while the Panhellenic games themselves find no antecedents in Mycenaean times, a number of the elements which came together at Olympia and later at Delphi can indeed be traced back to Mycenaean origins.

Conclusion

The Olympic Games, like the other great Panhellenic games, were at once a major athletic contest, a great religious celebration, and a social event of significance throughout the Greek world. Precursors, and perhaps origins, for each of these aspects can indeed be traced back into the Mycenaean period. Athletic sports, specifically boxing and wrestling, were already practiced in the Minoan world by 1450 B.C., and there are plausible suggestions that chariot racing may have been practiced at funeral games also in the Mycenaean period. Indeed, it is not impossible that the sports described by Homer in his account of the funeral games of Patroclus were indeed already practiced in Mycenaean times, although for a number of sports this remains doubtful. Likewise the origins of the religion of the Greeks can be traced back to the Minoan and Mycenaean periods, and specific features of the Mycenaean religion formed the basis, through a number of transformations, for the religion of the ancient Greeks of the first millennium B.C. What is altogether lacking, however, is any indication of Panhellenic gatherings until the period of the first Olympiad, although the *Homeric Hymn to Delian Apollo* suggests there may have been major religious gatherings there that early or even earlier and this is one sanctuary site whose Mycenaean antecedents can be demonstrated. This is emphatically not the case for Olympia itself or for Delphi.

Depending on the emphasis which is laid upon the early historical sources, it is possible to take two alternative views of the origin of the Panhellenic games. The first of these would accept the relevance of the Homeric account for the Mycenaean period and take it that a whole range of sports and games were already practiced in Mycenaean Greece, not least at funeral games in honor of a dead hero. From there it is but a step to accept some truth in the statements of Pindar and other Classical authors that the games were founded in the Mycenaean period, perhaps initially as the funeral games of some dead hero such as Pelops, and that they continued for some centuries, to be interrupted during the Dark Ages and resumed, as Hippias indicates, in the year 776 B.C.

Against this account is the total lack of any convincing evidence for a Mycenaean sanctuary at Olympia or Delphi and the indications offered by Mallwitz in this volume that Olympia functioned first as a sanctuary in the ninth and eighth centuries B.C. and only subsequently as a place where games were held. On this view the association of games with religious celebrations at a great Panhellenic sanctuary would only have occurred at Olympia either in the year 776 B.C., as Hippias indicates, or somewhat later. This second view in no way contradicts the possibility that games of various kinds took place during the Mycenaean period or indeed that they were held on occasions to honor a departed leader or hero. Evidence for the incorporation of the games as an institution in relation to the recognized cult of a deity at one of his principal sanctuaries is notably lacking until the eighth or seventh century B.C. I prefer the second of these alternatives and regard the Olympic Games, like the other Panhellenic games, as an institution developing in the eighth, seventh, and sixth centuries B.C. It was then that these various strands came together, although individually each may be traced back very much earlier. Indeed, the terracotta dancing group from the Late Minoan period at Palaikastro[28] reminds us that good evidence for the dance goes back into the Late Minoan period also, and the dance was a significant feature of the celebration at many of the Panhellenic games. Evidence for the kithara and the aulos, both instruments which featured in the Pythian contests at Delphi, can be traced right back to the Early Cycladic period to a date around 2,500 B.C., when delightful marble figures of kithara-players and pipe-players were produced.[29]

What we have not yet sufficiently emphasized, however, is the fundamental role of the Panhellenic games in the development of Greek ethnicity: that is to say, in the emergence of an awareness and self-consciousness that to be Greek was to be something special and different. Often it is assumed that the Olympic Games and the other periodic games were a reflection, an expression as it were, of the Greek spirit which somehow was inherent within the Greek way of life even at the very early date, perhaps in the eighth century B.C., when the games were first founded. But to say this is perhaps once again to project into an earlier period the reality of the fifth century B.C. I believe, on the contrary, that to a very large extent the Panhellenic games *were* the prime manifestations of the Greek spirit in those early times. It was there that the Greek poets and Greek historians first read their work publicly. And it was there and at the Panathenaic festivals that dramatic performances first took place in the theater. It was there that the Greek city states first peacefully competed, not only in the games themselves, but in the construction of treasuries and in the dedication of statues and monuments ostensibly to the glory of the relevant deity but in reality as much to the glory of the *polis* itself. Had it not been for the intense interaction between the different city states, these polities might have continued to be essentially independent and to some extent isolated, remote from the mainstreams of Greek culture to which so many of them contributed and yet which, in the early days, were dominated by none. This process of competition and emulation, by which independent states pull each other up by the bootstraps, as it were, I have termed "peer-polity interaction."[30]

It is also likely that the *active* role of the sanctuaries where games were held, where things *happened,* was critical in the wider dissemination and development of Greek religion. It is not only that the Greek games developed in a religious context: it may equally be true that the early Greek religion developed through the influence of the great Panhellenic sanctuaries in which *agones* (competitions) had a major role, harnessing the competitive spirit under the rule of the ten Hellanodikai, and the reign of the Olympic peace.

Notes

1. S. Marinatos and M. Hirmer, *Crete and Mycenae* (London, 1960) pl. 106.

2. Ibid. pl. 107b and c.

3. Ibid. pl. 107a.

4. S. Marinatos, *Excavations at Thera,* vol. 4, Archaiologike Etaireia (Athens, 1971) pl. 119; C. Doumas, *Santorini, A Guide to the Island* (Athens, 1980) pl. 25.

5. S. Marinatos, *Excavations at Thera,* vol. 6, Archaiologike Etaireia (Athens, 1974) pl. 6; Doumas (supra n. 4) pls. 27 and 28.

6. Marinatos and Hirmer (supra n. 1) pl. xvii.

7. R. W. Hutchinson, *Prehistoric Crete* (Harmondsworth, 1962) 265.

8. J. G. Younger, "Bronze Age Representations of Bull Leaping," *AJA* 80 (1976) 125–37.

9. Marinatos and Hirmer (supra n. 1) pl. 28.

10. Ibid. pl. xxxvi.

11. Ibid. pl. 233.

12. Ibid. pl. 147.

13. Ibid. pl. xxix.

14. C. Renfrew, ed., *The Archaeology of Cult: The Sanctuary at Phylakopi,* British School of Archaeology at Athens (London, 1985) pl. 44.

15. *Il.* 23, 653–99. Translated by Stephen G. Miller in *Arete* (Chicago 1979) 8–9.

16. R. Hampe and E. Simon, *The Birth of Greek Art* (London, 1981) pl. 160.

17. C. Renfrew, "Trade as Action at a Distance," in J. A. Sabloff and C. C. Lamberg-Karlovsky, eds., *Trade as Action at a Distance* (Albuquerque, 1975) 3–60, fig. 2.

18. Ibid. 16.

19. C. Renfrew, "Space, Time and Polity," in J. Friedman and M. J. Rowlands, eds., *The Evolution of Social Systems* (London, 1974) 89–114, quotation on p. 103.

20. A. Snodgrass, "Interaction by Design: The Greek City State," in C. Renfrew and J. F. Cherry, eds., *Peer-Polity Interaction and the Development of Sociopolitical Complexity* (Cambridge, 1986) 47–58.

21. H. Gallet de Santerre and J. Tréheux, "Depot égéen et géometrique de l'Artemision à Delos," *BCH* 72 (1948) 148–247.

22. For the treasury of the Siphnians at Delphi: R. Lullies and M. Hirmer, *Greek Sculpture* (London, 1960) pls. 48–53.

23. A. W. Lawrence, *Classical Sculpture* (London, 1929) pl. 5b.

24. M. P. Nilsson, *The Minoan-Mycenaean Religion and Its Survival in Greek Religion* 2, Skrifter utgivna av kungl. Humanistika Vetenskapssamfundet i Lund 9 (Lund, 1950).

25. C. Renfrew, "Systems Collapse as Social Transformation," in C. Renfrew and K. L. Cooke, eds., *Transformations: Mathematical Approaches to Culture Change* (New York, 1979) 481–506.

26. E. French, "The Figures and Figurines," in Renfrew, *The Archaeology of Cult* (supra n. 14) 208–80.

27. Renfrew (supra n. 14) pls. 67–70.

28. Marinatos and Hirmer (supra n. 1) pl. 132.

29. C. Zervos, *L'Art des Cyclades* (Paris, 1957) pls. 22 and 33.

30. In Renfrew and Cherry (supra n. 20) 1–18.

Jaan Puhvel

Hittite Athletics as Prefigurations of Ancient Greek Games

2

This chapter has to do with continuity, not forward in time from the traditional Olympic signpost zero of 776 B.C.E., but rather in retrograde fashion into an even dimmer past. Tales of origins are prone by nature to strike a stance *ab ovo,* and thus the Olympian Games were supposedly first launched in modest fashion, as extensions of cultic observances, with the *stadion,* something like a 200-meter foot race, as the sole athletic event. Perhaps this periodic Elean occasion truly had small beginnings and became a Panhellenic and indeed universal success by a singular conjunction of historical fortuity and shrewd promotion, similar to, but more lasting than, the parallel Pythian competitions at Delphi. But we should not equate the expansion of the Olympian Games with the development of Greek athletics. Apart from such combinatory specifics as the pankration and pentathlon, most of the common and customary events were included already in the Homeric tradition, as part of Achilles' one-man promotion following the cremation of Patroclus in *Iliad* 23—namely, horse racing, boxing, wrestling, running, jousting, weight-throw, archery, and spear-throw. There is no reason to assume that the Greeks suddenly turned athletic during the "Dark Ages," and the Homeric situation may be safely projected back to the Mycenaean period. Here written records fail us, apart from such indirect pointers as the Linear B chariot tablets from Knossos, and iconography is more explicit on Cretan bull-acrobatics than on normal athletics.

This retreat into prehistory would thus seem to reach a swift dead end, were it not for the written second-millennium records of another Indo-European conqueror nation newly ensconced in the cultural sphere of the Eastern Mediterranean and Asia Minor. Even a cursory look into the Hittite texts, especially the abundant tablets concerning rituals, brings to light evidence of clear relevance to what went on at Patroclus' funerary games in the northwestern corner of Asia Minor. Even as the cremation rites that precede the games are replicated in minute detail by the mortuary rituals for Hittite royalty, at least six of the eight athletic events that follow the cremation have clear parallels in Hittite texts. The ones I cannot document at the moment are athletic horse racing and spear-throw, although horses, chariotry, and spears are abundantly in evidence in military contexts and there are the famous hippological training manuals. Evidence for running, archery, jousting, weight-throw, boxing, and wrestling is reviewed below.

The description of a rite of spring (*KUB* X 18)[1] begins as follows (I, 1–18):

> When the king in the spring comes from Tahurpas to the Antahsum-festival (named after a plant) in Hattusas, as he arrives at Tippuwas, a tent and a *baitylos* (a sort of cultic stone) have already been left in place.
>
> Then the king steps down from the chariot and in Hattusas performs proskynesis. He also goes inside the tent and washes his hands. The king comes out of the tent and in front of the baitylos pours wine. Then the king steps into the chariot.
>
> He goes up to the upper baitylos. The bodyguards run (*pittianzi*), and he who wins, that one seizes the ass-bridle. Then the king steps down from the chariot, and before the baitylos breaks a breadloaf and libates.

The colophon to the same tablet (VI, 12–18) sums up the contents:

> First tablet finished. When in the spring during the Antahsum-festival he comes from Tahurpas to Tippuwas, the bodyguards have a race (*pittianzi*). He also comes to Hattusas, and in the palace compound the grand assembly (takes place).

This "earliest mention of an *agon* in cuneiform literature"[2] thus involves a foot race by the royal entourage, with the victor becoming what is designated sumerographically as *ŠA* ᴷᵁˢKA.TAB.ANŠU, "he of the ass-bridle," a title comparable to our "marshal" from Old High German *marahscalc*, literally "horse-keeper." That this was no menial appointment but rather a significant honorific is shown by the fact that it was the childhood title of the youngest son of Mursilis II, the future king Hattusilis III. Thus, a royal appointment and title constituted what Homer calls *tachutētos aethla*, "prizes of swiftness," while Achilles (*Il.* 23.740–51) posted a silver crater, a fat ox, and a half-talent of gold as rewards for his runners.

An Old Hittite text (*KBo* III 34, from perhaps 1600 B.C.E.) describes an archery contest (II, 33–34): "When they vie in shooting (*sieskanzi*) before the king, to him who scores a hit they give wine to drink . . . but to him who does not score they give (some kind of) cup, and naked he brings water."

The last feature is prescribed in a later text (*KUB* XIII 4 III, 32–34) as penal humiliation for malfeasance by temple officials. In our passage it is perhaps a more playful form of sanction in a mellower setting, possibly even a mirthful matter comparable to the lesser Ajax's ordurous discomfiture in his foot race against Odysseus, as he slips and falls face down into the excrement of slaughtered oxen (*Il.* 23.775–81). A cup as the booby-prize for the scoreless shot recalls Achilles' boxing trophies: an unbroken mule for the winner, and a two-handled cup for the battered loser (*Il.* 23.645–56).

At the games in memory of Patroclus, Achilles calls for a joust with spears. Whichever partner first draws blood will be awarded the silver-studded Thracian sword of Achilles' late enemy Asteropaios, but both combatants get to divide the weapons taken from Sarpedon, and Achilles will throw a party for them in his tent (*Il.* 23.798–810). Ajax and Diomedes volunteer, and matters are on the point of getting serious when the referees, fearing a killing, stop the fight, with Diomedes ahead on points and being awarded the sword of Asteropaios.

The Hittite parallel (*KUB* XVII 35 III, 9–15) is more in the nature of a ritual mock combat:

> They divide the young men into two halves and name them: one
> half of them they call Men of Hatti, and the other half they call
> Men of Masa. Men of Hatti have bronze weapons, whereas Men of
> Masa have weapons of reed. They wage battle. The men of Hatti
> are victorious; they take a captive and consign him to the deity.

This agonistic text has suffered various comparisons, from historical reminiscences of the Hittite conquest of Asia Minor[3] to folkloristic, Mannhardtian instances of ritual battles between the forces of summer and winter (or light and darkness, fertility and sterility), in ancient and modern Europe.[4] The most cogent parallels are those which, in contrast to the literary stylization of Homer, are anchored directly in cultic and mythic material, even if localized aetiologies may have conferred on them a quasi-historical tinge. Of this kind is Herodotus' account (2.63) of ritual battles of votaries versus priests at Papremis in the Nile Delta, involving wooden clubs and genuine head-bashing, or the cult myth of the Attic Apatouria, detailing a combat of the Boetian Xanth(i)os "Fair-haired" and the Athenian (really Messenian Neleid) Melanthos "Dark" in a border dispute about Oinoe-Eleutherai or Panakton-Melainai, presumably masking a myth of divine combat between the fair Apollo and Poseidon *kuanokhaites*. In the same way the Hittite ritual involving Hatti and Masa (the latter in western Asia Minor) may in the end be a localized mummery of a divine battle myth of deity against adversary, such as the Storm-god versus Illuyankas, or Zeus versus Typhoeus, or Apollo contra Python. Modern parallels would be the "good versus evil" folk plays pitting Christians against Turks in the Balkans. The "good" party naturally emerges victorious, and the Hittite adversary's reed weapons seem to doom him to engineered defeat from the start.

Boxing and wrestling, Homer's *pygmakhiē* and *palaismosynē*, are well documented in Hittite. The former is consistently expressed by the sumerogram GEŠPÚ, meaning "fist" and by extension "force," so that the Hittite term is still hidden. "Wrestling" is denoted by either the noun *hulhuliya-* (a reduplication of *hulaliya-*, "to wind") or the akkadogram *KIT-PALU* (an error for *kitpulu*), the literal verbal meaning of both stems being "entwine, wind around, embrace." Occasionally GEŠPÚ and *hulhuliya* occur in immediate juxtaposition, so that one is left to wonder whether the meaning is an asyndetic "boxing (and) wrestling" or rather a quasi-compositional "boxing-wrestling," something like the Greek pankration. An example would be (*KUB* XXV 23 I, 21–22) "they eat (and) drink, they fill cups, they go in for GEŠPÚ *hulhuliya* ("directive" case), they keep entertaining (*duskiskanzi*)." In a somewhat different context (*KUB* XVII 35 II, 26), "they entertain the deity (*duskanzi*, same verb in nondurative usage), they go in for *hulhuliya*, they throw the stone (NA₄-*an siyanzi*)." The weight-toss expressed by the last phrase corresponds to Achilles' *solos auto-khoōnos*, the "self-poured," natural lump of iron which will itself be the victor's valuable prize as a source of the metal (*Il.* 23.826–35). The incipient Iron Age still prized this metal as a mostly meteoric rarity, out of which Homer shaped a nice poetic conceit. Among the Hittites, too, iron was still a prized material for special gifts.

This brings us to the most elaborate, though unfortunately fragmentary, Hittite account of an athletic event (*KBo* XXIII 55 I, 2–27). A military gathering in the iconic presence of the solar deity seems to be the occasion. Throughout there is a dichotomy of "ours" (*anzel*) and "the enemy's" (sumerogram ŠA ᴸᵁ́KÚR). In the first scene the enemy's man falls down, but ours stays up; when he hits, the enemy's man is down, and all our troops applaud. In the sequel some wild animals (two leopards and two bears) are introduced, and later on bulls and black rams are mentioned in a sacrificial context. Thereafter "they put on the wrestlers (LÚ.MEŠ *KITP*[*ALU*)":

Ours and the enemy's man prostrate themselves to the deity three times, and then they proceed to wrestle (*KITPALU ti*[*yanzi*]). When our man topples (his opponent), they applaud, he (i.e., the opponent) prostrates himself to the deity, and our man squats. But afterwards the men likewise get into fisticuffs (GEŠPÚ). And after that they go to *tarpa* (*tarpa tiyanzi*). Four rams go to *tarpa*. Afterwards bulls (?) go to *tarpa*. After that they go before the deity.

What is the mysterious *tarpa-* to which men go after wrestling and boxing, followed (or accompanied?) by rams and bulls? There are no further attestations. The construction with the "directive" case is the same as with the agonistic terms *hulhuliya tiya-*, *KITPALU tiya-*, GEŠPÚ *tiya-* and the similar *argatiya-*, "turn to rage," *kāri tiya-*, "go to favor, humor." One can think of some kind of rodeo-type animal games,[5] but there is no other evidence of active participation by animals in the games. On the Homeric evidence domestic beasts figured rather as contest prizes, in combination with women and vessels. Thus, Achilles' first prize for horse racing was a woman plus tripod, followed by an untamed horse, a cauldron, two talents of gold, and a bowl (*Il.* 23.262–70). The wrestling champion got a tripod valued at twelve heads of cattle, and to the loser went a woman worth a mere four (*Il.* 23.702–5). Cattle were thus a form of value-unit, and so were sheep, as in many other cultures (cf., e.g., Latin *pecua: pecūnia*). It is hence conceivable that Hittite *tarpa-* denotes the awarding of prizes in terms of bulls and rams, and that men and beasts proceed to the award ceremony (*tarpa tiyanzi*). *Tarpa-* would then be the "pleasure part" of the event, the distribution, celebration, and enjoyment of winnings, perhaps even etymologically cognate with the Greek *térpomai*, "to delight," which crops up so often in the Homeric vocabulary of sports: e.g., δίσκοισιν τέρποντο καὶ αἰγανέῃσιν ἱέντες (*Od.* 17.168); ἐτέρφθησαν φρέν᾽ ἀέθλοις (*Od.* 8.131); ἐτέρφθητε φρέν᾽ ἀέθλοις (*Od.* 17.174).[6] It may thus be possible to throw even some etymological bridges form the Greek to the Hittite vocabulary of athletics: *tarpa-* would correspond to Greek *térpsis*, "enjoyment, delight," Sanskrit *tŕpti-* "satisfaction").

In any event it seems clear that many of the organized events which gradually were incorporated into the Olympic Games were neither new nor specifically Greek: they were fully present in the Hellado-Anatolian orbit of the second millennium before the common era. Their upswing, though, definitely owes a great deal to the new presence of Indo-European-speaking aristocratic warrior cultures, in contradistinction to the earlier Eastern Mediterranean and Near Eastern civilizations.

Notes

1. References are to: *Keilschrifturkunden aus Boghazköi (KUB)* and *Keilschrifttexte aus Boghazköi (KBo)*, in publication since 1921 and 1923 respectively.

2. H. Ehelolf, "Wettlauf und szenisches Spiel im hethitischen Ritual," *SB Preuss. Akad. der Wissenschaften, Phil.-hist. Kl.* (1925) 267–72, esp. 269.

3. Ehelolf (supra n. 2) 271; A. Goetze, *Kleinasien* (Munich, 1957) 163.

4. A. Lesky, "Ein ritueller Scheinkampf bei den Hethitern," *Arch RW* 24 (1926) 73–82 = *Gesammelte Schriften* (Bern and Munich, 1966) 310–17.

5. As H. A. Hoffner did in *BibO* 35 (1978) 247.

6. On *térpomai* in this and other uses, see J. Latacz, *Zum Wortfeld "Freude" in der Sprache Homers* (Heidelberg, 1966) 174–219.

Part Two

Olympic Ideals

Appearance and Reality

A. E. Raubitschek

The Panhellenic Idea and the Olympic Games

3

Born on the battlefields of the Peloponnesian War where Greeks were killed by Greeks in great numbers, formed by the Sophists and by other Greeks who by background and profession became conscious of the common bond among the Greeks, modeled after the organization in which Greek met Greek without regard to regional or political differences, the Olympic Games, the Panhellenic movement aimed from the beginning at friendship, harmony, and peace among the Greeks.

Unnoticed by Herodotus and Thucydides, it was proclaimed by the antiwar poet Aristophanes,[1] by the "Western" orators Gorgias and Lysias,[2] by the philosopher Plato,[3] and, above all, by Isocrates, who devoted much effort to it.

The link between the Panhellenic idea and the Olympic Games existed from the very beginning, or so it was claimed. Although our information comes from the *History of the Olympic Games* by Phlegon of Tralles,[4] a book written for the emperor Hadrian (the founder of the Panhellenion) and used by Pausanias,[5] the story was known already to such fourth-century champions of Panhellenism as Isocrates, and it may have been first recorded by Hippias of Elis.[6]

According to this account, the cult of Zeus, including the games, was neglected by the Peloponnesians during the ninth century, and as a result of this neglect strife and dissension broke out among the inhabitants of the peninsula. At this point Lycurgus the Spartan, a descendant of Herakles, who had originally founded the games, Iphitos the Elean, also a descendant of Herakles, and Kleosthenes of Pisa decided to restore harmony and peace among the Peloponnesians by reviving the Olympic festival according to the old tradition and to add the gymnic *agon* with its track and field events. They received approval from Delphi and were told to announce a truce *(ekecheiria)* to the cities wishing to participate in the contest; it was recorded on the famous discus which contained the rules of the Games. The Peloponnesians at first refused to accept the new order, and they were punished by Zeus with plague and famine. Once more called upon, the Delphic Oracle urged the Peloponnesians to restore the worship of Zeus and the games in his honor. They ultimately did this, and the Games were revived and placed in the care of the Eleans. For five Olympic Games no crowns were offered to the victors, but at the request of the Oracle crowns of wild olive were given to the victors beginning with the sixth Olympic Games (756 B.C.).

We do not know whether any of this actually happened in the eighth century B.C., but we may assume that the Greeks accepted this story from c. 400 B.C. on, and several of its elements do go back to that early period: the *ekecheiria,* the gymnic *agon,* the crowns as prizes. What is puzzling is the claim that Olympia discouraged warfare between Greek cities, since the excavations have brought to light enormous quantities of armor dedicated by Greeks after victories over other Greeks; the inscriptions and the character of the armor make this clear.[7] These were found in wells and in the debris of the older stadium and belonged originally to trophies. In the new stadium no dedications of captured armor were made. The literary evidence supports this historical analysis of the finds. Plutarch in his essay on the Oracles of Pythia denounces the beautiful dedications of weapons with their most shameful inscriptions, such as "Brasidas and the people of Akanthos from the Athenians" or "the Athenians from the Corinthians."[8] It is not impossible that Plutarch saw some of these ancient pieces of armor, since Pausanias reported that he saw them being excavated,[9] but the story itself is as old as the fourth century B.C. because Plato denounces not only warfare among the Greeks but especially the atrocious habit of dedicating armor captured from fellow Greeks in the Panhellenic sanctuaries.[10] Xenophon reports that the Eleans refused the Spartan King Agis permission to sacrifice in Olympia on behalf of a military expedition he was undertaking in Greece.[11] They said that the "ancient laws" forbade an appeal to the gods in a war between Greeks.

We have seen that there was indeed a close contact between the Panhellenic idea and the Olympic Games. This contact was the result of Greek yearning for peace, which grew during the horrors of the Peloponnesian War and which was in full force during the first half of the fourth century. Philip II of Macedon made use of this yearning in his day, and Sophists and orators gave added strength to it by claiming that the original purpose of the re-established Olympic Games in 776 B.C. was to promote friendship, harmony, and peace among the Greeks.

Notes

1. Aristophanes *Lys.* 1128–34.
2. Lysias *Olymp.* 1–2
3. Plato *Rep.* 5.469B–471C.
4. Phlegon of Tralles, *FGrH* 257 fr. 1
5. Pausanias 5.4.5. and 8.5.
6. See L. H. Jeffery, *Archaic Greece* (London, 1976) 24–25.
7. Deutsches Archäologisches Institut, *Die Funde aus Olympia: Ergebnisse hundertjähriger Ausgrabungstätigkeit,* ed. A. Mallwitz and H.-V. Herrmann (Athens, 1980) III: *Archaische Zeit,* 5: *Waffenweihungen,* by H. Koenigs-Philipp, 88–90.
8. Plutarch *De Pyth. or.* 15,410CD.
9. Pausanias 5.20.8–9
10. *Rep.* 5.469B–471C.
11. Xenophon *Hell.* III.2.22.

Wendy J. Raschke

Images of Victory

Some New Considerations of Athletic Monuments

4

When in April 1918 Lenin called for a plan for monumental propaganda that was to have created numerous statues and bas-reliefs of revolutionary and popular leaders in the main metropolitan areas of Soviet Russia, the head of the People's Commissariat for Enlightenment announced to an audience of painters and sculptors:

> I've just come from Vladimir Ilich. Once again he has had one of those fortunate and profoundly exciting ideas that have shocked and delighted us all so many times. He intends to have the squares of Moscow decorated with statues and monuments in honour of revolutionaries. . . . This denotes both agitation for socialism and a wide field for our sculptural talents to manifest themselves.[1]

This scene had its place, of course, in what could in no way be considered a politically unbiased situation; yet it illustrates a point and leads to a question which will be germane for the present discussion: what does a piece of sculpture communicate to its audience? And is it not true that the "message" delivered is greatly conditioned by the situation and experiences of the viewer?

Throughout its thousand-year history Olympia was, unlike any other place in Greece, the cultural, religious, and political forum of Hellenism, and the natural site for the communication of messages through the language of sculpture. Monuments commemorating an athlete's victory and honoring his fatherland were important because of their mere visibility in the Olympic sanctuary. The temple sculpture, specifically that of the Zeus temple, not only conveyed an agonistic motif and athletic style appropriate to the Olympics, but can also be seen as promoting the local and national political ideals of Classical Greece. After some general considerations regarding the heroization and politicization of athletic victors through sculpture, an investigation will be made of the ways in which the Zeus temple exploits important images of victory to associate the mythical and athletic message with that of contemporary democracy.

It was once commonly asserted and accepted that the earliest form of freestanding full-size male statue in ancient Greece, the kouros, was a representation of a deity, specifically Apollo. More careful investigation has revealed that kouroi were equally commonly used as representations of human beings—of youths who died prematurely (many have been discovered in cemeteries as tombstones), or of victorious athletes.[2] The latter are, naturally, of particular interest for the present investigation, and our evidence comes from Pausanias, who describes the statue of Arrichion, a three-time victor in the pankration at Olympia, as "ἀρχαῖος καὶ οὐχ ἥκιστα ἐπὶ τῶι σχήματι· οὐ διεστᾶσι μὲν πολὺ οἱ πόδες, καθεῖνται δὲ παρὰ πλευρὰν αἱ χεῖρες ἄχρι τῶν γλουτῶν" ("archaic in attitude, with the feet not much separated and the arms hanging down by the sides to the buttocks").[3]

In short, then, the same image, the kouros, could in the Archaic period appear as a representation of a god or of a heroized man, "hero" status being attained either through success in the athletic field or by a premature death in line with the traditional notion that it was most glorious to die at the height of one's powers and in the flower of manhood (cf. "Kleobis and Biton" at Delphi, whose reward for drawing the cart of their mother, the priestess of Hera, to the Heraion at Argos was to die in the hour of their triumph).[4] This ambiguity between representations of god and man may perhaps at least partially account for early Greek diffidence toward the erection of portrait statues per se. The early kouroi cannot be said to be iconic; they are the expressions of an ideal—an aristocratic ideal, moreover—the *kalos kagathos,* which becomes democratized with the development of the *polis,* the city state (one finds dedications by manual laborers, for example).[5] The kouroi can also become "personalized" by the presence of inscriptions or occasionally by the addition of individual attributes.[6]

There must have been a public awareness of the "danger" of erecting statues to individuals. The danger is the implication of at least heroization and possibly effective apotheosis; hence the rule at the athletic festivals even in the Classical period that "iconic" statues are a privilege afforded only to triple victors.[7] Even in the context of the city, statues of individuals appear exceptional in the Archaic period—Pliny, in fact, informs us that the first portrait statues officially erected at Athens were those of the tyrannicides Harmodios and Aristogeiton, raised in the same year that the kings were expelled from Rome (510).[8] Statues as the embodiment of ideals and as reminders of exceptional individuals easily become objects of reverence, and this is especially true for athletic victors. Thus, in Herodotus we learn how Philippos of Croton, a victor in the Olympiad of 520, had a heroön erected in his honor by the people of Egesta in Sicily on account of his beauty and was worshipped after his death as a hero.[9] The boxer Euthymos of Locri Epizephyrii was worshipped and sacrificed to in and after his lifetime, and Theogenes of Thasos, also a boxer, was heroized after his death.[10] Moreover, we learn from Pausanias that the statue of Theogenes by the sculptor Glaukias at Olympia and what were probably copies of it erected in and beyond Greece were believed capable of healing sickness;[11] Lucian indeed records that his image could cure fevers.[12] Clearly, success in athletic competition could lead to intense glorification of the individual in his home city and even farther afield, and could potentially provide him with considerable political influence, which in the hands of an opportunist could pave the way to power. An immediate example suggests itself in the figure of Kylon of Athens, victor in the *diaulos* at Olympia in 640 B.C., who within the decade seized the Acropolis in an attempt to establish himself as a tyrant at Athens; as it happened, he apparently miscalculated the extent of popular support![13] The prestige derived from athletic success may be readily illustrated by the record in Herodotus of the successes of Kimon in the quadriga in the sixty-first, sixty-second, and sixty-third Olympiads: his first victory (536) was won during the period when he was exiled from Athens by Peisistratus, a victory whereby, our source indicates, "he gained the very same honor which before had been carried off by Miltiades, his half-brother on the mother's side. At the next Olympiad [532] he won the prize again with the same mares, upon which he caused Peisistratus to be proclaimed the winner, having made an agreement with him that on yielding him this honor he should be allowed to come back to his country. Afterwards, still with the same mares, he won the prize a third time, whereupon he was put to death by the sons of Peisistratus, whose father was no longer living."[14] We may assume that by this time he presented too great a political threat to the Peisistratids.

Political ramifications, then, are apparent, and these extend in various directions. Quickly athletes became the political representatives of their cities and the focus of civic consciousness. The cost of having a victory monument made could be prohibitively high for an individual, and often in such cases the city of origin provided the resources to pay for the monument.[15] The importance of the statue is evidenced in the story of Oibotas of Dime in Achaia, victor in the *stadion* in 756: because he was not rewarded by the Achaeans for his success (the implication surely is that no statue was financed for him, although a life-size monument would be unusual at this early date), he pronounced a curse that no Achaean in future should win an Olympic victory. This came to pass. The distraught Achaeans asked the Delphic Oracle why they had been unsuccessful, and after they had subsequently dedicated a statue, they again attained success. Thereafter Achaean competitors were accustomed to sacrifice to Oibotas as a hero before entering competition at Olympia.[16] A similar tale is attached to the name of Orrhippos (?Orsippos) of Megara, victor in the fifteenth Olympiad (720).[17]

Repeatedly successful and therefore celebrated athletes would be sought after by cities other than their own. Athletes were aware of the possible benefits to be derived from their successes, not surprisingly. Astylos of Croton, for example, victorious in three or perhaps four sequential Olympiads and celebrated by the establishment of a statue at Olympia (the work of the leading sculptor Pythagoras of Rhegion), and by a second statue near his home in Croton (probably a copy of the one at Olympia), sought to ingratiate himself with Hieron, tyrant of Syracuse, by having himself proclaimed Syracusan in two later contests. The response of the citizens of Croton was immediate—they condemned his house to be a prison and pulled down his statue![18]

From the foregoing discussion it will have become apparent that victory monuments, and specifically statues, were of considerable significance to the people in the cities, not only as a reminder of their hero, but as the focus of civic and therefore political pride. This point may be further illustrated by two observations. First, our evidence indicates that once the dedication of victory statues became acceptable usage in the fifth century, a number of dedications were made by cities in celebration of athletes who had in some instances been victorious as much as two centuries earlier. There is some indication of rivalry in this connection: the victory of the athlete Chionis of Sparta in the twenty-ninth Olympiad (664) was memoralized by stelai in Sparta and Olympia and by a statue, the work of Myron, whose floruit was c. 480–450 B.C.[19] It has been suggested—and the suggestion is an attractive one—that since Chionis' statue was set beside that of Astylos of Croton in the Altis, the motivation of Sparta in erecting this latterday memorial was largely political.[20]

Second, there is some indication that attention might be given to the place of origin of the athlete or his kinship when monuments were placed in the Olympian sanctuary; thus, later Achaeans had theirs near to that of their countryman Oibotas (discussed above) and Spartans near that of Chionis. (It would, incidentally, be of considerable interest to investigate what were thought to be the "choice" locations and whether influence could play any part in obtaining them. Ridgway, in her lucid examination of the setting of Greek sculpture, has recently demonstrated how great a part the proposed site might play in determining the form of the work: thus, a unified group would be an unsuitable choice for a location beside a thoroughfare, since the viewer could not absorb it *en passant*.)[21]

Perhaps the greatest form of flattery paid to the victorious athletes of the era was the imitation of their statues in the sculptures on the Temple of

Zeus. There the mythical contests literally and figuratively lift the heroes from the ground level of the Altis to the idealized Olympian heights, where both agonistic imagery and athletic forms proclaim the eternal nature of human competition.

The common bond between the pedimental and metope sculpture on the Temple of Zeus is the agonistic theme: in the west pediment the struggle between the Lapiths and the Centaurs; in the east pediment the beginning of the race of Pelops and Oinomaos; in the metopes the labors *(athloi)* of Herakles. The competitive spirit finds a place in several levels of Greek life; traditionally *arete,* an aristocratic ideal, involved physical prowess—in battle in time of war, in athletics in peacetime. The two appear in happy juxtaposition in a building erected not long before the Temple of Zeus: namely, the Temple of Athena Aphaea at Aegina. The warriors in these pediments are commonly perceived to be modeled on athletic figures, as can be readily exemplified by considering one figure from the east pediment who springs forward in a wrestling pose which is easily paralleled in freestanding athletic sculpture,[22] as will be presently observed.

Freestanding athletic statues, the majority of which are victor monuments, have on occasion been divided into two types: those depicting the athlete at rest, and those depicting the athlete in action, usually performing his characteristic sport. Of necessity the latter type can display only one phase of the activity, or in some cases the artist prefers to show the moment before the action, a quite characteristic election for early sculptors. In the east pediment at Olympia, the "moment before" is depicted. The contestants wait on either side of the judge, Zeus, the central figure in the pediment. The chariots are drawn up on either side, ready for the contest and with their drivers or grooms. The anxiety of the moment is communicated to us by the onlookers, especially the seer, who apparently foresees the outcome. The race of Pelops and Oinomaos is one of local interest and color.

The west pediment is of more immediate interest here because not only is the theme agonistic, but the activities of the figures more poignantly reflect the activities of the athletic festival, since their poses seem directly borrowed from the field of sports and from athletic art. The central figure is commonly identified as Apollo, though at least one authority sees here Zeus Areios (warlike Zeus), an early local form of Zeus, youthful in appearance and, in relation to the Centaurs and Lapiths scene, meant to illustrate "the crushing of the brutal violence of the early period of man's development, the predominance of moral principles and the establishment of Law and Standing Order of Zeus." On this rationale the east pediment has an older Zeus glorified as an austere and unbribable judge.[23] But if the east pediment represents Zeus as a judge, perhaps the west pediment "Apollo," the son of Zeus and himself a patron deity of athletic festivals, might also be deemed a judge. This would be a possible explanation of the gesture of the right hand, for long an object of concern to art historians.[24] Comparison with a number of athletic scenes from vases provides similar instances in which a trainer or judge instructs or disciplines an athlete.[25] Of further assistance in this "athletic" interpretation of Apollo is the appearance of his head, which is readily paralleled in the Blond Boy in Athens, originally part of an athletic statue of the same period and "Severe" style.[26]

A number of parallels between the figures of the west pediment and extant athletic illustrations or records of athletic statues might well be adduced. One or two will suffice. The group of Deianeira and the centaur Eurytion (figures H and I in the standard arrangement) find comparison in contemporary or earlier vases—for example, a red-figure amphora by the Andokides Painter (c. 530–520)[27] shows a similar waist-hold. The Centaur-Lapith group in which the neck-hold is applied and the Centaur is committing a foul by biting the Lapith's arm (figures P and Q) can be paralleled in a red-figure cup from Vulci illustrating the pankration.[28] In addition, the youth portrayed in a wrestling position (figure C) finds a ready comparison first in the warrior from the Aegina pediment mentioned earlier, and second in a mid-fifth-century bronze statuette of an athlete allegedly from Dodona.[29] Such postures appear similarly on black-figure vases of the late Archaic period—for example, an amphora of Psiax (c. 520) which shows two wrestlers in action.[30]

Clearly in the pediments at Olympia the connection between the architectural sculpture and the athletic festival celebrated at the sanctuary is not simply a thematic one; rather, there has been a conscious borrowing of the poses and physical forms of athletic figures either from contemporary artistic productions or, less likely, from reality.[31]

The metopes remain for consideration. Twelve of them, displayed on the exterior of the east and west walls of the cella, portrayed the canonical labors of Herakles.[32] Herakles as the hero of athletes is obviously a suitable subject. It is still more interesting to note that his labors ultimately brought him immortality, a reward indicated, as we shall see, in the metopes, and an appropriate lesson for the athletes who will compete in the games and thus have an opportunity to attain their own version of immortality and/or heroization. Three metopes are here selected for inspection. The Stymphalian birds metope is a peaceful scene in which Herakles comes to display his spoils to his patroness Athena, pictured as the goddess of the rock (i.e., citadels in general, so it is asserted). Clearly one may feel the religious aspect of this scene and the relevance to the athletes, who are made ever mindful in the course of the festival of its religious basis and who give thanks to the gods at the successful completion of their labors. But there is a further kinship here: Herakles adopts a stance which can be observed in a number of victory statues. In the period contemporary with the temple, the so-called Choiseul Gouffier Apollo, now in London, and a reconstruction thereof show the same elemental form: one leg is taut, one relaxed; there is a resulting shift in the position of the hip which bears the weight, and the arms are one to the side, the other rather diffidently extended forward. The pose is similarly witnessed in coins, as on the reverse of a coin from Pandrosia in Bruttium dated to c. 430, in which the youth holds a *patera* or a wreath in his right hand and in his left a laurel branch; and a fifth-century coin from Selinus displays the same characteristics.[33] And from the period 440–430 might be adduced the well-known "Idolino" bronze, which repeats the form.[34]

The Cerberus metope exhibits a generally acknowledged new concept in representing an old story. Whereas some earlier illustrations of this labor show almost comical scenes of Herakles rather gingerly luring the three- (or often two-) headed monster from Hades, with the hero sometimes on his knees (as in the Andokides Painter's rendering, c. 510), or in retreat (as in the Boston plate of Paseas, floruit 510),[35] in the Olympia metope Herakles is shown with hound on leash, focusing his whole mental effort on the wary extrication of the beast from the Lower World. The stance of Herakles easily recalls a number of illustrations of athletes preparing to throw the javelin, as on a statue base from Athens (c. 510) or on a red-figure calyx krater of Kleophrades (500–490).[36]

A third metope depicts the delivery of the golden apples from the Garden of the Hesperides. One version of the legend tells how Herakles persuaded the giant Atlas to fetch the apples for him, offering to bear the burden of the heavens while Atlas was away. The apples were the symbols of the immortality which Herakles had been promised when his labors were accomplished. This is of considerable pertinence to the athletic tradition, for at Delphi apples were given as prizes in athletic competition. Moreover, in Pliny appears the record of a victor statue by the early fifth-century sculptor Pythagoras in which the nude athlete is represented holding apples *(mala tenentem).*[37] The same posture is adopted not only by an early fifth-century bronze statuette of a rather stocky athlete, a close prototype of the Canon of Polykleitos, who holds a ball in his left hand in precisely the position of the Atlas in our metope,[38] but also finds comparison in other small bronzes, including an example from the Acropolis c. 500,[39] and in a red-figure amphora (c. 490) in Leningrad, in which the victorious athlete holds branches and leaves in his hands.[40] As to the pose of Herakles, it will be of interest to note a comparable position of the arms in a figure of a javelin-thrower in a mid-fifth-century red-figure oinochoe now in Paris.[41]

Further comparisons could readily be drawn, but this brief encounter is, I believe, sufficiently persuasive of the conscious incorporation of the forms of athletic monuments—frequently enough those of victor statues—into the decoration of the Temple of Zeus. In this particular sense, then, the Olympia sculpture can be said to offer the viewer a variety of images of victory. But, just as victor monuments for individual athletes inevitably took on a greater political significance in the Panhellenic sanctuary, so, too, the Temple of Zeus itself could not but invite the visitor to Olympia to see beyond its mythical symbols and agonistic motifs to a political message conveyed by the statuary.

Political implications and applications are readily acknowledged in a number of examples of major architectural sculpture in the late Archaic and Classical periods, from approximately 525 to 420 B.C. The Siphnian Treasury (c. 525), which has in its east pediment the depiction of the struggle between Herakles and Apollo for the Delphic tripod, has been judged to be a memorial of the victory of the Amphictiony (Thessaly, Sicyon, and Athens) over Krisa in the First Sacred War, which led to Delphi's independence.[42] The Hephaisteion (traditionally dated 449–444), which is believed to have been erected on the initiative of Cimon, shows both Herakles and Theseus in its sculpture in a manner comparable to the Athenian Treasury at Delphi (infra).[43] And the Parthenon (447–432) is in itself and in its decoration a monument to Athenian reconstruction and self-confidence after the Persian Wars.[44] It is not, however, my purpose here to reiterate earlier discussion at length, merely to recall a number of pertinent conclusions.

Boardman, in an examination of Attic art of the second half of the sixth century, identifies Herakles as a symbol and favorite of the Peisistratid era and notes his "special association with Athens' ruling family, an association fostered by act, story and art for some fifty years." This Heraklean predominance in Attic art is subsequently countered, but not supplanted, by the appearance of a second hero, Theseus.[45] Theseus' arrival is associated with the political changes in Athens, the establishment of Cleisthenes' power, and the initiation of democracy, and Theseus is transformed into a national hero, protector of the people and their liberator from dangerous figures.[46] Thus, it is less than surprising to discover Herakles and Theseus side by side on the Athenian Treasury at Delphi (c. 510), a monument to the new democracy.[47]

The popular heroization of Theseus persists well into the fifth century: the 470s bring Cimon's mission to Skyros to retrieve the bones of Theseus and Theseus' "return" to Athens, where he was welcomed with procession and sacrifice and laid in a shrine in the midst of the city—the so-called Theseion, to be dated 476/5.[48] If this all seems rather removed from Olympia, it will soon become clear that it is not.[49] A red-figure volute krater from the middle years of the fifth century, now in New York, the work of the Painter of the Woolly Satyrs, shows on its neck Theseus fighting in the struggle of the Centaurs and Lapiths at the wedding of Peirithous[50]—the same scene which is attested by Pausanias as the subject of one wall of the Theseion[51] and which appears in the west pediment of the Temple of Zeus at Olympia, constructed 470–457 B.C.[52] Barron's work on the murals of the Theseion has revealed that the "Theseus" on the New York vase and the Theseus at Olympia share a common original: namely, the mural painting at Athens.[53] For us the interest here lies in the adoption of the Athenian hero from an Athenian mural celebrating Theseus into the west pediment at Olympia. It is the more fascinating because of the pose, which, together with that of Peirithous, is an apparent adaptation of the Tyrannicides' group, originally the work of Antenor in the last part of the sixth century, subsequently removed by the Persians and replaced by a second group in 477, this the work of Kritios and Nesiotes.[54] They stood for the Athenian people as a symbol of the end of tyranny and the establishment of democracy, as did Theseus.

One could at this point indulge in fine speculation about the implications of the presence of this strangely Athenian symbolism in the west pediment at Olympia.[55] After all, does not Pausanias, in a passage as yet not satisfactorily explained because of problems of the chronology of the artist's floruit, inform us that Alkamenes was the sculptor of the west pediment, and was not Alkamenes an Athenian? And one might also recall here that the subject of the metopes is Herakles, another Athenian favorite. Certainly later in the Classical period Athenian artists introduce Athenian themes into their work at Elis; for example, one historical scene represented on the screens of the Throne of Zeus was the sea fight at Salamis. Moreover, the other painted screens of the throne represented Herakles and Atlas, Theseus and Peirithous, and Herakles and the Nemean Lion, the work of the Athenian Panainos, brother of Pheidias and artist of the Marathon mural in the Stoa Poikile (the Marathon mural depicted *inter alia* Theseus rising out of the ground!). Clearly ideas are readily transferred from walls at Athens to religious sculptural contexts at Olympia.[56] Furthermore, there might be raised the question of the possible relevance of Cimon, who had been responsible for the revitalization of the Theseus cult by retrieval of the bones of Theseus from Skyros (supra) and their placement in the Theseion and who is connected through his brother-in-law Peisanax with the erection of the Stoa Poikile, perhaps as part of his grand plan for the embellishment of Athens.[57]

More pertinent would be reflection on the historical developments immediately prior to the building of the Temple of Zeus. Up to the period of the Persian Wars, Elis had been governed by an oligarchy, who at the time of national crisis had shown little concern for the national cause. The Elean contingent had arrived too late at the battle of Plataea. Returning home in shame, they dismissed their generals, and in 471 the small communities of Elis coalesced into a single city *(synoikismos)* which became the capital of a more strongly centralized state and apparently adopted a democratic form of government after the Athenian pattern.[58] Could it then be that at this time was adopted not only the Athenian form of government, but also the symbols of Athenian democracy—hence the presence of Theseus and the reminiscence of the Tyrannicides?

This is not to suggest, of course, that Elis had "gone Athenian" or that it was blatantly promoting a narrowly democratic partisanship at the Panhellenic sanctuary. One need only look at the subjects of the pediments and the metopes of the Temple of Zeus, which give voice to the triumphant Greek attitude of the post–Persian War period; they are a statement of the triumph of civilized Greeks over barbarians, of law and order over chaos. In terms of levels of interpretation, this might well be expressed as the *national* level. The race of Pelops and Oinomaos (east pediment) has obvious interest for the Eleans and might be thought (with one or two other allusive details) the extent of *local* color;[59] but there may be more.

The political aspects and applications of the games both at Olympia and elsewhere may be illustrated already in the sixth century by Cleisthenes of Sicyon's manipulation of them for political ends.[60] Moreover, Elean athletes found themselves ousted from the Isthmian Games as a result of political differences with Corinth'[61] and earlier in this discussion some elucidation has been offered of the extent to which civic pride and civic rivalries were involved in the performances and victories of the athletes at the Panhellenic games.

At the end of the Archaic period and in the first decades of the fifth century, the mood was democratic. At Athens, with the tyranny overthrown and Cleisthenes' reforms in place, a new hero, Theseus, appears, though not to the exclusion of the well-established national hero, Herakles. Elis, too, saw the overthrow of her oligarchy and the establishment of an Athenian-style democracy. The games, originally an aristocratic activity of Homeric heroes, had already in the Archaic period begun to attract a few nonaristocratic participants. Certainly is is clear that the fifth century saw a change in the sociological balance, the effect of which is underlined by Alcibiades' complaint (as if it were a recent development) that some of the athletes were of low birth—and his subsequent retreat into the almost exclusively aristocratic hippic events.[62]

The question arises whether the democratization of the Games and the democratization of Elis are to be envisaged as progressing hand in hand—which seems not improbable—and, if so, whether the introduction of recognizably athletic figures into the sculpture of the Zeus temple may not be interpreted on a political level as a symbol of democratization. There is perhaps further support for this notion in that, particularly in the metopes, the popular athletic hero Herakles is portrayed as moving through his labors in the pursuit of the ultimate promise of immortality symbolized by the apples of the Hesperides. This is surely an idea with which the athlete would identify, for varying forms of "immortality" were available to the victorious athlete: the Games were a splendid opportunity for "upward social mobility"!

The sculptural artistry of Olympia has, then, something for everyone—not in a Panhellenic sense, but because it speaks to national, local, political, and athletic interests. It was (to borrow a phrase) a "profoundly exciting idea" which in this case not only offered a wide field for sculptural achievements but also permitted some "agitation" for an as yet fresh and vital democracy.

The Temple of Zeus, like the honorary statues over which it towered, offered to the pilgrim an aesthetic experience of victory on several levels at once. Both the temple and the statues showed anthropomorphic demigods who inspired the viewer to emulate an idealized *arete*. Both illustrate an agonistic spirit which pervaded many aspects of Greek life. And both paid tribute to an increasingly democratic feeling which allowed to the individual the freedom to compete and cooperate with other free Greeks in their daily exchanges. The temple is thus a synthesis or even the epitome of the religious, the agonistic, and the political ideals espoused by the Classical Greeks, and its sculptural decoration the clearest focal point in which these ideals converge at Olympia.

Notes

1. The head of Narkompros (the People's Commissariat for Enlightenment) was Anatolii Lunarcharsky. The speech, cited originally in I. Grabar, "Aktualnye zadachi sovetskoi skuptury," *Iskusstvo,* Nos. 1–2 (1933) 155, is quoted *apud* John E. Bowlt, "Russian Sculpture and Lenin's Plan of Monumental Propaganda," in Henry A. Millon and Linda Nochlin, eds., *Art and Architecture in the Service of Politics* (Cambridge, Mass., 1978) 184.

2. On the application of the kouros type see G. M. A. Richter, *Kouroi*[3] (London and New York, 1970) 1–2. On the kouros as Apollo: Diodorus Siculus 1.98.9 on the *xoanon* of Pythian Apollo at Samos by Theodoros and Telekles; cf. the red-figure Nolan amphora in London, British Museum E336 = *ARV*[2] 1010, no. 4; the earliest representations of athletes reported in Pausanias (6.18.7) are those of Praxidamos of Aegina, winner of the boxing competition in the fifty-ninth Olympiad (544 b.c.,) and Rhexibios of Opous, winner of the pankration in the sixty-first Olympiad (536 b.c.)—both made of wood. For the best modern discussion of the relationship of kouroi to athletic statues, see B. S. Ridgway, *The Archaic Style in Greek Sculpture* (Princeton, 1977) 49–59

3. Pausanias 8.40.1, and see discussion of the MS variants for the name in Richter (supra n. 2) 1 n. 4

4. On the story of Kleobis and Biton: Herodotus 1.31; cf. W. Helbig, *Führer durch die öffentlichen Sammlungen klassischer Altertümer in Rom,* 4, 3 (1969) no. 2414; C. Caprino, s.v. Cleobi e Bitone, *EAA* 2 (1959) 713–14 and refs. there cited. Note that "Kleobis and Biton" have recently been reidentified as the Dioscuri; see C. Vatin, "Monuments votifs de Delphes, V: Les couroi d'Argos," *BCH* 106 (1982) 509–25.

5. On the "democratization" of the kouros: V. Zinserling, "Zum Bedeutungsgehalt des archaischen Kuros," *Eirene* 13 (1975) 26–27.

6. Ibid. 25 and 28. On victor statues, most recently S. Lattimore, "The Nature of Early Greek Victor Statues," in *Coroebus Triumphs* (San Diego, 1987, in press). I would like to express my gratitude to Dr. Lattimore for allowing me access to his paper prior to publication.

7. Pliny *NH* 34.16 On "iconic" statues see W. H. Gross, *Quas iconicas vocant: Zum Porträtcharakter der Statuen dreimaliger olympischer Sieger,* Gött-Nachr. Phil-hist. Kl. (1969) No. 3, who concludes that such statues were not portraits per se, but represented an athlete engaged in the discipline characteristic of the individual honored. The distinction is still not valid for the fifth century and admits of exceptions later. Note also W. W. Hyde, *Olympic Victor Monuments and Greek Athletic Art* (Washington, D.C., 1921) (hereafter cited as *OVM*) 54–57.

8. That is, 510–509 B.C.: Pliny *NH* 34.17.

9. Philippos of Croton: Herodotus 5.47; cf. Hyde, *OVM* (supra n. 7) 35, 57, 363; L. Moretti, *Olympionikai: I vincitori negli antichi agoni Olimpici,* Mem Linc ser. 8, vol. 8.2 (Rome, 1957) 76, no. 135.

10. Euthymos, worshipped and sacrificed to: Pausanias 6.6.4f; Callimachus fr. 98 (Pfeiffer); Pliny *NH* 7.152; Moretti (supra n. 9) 86, no. 191 (cf. nos. 214, 227). Theogenes: Pausanias 6.11.8. On Theogenes and Euthymos: Hyde, *OVM* (supra n. 7) 35; idem, *De Olympionicarum statuis a Pausania commemoratis,* Diss. Halle, 1903, 13, no. 56.

11. Pausanias 6.11.9.

12. Lucian *Deor. Conc.* 12. On the subject of the heroization of athletes in general, see J. Fontenrose, "The Hero as Athlete," *CSCA* 1 (1968) 73–104.

13. The masses did not follow him, and he was besieged. He himself escaped, but his friends were surrounded and killed. See the detailed account in Thucydides 1.126, Herodotus 5.71. Also Pausanias 7.25.3; Aristotle *Ath. Pol.* fr. 8, ch. 1; Plutarch *Sol.* 12; schol. Aristophanes *Eq.* 445. On Kylon's date: F. Jacoby, *Atthis* (Oxford, 1949) 366, no. 77.

14. The evidence of the victories of Kimon is collected in Moretti (supra n. 9) 72, 74, nos. 120, 124, 127. The story is preserved in Herodotus 6.103, trans. G. Rawlinson (adapted). Bronze statues of the winning mares were subsequently created: Aelian *VH* 9.32. On the graves of the mares nearby the family tomb of Kimon, see Plutarch *Cat. Min.* 5.

15. E.g., Pausanias 6.3.8, 6.2, 17.2, 17.4; and Hyde, *OVM* (supra n. 7) 27, 30.

16. So Pausanias 7.13. On Oibotas, Moretti (supra n. 9) 60, no. 6; Hyde (supra n. 10) 10, no. 29.

17. Pausanias 1.44.1; cf. Moretti (supra n. 9) 61, no. 16.

18. Astylos: Hyde (supra n. 10) 19, no. 110 and refs.; Moretti (supra n. 9) 82–85, 87, 90, nos. 178–79, and cf. 186–87, 196–98, and possibly 219. For the story of the house and statue, see Pausanias 6.13.1; Pliny (*NH* 34.59) calls the statue of Astylos at Olympia that of a *stadiodromos.* On the victories of Astylos: Dionysius of Halicarnassus 8.1. 77; Callimachus fr. 666 (Pfeiffer); Diodorus Siculus 11.1; Dionysius of Halicarnassus 9.1; *POxy.* 222. Discus-

sion of the sources and the details of the victories in Hyde, *OVM* (supra n. 7) 363, no. 10.

19. Chionis of Sparta: Hyde (supra n. 10) 19, no. 111; Moretti (supra n. 9) 64, nos. 42–43; Pausanias 6.13.2; 3.14.3; cf. Hyde, *OVM* (supra n. 7) 362, no. 1 (also 32), who believes that the monuments at Olympia and the stele at Sparta were erected around 472–468 B.C.

20. See Hyde (supra n. 10) 19, no. 111, discussed by Moretti (supra n. 9) 64, nos. 42–43.

21. B. S. Ridgway, "The Setting of Greek Sculpture," *Hesperia* 40 (1971) 336–56, esp. 338 and 340–41.

22. As has been observed by E. N. Gardiner, *Athletics of the Ancient World* (Oxford, 1930; repr. Chicago, 1980) 56 and fig. 19, who, however, strangely identifies the figure as "that of an attendant who rushes forward to help his fallen master."

23. Cf. C. Kardara, "Olympia: Perithoos Apollo or Zeus Areios," *ArchDelt* 25.1 (1970) 19. Kardara imagines a sword in the left hand of the "Apollo" figure, but while the position of the hand would be suitable for a "grasp," is is hard to imagine the sword projecting forward from the pediment directly toward the spectator.

24. On the gesture of Apollo's right hand: for example, B. Ashmole, *Architect and Sculptor in Classical Greece* (New York, 1972) 44.

25. E.g., a red-figure kylix of c. 480 B.C. from Cerveteri, *ARV*[2] 340, no. 65 = Baltimore (n.n.): *CVA* Baltimore 2 Collection 3.1 pl. 18, fig. 1b; or a red-figure kylix from Vulci, Munich 2649 = *ARV*[2] 418, no. 25; cf. R. Patrucco, *Lo sport nella Grecia antica,* Arte e Archaeologica, Studi e Documenti 1 (Florence, 1972) figs. 117 and 157.

26. Blond Boy: Athens, Acropolis Museum no. 689 = H. Payne and G. M. Young, *Archaic Marble Sculpture from the Acropolis* (New York, 1950) pls. 113–15; Richter (supra n. 2) fig. 570 (figs. 572–74 show fragments of a torso which may belong); J. D. Beazley and B. Ashmole, *Greek Sculpture and Painting* (Cambridge, 1966) fig. 68; B. S. Ridgway, *The Severe Style in Greek Sculpture* (Princeton, 1970) pls. 72 and 74 and pp. 56–57 compares and points up differences between the Blond Boy and the Olympian Apollo.

27. Red-figure amphora by the Andokides Painter, Berlin Museum F2159 from Vulci, c. 530–520 B.C. : *ARV*[2] 3, no. 1; P. Arias, M. Hirmer, and B. Shefton, *A History of Greek Vase Painting* (London, 1962) (herafter cited as *AHS*) pl. XXIX.

28. Red-figure cup by the Foundry Painter, London, British Museum E78 = *ARV*[2] 401, no. 3; cf. J. Boardman, *Athenian Red-Figure Vases: The Archaic Period* (Oxford, 1975) fig. 263.

29. = D. G. Mitten and S. F. Doeringer, *Master Bronzes from the Classical World* (Mainz, 1968) no. 97. Traces of the opponent remain along the inside of the left arm, left chest, and right fist.

30. Black-figure amphora by Psiax from Vulci, c. 520, Brescia, Museo Civico (n.n.) = *ABV* 292, no. 1; *AHS* (supra n. 27) fig. 68. There exists for the Archaic period a comprehensive typological study of athletic scenes on

red- and black-figure vases by B. Legakis, *Athletic Contests in Archaic Greek Art,* Diss. University of Chicago, 1977, which categorizes the types of events and the moment of action portrayed.

31. The borrowing of sculptural forms for architectural compositions from earlier or contemporary freestanding and related statuary can be paralleled subsequently in the Parthenon frieze, whose figures are judged to reflect sculptural dedications on the Acropolis in the pre-Persian period; see R. R. Holloway, "The Archaic Acropolis and the Parthenon Frieze," *Art Bulletin* 48.2 (1966) 223–26.

32. Pausanias' description (5.10.9) mentions only eleven, omitting the Cerberus metope.

33. For a full discussion of the reconstruction of the Choiseul Gouffier Apollo, the numismatic evidence, and the identity of the sculptor, see C. Waldstein, "Pythagoras of Rhegium and the Early Athlete Statue," *JHS* 1 (1880) 179–201 and 2 (1881) 332–51.

34. The Idolino, Florence, Museo Archeologico = W. Amelung, *Führer durch die Antiken in Florenz* (Munich, 1897) no. 268; G. M. A. Richter, *The Sculpture and Sculptors of the Greeks*[3] (New Haven, 1950) figs. 43, 44 (= ibid.[4] figs. 47, 48).

35. Bilingual amphora by the Andokides/Lysippides Painter, c. 510, Paris, Louvre F204 = *ARV*[2] 4, no. 11; *ABV* 254, no. 1; *AHS* (supra n. 27) pls xxix and 88; see note on p. 317 concerning "dragging" Cerberus out of Hell into captivity. Paseas' plate, Boston, Museum of Fine Arts 01.8025 = *ARV*[2] 163, nos. 6 and 1630: Boardman (supra n. 28) fig. 16; cf. idem, "Herakles, Peisistratus and Eleusis," *JHS* 95 (1975) pl. 1c.

36. Base of kouros with athletic reliefs on three sides, Athens, NM 3476 = R. Lullies and M. Hirmer, *Greek Sculpture* (New York, 1957) pls. 58–61; J. P. Barron, *Greek Sculpture* (London, 1965) 45 (cast).

37. Apples at Delphi: Lucian *Anach.* 9. On the "nude holding apples," Pliny *NH* 34.59; cf. Hyde, *OVM* (supra n. 7) 182 on the unlikeliness of the identification of this work with the statue of Dromeus at Olympia.

38. The Ligurio Bronze, Berlin Museum (n.n.) = Hyde, *OVM* (supra n. 7) 112, fig. 16; cf. p. 111 for discussion; also Gardiner (supra n. 22) 60, pl. 25, who believes the object in the youth's left hand to be an apple.

39. Bronze statuette from the Akropolis: Athens, NM 6445, c. 500 B.C. = Hyde, *OVM* (supra n. 7) fig. 15; cf. N. Yalouris, ed., *The Eternal Olympics* (New Rochelle, N.Y., 1979) fig. 63, though here the youth may be holding *halteres.*

40. Red-figure amphora; c. 490 B.C. in Leningrad, Hermitage = Yalouris (supra n. 39) fig. 56; cf. psykter by Oltos, New York, Metropolitan Museum 10.210.18 = *ARV*[2] 54, no. 7; G. M. A. Richter, *Attic Red-Figured Vases: A Survey* (New Haven, 1946) fig. 35.

41. Red-figure oinochoe, mid-fifth-century, Paris, Louvre = Yalouris (supra n. 39) fig. 104.

42. Cf. H. W. Parke and J. Boardman, "The Struggle for the Tripod and the First Sacred War," *JHS* 76 (1957) 276–82. For a different, but nevertheless political, interpretation, see L. V. Watrous, "The Sculptural Program of the

Siphnian Treasury at Delphi," *AJA* 86 (1982) 167, who argues that the east pediment provides a reference to "the contemporary rivalry between Peisistratus (Herakles) and Delphi (Apollo) and to the tyrant's attempt to usurp the god's authority by setting up a rival oracular establishment at Athens"—this as part of a plan devised by the local priesthood to justify Delphic pre-eminence.

43. On this question: J. S. Boersma, "On the Political Background of the Hephaistion," *Bulletin van der Vereeniging tot Bevordering der Kennis van de Antieke Beshaving* 39 (1964) 101–106. On the dating of the Hephaistion see n. 52 infra.

44. Cf. J. J. Pollitt, *Art and Experience in Classical Greece* (Cambridge, 1972) 66; R. R. Holloway, *A View of Greek Art* (Providence, R.I., 1973) 123–32 passim; cf. Ashmole (supra n. 24) 142–44 with notes. The essentially democratic basis of the construction of the Parthenon is emphasized by R. Meiggs, "The Political Implications of the Parthenon," in G. T. W. Hooker, ed., *Parthenos and Parthenon, Greece and Rome* 10 (Suppl.) (1963) 36–45, reprinted in V. J. Bruno, ed., *The Parthenon* (New York, 1974) 101–111.

45. J. Boardman, "Herakles, Peisistratos and Sons," *RA* (1972) no. 1, 57–72, esp. 70; cf. idem, "Herakles, Peisistratos and Eleusis" (supra n. 35) 1–12. Also, more recently, J. Boardman, "Herakles, Theseus and Amazons," in D. Kurtz and B. Sparkes, *The Eye of Greece: Studies in the Art of Athens* (Cambridge, 1982) 1–28, esp. 1–15. Cf. Plutarch *Thes.* 29 on the development of the proverbial saying ἄλλος οὗτος Ἡρακλῆς.

46. See C. Sourvinou-Inwood, "Theseus Lifting the Rock and a Cup near the Pithos Painter," *JHS* 91 (1971) 98–99.

47. J. Boardman, "Herakles, Delphi and Kleisthenes," *RA* (1978) no. 2, 227–34, esp. 234. On Theseus' association with the establishment of a democratic form of government, see H. W. Parke, *Festivals of the Athenians* (Ithaca, N.Y., 1977) 81–82. In the fourth century Theseus appeared with Demos and Demokratia in a famous painting by Euphranor, which, according to Pausanias (1.3.3), clearly indicated that Theseus established democracy for the *demos.* On this passage and both the earlier and later traditions of Theseus as founder of Athenian democracy see A. E. Raubitschek, "Demokratia," *Hesperia* 31 (1962) 238–39. That Herakles, like Theseus, was a democratic hero ("a champion of the middle class") in the fifth century is suggested by W. G. Moon, "The Priam Painter: Some Iconographic and Stylistic Considerations," in W. G. Moon, ed., *Ancient Greek Art and Iconography,* Wisconsin Studies in Classics (Madison, 1983) 101.

48. Plutarch *Thes.* 36.1.4; J. P. Barron, "New Light on Old Walls: The Murals of the Theseion," *JHS* 92 (1972) 20–21, discusses Cimon's mission, the "return" of Theseus, and the Theseion.

49. The establishment of athletic games in association with the festival of the Theseia at this time makes Theseus' appearance at Olympia all the more pertinent; cf. Parke (supra n. 47) 81.

50. Red-figure volute krater, New York, Metropolitan Museum 07.286–84, dated c. 450: *ARV*² 613, no. 1; Richter (supra n. 40) pl. 74; G. M. A. Richter and L. F. Hall, *Red-figured Athenian Vases in the Metropolitan Museum* (New Haven, 1936) vol. 2, pls. 97–98. Cf. a fragmentary volute krater by the

Niobid Painter, Berlin 2403, c. 460 = *ARV*[2] 599, no. 9; T. B. L. Webster, *Der Niobidenmaler* = J. D. Beazley and P. Jacobsthal, eds., *Bilder Griechischer Vasen,* Vol. 8 (Leipzig, 1935) pls. 24b and c.

51. Pausanias 1.17.2; Pausanias does not, however, give a detailed description of the pose of Theseus. On the relationship of the Olympia centauromachy to the New York vase of the Painter of the Woolly Satyrs, as part of his discussion of Agora P 12641, see B. B. Shefton, "Herakles and Theseus on a Red-Figured Louterion," *Hesperia* 31 (1962) 360–62, and critique by Barron (supra n. 48) 28–29.

52. The Theseus figure also appears on the west frieze of the Hephaistion, for which an earlier date (c. 460) than previously offered has now been advanced (though the exact chronology of the sculpture is still elusive); see W. F. Wyatt, Jr., and C. N. Edmonson, "The Ceiling of the Hephaisteion," *AJA* 88 (1984) 135–67, esp. 167.

53. Barron (supra n. 48) 25–27; cf. K. Schefold, *The Art of Classical Greece* (New York, 1967) 63–70, esp. 65–67 and 80.

54. Compare, for example, the adaptations of the Tyrannicide poses on a red-figure kylix in the British Museum (BM E84), for which see C. P. Kardara, "On Theseus and the Tyrannicides," *AJA* 55 (1951) 293–300. On the frequent application of the Tyrannicide motif in scenes of violent action in this period, see Barron (supra n. 48) 39–40, and B. B. Shefton, "Some Iconographic Remarks on the Tyrannicides," *AJA* 64 (1960) 174 n. 10; idem (supra n. 51) 358.

55. It is interesting to note that the Tyrannicides appear in close connection with athletic games again as the shield device of Athena on a Panathenaic amphora of the Kuban group, London, British Museum B605 = *ABV* 411, no. 4; *AHS* (supra n. 27) pl. xxviii; the vase is usually dated to 402 B.C. on the basis of the shield device, which is considered symbolic of the re-establishment of democracy at Athens in 403; cf. K. Peters, *Studien zu den Panathenaischen Preisamphoren* (Leipzig, 1942) 97 no. 1, 99.

56. On Alkamenes: Pausanias 5.10.8; Alkamenes as an Athenian: Pliny *NH* 36.16. On the throne Pausanias 5.11.4-6; cf. E. N. Gardiner, *Olympia: Its History and Remains* (repr. Washington, D.C., 1973) 110.

57. Plutarch *Cim.* 4.5–6; Pausanias 1.15.1–3; Arrian *Anab.* 7.13.5 On the "Kimonian climate" of the paintings in the Stoa Poikile, see L. H. Jeffery, "The Battle of Oinoe in the Stoa Poikile," *BSA* 60 (1965) 42 and refs.

58. On the establishment of democracy at Elis: Swoboda, s.v. Elis, *RE* 5.2 (1905) 2392–93, who gives sources. Also, N. G. L. Hammond, *A History of Greece to 322 B.C.* (Oxford, 1959) 262; Gardiner (supra n. 56) 103; A. Mallwitz, *Olympia und seine Bauten* (Munich, 1972) 94. Of the sources, Diodorus Siculus 9.54 and Strabo 337 describe synoecism; and Herodotus 9.77 the banishment of the generals, which appears to imply the creation of democracy; see How and Wells ad loc. and J. A. R. Munro, "Some Observations on the Persian War," *JHS* 24 (1904) 148.

59. One interpretation which seeks to identify various parts of the sculpture as purely geographical references to specific areas of the Greek world is offered by R. R. Holloway, "Panhellenism in the Sculptures of the Zeus Temple at Olympia," *GRBS* 8 (1967) 93–101.

60. Cf. M. F. McGregor, "Cleisthenes of Sicyon and the Panhellenic Festivals," *TAPA* 72 (1941) 266–87.

61. Various versions of the tradition of the exclusion of the Eleans are given by Pausanias 5.2.2–5.

62. Isocrates *Peri Zeug.* 33; cf. H. W. Pleket, "Games, Prizes, Athletes and Ideology," *Stadion* 1 (1975) 72–73. D. C. Young, *The Olympic Myth of Greek Amateur Athletics* (Chicago, 1984), argues convincingly against the generally held view that non-nobles did not compete in athletics until the late Classical period, but admits that there was "extensive participation of the nobility" in the Archaic and later ages and that "no reliable proportion of nobles to non-nobles can be established at present" (p. 163). Given that Archaic Greece lacked professional athletic organizations such as the later *xystoi,* it may well be that the proportion of non-noble participants in pre-Classical Greece was low. In any case, one may argue that the advent of honorific victor monuments for athletes in the Classical age heralded a *spirit* of democratic competition in which individuals were honored for their personal achievement, no matter what their status.

David C. Young

How the Amateurs Won the Olympics

5

At the 1912 Stockholm Olympics, James Thorpe won both all-around events, the pentathlon and the decathlon.[1] It was a magnificent perform-ance. The king of Sweden gave him his medal, saying, "Mr. Thorpe, you are the greatest athlete in the world." Thorpe, the story goes, gave the immortal reply, "Thanks, King." But in January 1913 Thorpe's delin-quent past was exposed. He had pitched semipro baseball two summers before for fifteen dollars a week! He was *not* a purely amateur athlete. A penitent Thorpe apologized in writing: "I did not know that I was doing wrong."

The International Olympic Committee (IOC) seized the oppor-tunity to make an example of Thorpe, to warn the many athletes, clubs, and colleges that habitually winked at amateur rules. Baron Pierre de Coubertin, founder and president of the IOC, was quick to cite the fabled purity of ancient Greek Olympians as precedent—indeed, as cause—for disqualifying the great Carlisle athlete:

> It is enough to remember the careful way antiquity allowed par-ticipation in the Olympics only to those athletes who were irreproachable. Ought it not to be the same in the modern world? . . . If the Thorpe case convinces the whole world of the need for a change, it will undeniably have rendered sports an invaluable service.[2]

Thorpe's medals were called back and his Olympic victories were expunged from the record—an event unique in Olympic history.

Years later Thorpe was voted the outstanding American athlete of the first half of the twentieth century. Some sportswriters tried to get the

Olympic officials to reconsider his disqualification. But Avery Brundage of the United States Olympic Committee (and later president of the IOC) held firm. A rule was a rule. Many thought old Avery a bit harsh, but they had to admire his devotion to principle. After all, Brundage stressed, there was that ancient Greek model of pure amateurism to live up to. Who could argue with Avery Brundage and the Greeks? Many people know that much of the story, and perhaps even the IOC's surprising change of heart in 1983, seventy years after its harsh decision. But to understand the Thorpe story in full is another matter. For the case of James Thorpe resulted from an almost incredible sequence of events; from a truly odd coincidence of classical scholarship, national and personal ambitions, class warfare, and the athletic renaissance that came with the Industrial Revolution. Even the traditional enmity of Greeks and Turks played a role.

It all happened very fast. Athletics as we know them did not exist as the nineteenth century began. Amateurism itself is a strictly modern concept born not much more than a century ago. It began as the ideological means to justify an elitist athletic system that sought to bar the working class from competition. Most people think that amateurism was the original state in our own sports, that professionalism encroached on an earlier amateur system. The opposite is true. Amateurism was the late-comer.

In the early nineteenth century, competitive sport began to grow in England, Scotland, and America. Professionalism—that is, money prizes, cash payments, and wagers—was the standard in most competitions of public note, such as prize fights, rowing matches, and foot races. The purses were often large. In a Long Island foot race in 1835, a farmer beat a butcher, a carpenter, and a house painter to win a $1,300 cash prize—a fortune in those days, several years' wages for a working man. In Scotland, the Highland Games began. These games were the forerunner of modern track and field, and they regularly offered cash prizes in each event. About mid-century they spread to Scottish immigrant communities in America, where they were called "Caledonian Games." Competitors traveled a circuit from town to town, the better ones collecting large amounts of money. In England, too, foot racing held its place and its rewards, often connected with pub life. The upper classes generally frowned on such sports; they preferred hunting and cricket.[3]

But in the early 1860s some Oxford and Cambridge students held some contests in track and field, and similar meets sprang up here and there. At first the upper classes contended side by side with the others. Yet many who called themselves "gentlemen" (often, in fact, bourgeois parvenus) found it distasteful to compete—and to dress—with members of the working class. They also found it difficult to win. Preferring to contend only against one another, they started to form limited-membership clubs in order to keep their contests away from others. These exclusive clubs were the very origin of "amateur" athletics.

The first amateur athletic club in history, suitably named the Amateur Athletic Club (AAC), was founded in London in 1866. But it did not define the words "amateur" and "professional" as we do now—that is, in terms of money or athletic profit. It was mainly a question of social class. "Gentleman" and "amateur" were synonyms; and "professional" simply *meant* "working class." Besides nominally barring athletic profit, the AAC excluded as a "professional" any man who "is a mechanic, artisan, or labourer."[4]

Soon other athletic clubs formed along these lines, and some older rowing clubs became even more cautious. The "amateur" rules for the famous Henley Regatta excluded anyone who had *ever* "engaged in any menial duty."[5] In practice, rules against money prizes were not enforced against Gentlemen athletes, and a working-class athlete, no matter how pure of athletic gain, could never gain amateur standing. As one English sportsman put it in 1872: "Men of a class considerably lower must . . . understand that the facts of their being civil and never having run for money are *not* sufficient."[6] In 1880 the *Times* of London strongly endorsed the amateur policy that barred, as the *Times* called them, "outsiders— mechanics, artisans, and such like troublesome persons. To keep them out," the *Times* snapped, "is a thing desirable on every account." The *Times* also explained that if a mechanic won one of the valuable prizes given at amateur meets, there was a dangerous redistribution of wealth— "to say nothing of the social degradation involved in such a victory."[7]

Here lies the main question. If a Gentleman amateur lost to a man from the working class, he lost more than the victory and the valuable cup. He lost his identity, the very premise on which his life was based: namely, that he was *innately* superior to the working man, and could win even without practicing. Only in this light can we understand the amateur's vehement need to win—to win, despite his code, at almost any cost or else to abstain from the lists.

Yet in that same year, 1880, the AAC collapsed under pressure from northern clubs. It was replaced by the present Amateur Athletic Association (AAA). The term "amateur" itself was redefined. In AAA rules *all* athletic money was strictly forbidden, and social class left unspecified. But it was understood. The total ban on money would tend to achieve de facto what the older 1866 rule achieved by fiat, the exclusion of the laboring class, who could hardly afford the time to train and travel with no hope of remuneration.

When it was born in 1866, the amateur movement spread quickly to America, but met total defeat in baseball by 1869. Our first amateur athletic club, the New York Athletic Club, was founded in 1868. Others formed soon. But at first the New York club, with no other amateur club to contend against, competed against a long-established Scottish-American club, which had always given cash prizes. Amateurism made its best inroads in the universities. The first track contests among American university teams, mostly Ivy League, took place in the early 1870s. They offered cash prizes, both on and off campus. But when Yale one year offered cash prizes for its annual games, a howl came from the press, and the cash prizes were changed to medals. Soon Caledonian athletes began to reject their ancestral games in order to meet the new amateur standards. By 1879 the universities had turned amateur.

But "amateur" was always hard to define in America, where class lines were never so clearly and quietly drawn as in England. Amateur sport in the private athletic clubs soon became chaotic. Club members competed for prizes and made large side bets on club contests. The amateur clubs themselves hired professional athletes to compete under their colors.

> While some of the socially elite were top-flight performers, most were not. . . . in amateur sports, like track and field, . . . athletic clubs began to hire the best athletes, including collegians, by offering them free room and board, and giving them valuable prizes including cash.[8]

In 1888 the quarrels, power plays, and bidding wars among the amateur clubs led to the fall of the first American umbrella organization and to the birth of another, the Amateur Athletic Union (AAU). The AAU patterned its strict rules after the 1880 British revised definition: *no* athletic money of *any* kind. But the AAU, it turned out, simply wanted to control the sport. The AAU itself offered lucrative cash prizes. "Athletic clubs bid for recognized talent helping further to debase the concept of amateurism with their hypocritical policies."[9] The chaos continued, and by 1895 amateurism—then only twenty-nine years old—seemed near collapse. Professional soccer had won out in England in 1885, a crippling blow to amateurism like that delivered by American baseball in 1869. Now, even in its strongholds, the universities and track and field, amateurism seemed to gasp its last gasp. It had never really existed much. It was mostly a brief fond dream dreamed by a privileged few in the 1860s and 1870s—almost a Platonic *idea,* which a few glimpsed now and then but never found in authentic form in this imperfect world.

I introduce here Caspar Whitney, the most influential American sportswriter of his time and America's most dedicated apostle of amateurism. He took a trip to England and wrote up his experience and his opinions in a book called *Sporting Pilgrimage.* The date was 1895. Whitney was zealously dedicated to English class-exclusive sport. He was also a racist and an open elitist. He spat out his contempt at working-class athletes, the "great unwashed," as he called them. He complained that they were competing in amateur sports in England as well as America. They were, he said, "vermin" and wholly lacking in "the true amateur instinct of sport for sport's sake." He pleaded for a return to the "halcyon days"—the 1870s—when "amateur" was still defined by class. America should have a rule excluding "mechanics, artisans, and laborers." "Amateur contests" should be restricted to "the better element." In 1895 he made a plea for a separation of the classes in all future American sport. It was only evil, he said,

> to bring together in sport the two divergent elements of society that can never by any chance meet elsewhere on even terms. . . . The laboring class are all right in their way; let them go their way in peace, and have their athletics in whatsoever manner suits their inclinations. . . . Let *us* have *our own* sport among the more *refined* elements.[10]

Whitney did not know that he would soon find his dream-world of sport, a magnificent athletic festival intended for "the more refined elements." He would find it in the modern International Olympic Movement of Baron Pierre de Coubertin. Whitney was to become, in fact, the second American ever appointed to the IOC and was president of the United States Olympic Committee from 1906 to 1910.

But the stage is not yet set for the IOC or for Coubertin—whom we always credit with reviving the Olympic Games. We must go back in history to Greece, already left unfairly behind. Not ancient Greece, but modern Greece. The credit we give Coubertin for the Olympic revival comes by Coubertin's own design. The Greeks themselves revived the Olympics. Coubertin covered that fact up, for he wanted the title of *renovateur.* What he wrapped in darkness was a series of modern Olympic Games that began in Athens in 1859—several years before Coubertin was born; several years before amateurism itself was invented. I call them the "lost Olympics" because no one today knows anything about them. Even the Greeks have forgotten.

As the nineteenth century began, Greece was still under Turkish rule, but by 1829 their War of Independence had put much of southern Greece in Greek hands. Their paternalistic allies, France and Germany, installed a teenager from Bavaria, Otto the First, as King of the Hellenes. In 1858 a wealthy Greek veteran of the war, Evangelis Zappas, gave Otto a sum of money for "the restoration of the Olympic Games, to be celebrated every four years, following the precepts of our ancestors."[11] Zappas thought restoring the Olympic Games would restore Greek national pride. The 1859 modern Greek Olympics were no great success. An anti-athletic faction among Otto's advisers tried to divert the money to what they called "Industrial Olympics," contests in manufacturing and agriculture. They said athletics were an anachronism. But athletic Olympics were held in Athens in 1859, not far from what is now Omonia Square. People could not see well and crowded the site. Police removed them roughly. But the events were held, and the victors were rewarded with cash prizes, as Zappas had specified. An Olympic revival had indisputably occurred.

Zappas soon died, leaving his immense estate to fund the Olympic Games. The Greeks' allies replaced the embattled Otto with another unemployed prince from the north, this time a teenager from Denmark. To hold Olympics every four years was impossible. But the Greeks held another edition of the restored Olympic Games in Athens in 1870. The ancient Panathenaic stadium was excavated and prepared for the events, just as specified in Zappas' will (but the marble seats he paid for were omitted). These 1870 games were an outstanding success. By today's standards the 1870 Olympic program was the most sophisticated athletic program that the world had ever seen to that date. It combined ancient Olympic events (discus, javelin, foot races, long jumps, and wrestling) with modern gymnastic events. Contestants came from all around the Greek world. The winners received their cash prizes before an immense and approving crowd of 30,000 spectators (Coubertin's non-Athenian Olympics drew smaller crowds until the Paris games of 1924). There was perfect order and dignity both on the stadium field and in the stands. The 1870 Greek Olympics mark a high point in Olympic revivals before 1896, perhaps a real ancestor of our own Olympic games. Virtually every Greek joined in their praise.

But not *every* Greek. It seems that an ordinary laborer won the wrestling, victory in the pole climb fell to a stone-cutter, and a butcher won the 400-meter dash. Even in Greece there rose men to complain. Philippos Ioannou, a university professor, one of the Olympic judges, and a member of the antiathletic faction, led a movement to change the nature of the Olympic Games. "Some laboring men," he wrote contemptuously, had competed "scarcely pried away from their wage-earners' jobs, and, for the most part, for the money prize."[12] Even worse, I might inject, they had won. Future Olympics, Ioannou urged, should exclude the working class, even the general public, from eligibility. They should be restricted to "the educated youth": university and upper-school students from "the cultured class." The date, I repeat, was 1870. News of amateurism had traveled fast from London, both west and east.

Ioannou's party carried the day. Olympic funds paid for a corps of gymnastic teachers, headed by Ioannis Phokianos, a devotee of calisthenics who rather disliked competitive athletics, ancient or modern, and even some of the modern gymnastic events, such as the parallel bars. He produced Olympics in 1875. But they were a dismal failure beside the previous, 1870 edition. Money prizes were rewarded as before, the events were much the same, and the site was that same Panathenaic stadium in Athens. The contestants, the newspapers noted, were of "a much higher social class" than before. But neither the contestants nor the officials took the games seriously. Athletes did not come when their event was called. There was disorder on the field and in the crowd. Instead of Greek music, the band played polkas. In between events, the judges made long, boring speeches. The patient crowd grew impatient, and the games ended without the scheduled contests in the horizontal and parallel bars. The newspapers called the 1875 Olympics a clear failure. Phokianos resigned and left Athens in disgrace.

He returned fourteen years later to preside over one last Olympic disaster, again games for an elite (1889). This time, though, the spectators as well were of the elite, for Phokianos produced these games in an indoor gymnasium for a chosen few, away from the stadium and the public. First the Greek people, to whom Zappas had given the games, were forbidden to compete. Now they were not even allowed to watch. No doubt it was a good thing. For some reason the contestants, the "cultured youth" of Greece, suddenly ran amuck among the cultured but tightly packed spectators, and the games were stopped almost before they began. In short, the modern Greek Olympics had turned "amateur" and run aground.

The 1889 Games amounted to little or nothing. But history calls us back to those last Games in the Panthenaic stadium, the 1875 Olympics. They were fated for more than failure. In the stadium that day in 1875 sat a fateful figure, John Mahaffy—classical scholar and prolific author of books on Greece. He was Irish, but worshipped the English upper class. He contemned all else—the Irish, the working class, the French, the Germans, and particularly the Greeks. Even his supporters agree that he was a pretentious social snob. He disliked track and field athletics. They were not aristocratic enough. The track, he said, was no place for a "Gentleman." The only "proper" sports were cricket and fox-hunting with hounds.

The 1875 Greek Olympic Games were themselves bad enough. But Mahaffy wrote them up with brutal satire and derision in the 1875 *Macmillan's* magazine. "Were *we* to propose the resuscitation of the Olympic Games in the Panthenaic stadium, we should fear an accusation of absurdity. . . ." But "the burden of great names and of a noble past seems to sit lightly on the modern Greeks."[13]

Mahaffy knew nothing about the successful 1870 Games, nor that what he had seen in 1875 was a demonstration of upper-class athletics. He ridiculed the Greek Olympics for all the wrong reasons. There were as yet no stadia in Britain or America or anywhere else outside of Greece. Mahaffy had never seen one before. He found the basic stadium shape ludicrous, "like a huge oblong stewpot." He ridiculed the Greeks for reviving the discus throw, an impossible anachronism, he thought. "We English never throw the discus," he proudly observed. He thought the dogs which came on the field more interesting than the athletic events, and gave them equal space. And he ridiculed the coach, again for the wrong reason. "We could not help wishing," Mahaffy wrote, "that some slight flavour of English system had been known to him." Finally, Mahaffy said, "There were horse races, *monozogoi* and *dizygoi,* announced, but had to be postponed to another day." But Mahaffy should never have expected to see horse races that day. *Monozygon* and *dizygon* (Mahaffy could not spell in Greek) are the modern Greek words for horizontal bar and parallel bars, respectively. They have nothing to do with horse races.

Mahaffy's scholarship was no more accurate in other matters. And Mahaffy, it seems, is the one who invented the notion that the ancient Greeks were somehow *amateur* athletes. He soon followed his article in *Macmillan's* with a companion piece, this time on ancient Greek athletics.[14] The ancient Greeks, too, were inferior to the English. "The Eton and Harrow match at Lords," he wrote, "is a far more beautiful sight than [was] the wrestling or running at Olympia." But ancient Greek athletics had one saving grace: at first they were "amateur performances," "sport for sport's sake." Only later were they corrupted by the professional spirit.

There has never been any evidence for amateurism in ancient Greece, whether of the 1880 or the 1866 kind. All Greek athletes from the start collected as much prize money as they could win. The Greeks had no word or concept for "amateur." Furthermore, athletes from the working class participated from the start. The earliest Olympic victor, Koroibos, was reportedly a cook. Other early Olympic victories were won by an ordinary farm boy, a cowherd, and a young goatherd. Among his peers, Mahaffy's scholarship was infamous for its inaccuracy, but he said that he did not really care: "Works of genius" necessarily contained many little mistakes. Besides finding amateurs in Greece who rejected "the spirit of lucre," Mahaffy found another redeeming quality. The more intelligent Greeks, he claimed, viewed athletics with as much "highbred contempt" as he. "Athletic," he says, "was a rather low thing among the Greeks." Even in Pindar's time, "men began to think of *more serious* rivalries, and more exciting spectacles . . . than Olympia." I add emphasis to draw attention to the word "serious." Athletics, the amateur partisans tell us, are not a very serious activity.

Mahaffy's influence on classical scholarship was profound, and his influence on twentieth-century sports perhaps even more profound. In ancient Greece he saw a chance to belittle the French and the Germans, as well:

> The finest English schoolboy is not inferior to the best Greek types
> in real life. . . . The Greeks were like the French and the Germans,
> who always imagine that the games and sports will not prosper . . .
> without the supervision of a *Turnlehrer* [coach, or overseer]. . . . If
> the zealous and learned reformers who write books on the subject in
> modern Europe would take the trouble to come and see [English
> sport] for themselves, it might modify both their encomia on Greek
> training and their suggestions for their own countries.[15]

Mahaffy did not know that a zealous French reformer would actually
answer his call and come to view English sports with all the reverence and
awe that Mahaffy thought they deserved. But our stage is still not quite set
for the entrance of the French reformer, Baron de Coubertin, *renovateur* of
the modern Olympics.

As Coubertin visited England in 1883, to see English sports for himself, a real Englishman, Percy Gardner, read Mahaffy's piece on ancient
Greek athletics and then wrote his own version. He too was a classical
scholar. Gardner shared all of Mahaffy's aristocratic preferences, but not
his contempt for ancient Greece. The Greeks were as good as the English,
Gardner believed. Mahaffy founded the myth of Greek amateurism, but
he never idealized Greek athletics. It was Percy Gardner who created our
fully idealized picture of the ancient Greek amateur athlete, whose noble
world of amateur sport crumbled and collapsed at the advent of a creeping
and sordid professionalism. But Gardner's scholarship was no better then
Mahaffy's. His ancient Greek could be the Victorian amateur's equal for
only one reason. His ancient Greek *was* a Victorian amateur. All the best
Greeks, the Victorians had decided, were really nineteenth-century Eng-
lishmen. Sophocles was an "amateur" playwright, Thucydides an "amateur" historian. And an ancient Athenian, according to another
Englishman, would have felt at home with "the athletic grace" and "easy
condescension" of the gentleman students at Oxford and Cambridge.[16]
Now sixth- and fifth-century Greek bruisers such as Milo the wrestler
and Theogenes the boxer were to walk the High Street at Oxford, and to
stroll along the Cam.

Ancient Greek history needed to be rewritten to follow its English
prototype. With no relation whatsoever to the ancient evidence, Gardner
paints a vivid picture of what he calls "the rise and fall of Greek athletic
sports":

> The chapter is a short one. The bloom of all the promising institu-
> tions of Greece was short. Abuse soon succeeded use; excess
> supervened on moderation; and the same causes which had made
> the greatness of the people, in matters athletic as in other matters,
> also caused its decline and eclipse.[17]

In reality Greek athletics lasted more than eleven hundred years, hardly a short chapter. They went on for eight hundred years after their supposed "brief bloom" and "decline"—eight hundred years in which they somehow stayed alive in a state of "degradation" and degeneration. But "decline" means here simply the participation of the working class.

In the early days, Gardner writes, "when the Olympic festival was at its best," all the contestants were from the noble class. The aristocratic victor returned to his home city through a breach in the walls. (This claim is nonsense; the only Greek athlete to do that was the Roman emperor Nero.) In his Pindaric or Simonidean victory ode, this early aristocratic victor was sung by "the noblest born" of the city. The "proudest and wealthiest houses sought a marriage alliance with him." But "it was not long until evil days came"—the "degradation" of Greek athletics. By degrees the "professional element" came in among the competitors and the "gentlemanly spirit" went out. "The competitors ceased to be drawn from the better classes. . . . Olympic victory went more and more to the professional. . . . Surely we need not apply the lesson to English sports."[18]

Most of this comes directly from Mahaffy. But Gardner's term the "better classes" recalls Whitney and his concern for the "better element." So does Gardner's history of Greece. I certainly cannot find in the annals of Greece the "history" from which Gardner draws his lesson. But it is all right there in Whitney's *Sporting Pilgrimage.* Gardner's history of the brief "bloom" of Greek athletics is really nothing other than the history of Anglo-American sport from the 1860s to the 1890s, seen through the Gentleman Amateur's eye.

Despite a common cause and vocabulary, Gardner, the Oxford don, and Whitney, the American sportswriter, were worlds apart. It took a third element to unite their ideas into a successful institution. The catalyst was that idealistic Frenchman, who had the money, the ability, and the obsession to achieve what others could only dream. Amateurism had not, after all, shouted its last hurrah. I quote from the Frenchman, Baron Pierre de Coubertin:

> Games for the elite. An elite of contestants, few in number, but consisting of the champion athletes of the world; an elite of spectators, sophisticated people, diplomats, professors, generals, members of the institute. For these people, what could be more refined, more ravishing than a garden party at Dampierre?[19]

Here is more Coubertin, the conclusion of an article entitled "Why I revived the Olympic Games":

> Such is the . . . development which ought to take place in the . . . modern Olympic Games. . . . to exercise over the sports of the

future that necessary and beneficent influence which shall make them the means of bringing to perfection the strong and hopeful youth of our white race,[20] thus again helping towards the perfection of all human society.[21]

Those are surely games of the kind which Caspar Whitney had in mind.

Now enter Baron Pierre de Coubertin, born to great wealth and a family titled since 1477. He did not start out to revive Olympic Games but to rebuild the youth of his native France, which still reeled from losing another war to Germany. Unlike the rest of Mahaffy's "zealous and learned reformers" on the continent, Coubertin took "the trouble" to visit England in 1883 and see for himself the phenomenon of English amateur sports. He became a true believer, even experiencing a "vision" at the tomb of Thomas Arnold of Rugby. In France he began a campaign to reform French education, to introduce English-style athletics into French schools, and to form French amateur clubs after English models. He was following Mahaffy's prescription to the letter.

But he had little luck in a rather Anglophobic France. Athletics seemed ill-suited to Gallic refinement, and Coubertin's frequent praise of what he called "the Anglo-Saxon" race did not help his cause. He went to America in 1889, and England again in 1890. There he saw his first Olympic Games, or rather some traditional English village games called "Olympics" by their sponsor, Dr. W.P. Brookes of Shropshire. Two years later he staged the Jubilee of his faltering organization of French athletic clubs—not yet five years old at its Jubilee. But he had a surprise up his sleeve. A woman sang some Sophocles, Coubertin's friend Georges Bourdon read some translations of Pindar, and Coubertin blurted, "Let us reestablish the Olympic Games." But no one took him seriously. Mahaffy had already predicted the scenario. Absurd.

Coubertin, however, became obsessed with the idea of a grand international sporting festival. When the august name "Olympics" failed to excite support, he turned to the fetish of the aristocrats whom he regularly courted—"amateurism." In early 1894 amateur athletic clubs around the world received invitations to an "International Congress of Amateurs" to be held at the Sorbonne that summer. The stated aim of the congress was to consider "the principles which underlie the idea of amateur sports." Since the revised 1880 definition of "amateur" had led to many controversies, the congress would focus on questions of amateur eligibility. The invitation listed eight "points" for the meeting's agenda. The first seven of these items were indeed questions of amateur eligibility, such as: "Can a professional in one sport be amateur in another?" "Should the value of prizes be limited?" "Does betting on himself disqualify an amateur?" But buried at the end, literally last on the agenda, was a brief, innocuous-looking item awkwardly appended to the rest: "The possibility of reestablishing the Olympian Games. Under what conditions would it be feasible?" It was intended, Coubertin later confessed, to appear innocuous, lest it make his conference appear absurd and dissuade delegates from coming.

Yet when delegates arrived in Paris for the Congress of Amateurs, they found that their tickets read instead "Congress to Re-establish the Olympic Games." Minor item number eight had become major item number one. The questions of amateurism were quickly resolved. The strict 1880 definition would apply. No amateur can ever profit from athletics in any way. The English delegates in Paris lost their bid to restore the 1866 definition and define amateurism in terms of social class. A no-money rule would obviously limit those who could enter international competition anyway.

But amateurism was never Coubertin's main goal for the conference. He later said it was just a camouflage.[22] The delegates were wined, dined, and entertained lavishly—with refinement. Almost without noticing it, they found that they had voted to re-establish the Olympics, Games open only to amateurs. Coubertin had already formed an International Olympic Committee to administer the revival. Demetrios Vikelas, a Greek, was at its head, and Coubertin was the secretary. Others had come to haggle over definitions of "amateur." Vikelas, like Coubertin, had come to deal in modern Olympic Games, something which he, as a nineteenth-century Greek, already knew something about.

On the final day Vikelas made a surprise proposal, and Coubertin announced that the first of the revived Olympic Games would not take place in Paris in 1900 as he had already suggested in print. The Olympics could sprout up even sooner, and on their native soil. *Athens in 1896!* In a euphoric state Coubertin closed his speech. "We voted unanimously for the restoration of an idea that is two thousand years old. . . . I raise my glass to the Olympic idea which, like a ray of the all-powerful sun, has pierced the mists of the ages."

The course was clear. As Coubertin had used amateurism as a devious means to achieve his ends, he would now use the appealing aura of Greece the same way.

"The mists of the ages." Suddenly amateurism, now twenty-eight years old, had come of age—had aged beyond its fondest hopes. The legitimacy, the history, the priority which amateurism sorely lacked had been found in ancient Greece, in arcane, archaic texts that few could or cared to read. Some classical scholars were already allies. The hybrid seed which Mahaffy had planted and Gardner nurtured would now bloom as a lovely flower, no longer the conceit of a few second-rate academics. *Myth was now reality.* In two years the ancient Greek Victorian amateurs would perform once more and in their spiritual homeland. It was time for all good amateurs to come to the aid of their cause.

The American classicist Paul Shorey quickly adapted (some would say plagiarized) Gardner's Olympia chapter for an article in the Philadelphia *Forum*.[23] There he lectured the ancient Greek Victorians of Chicago, Boston, and Philadelphia on the "chief lessons" they had to learn from ancient Olympic history. *No money of any kind.* The place of the "amateur" athletes of Pindar's day, he sadly noted, was "usurped" by the later "professionals" whose commercial spirit caused the "degeneration" of Greek athletics. To demonstrate this lesson from Greek history, Shorey used a method already employed by Mahaffy and Gardner. He violently misdated pre-Pindaric, sixth-century B.C. evidence to the A.D. Roman empire, then used it to illustrate the very deterioration which he deplored. His argument is literally preposterous.

Whether Shorey's regurgitated Gardner helped to induce any Americans to go to Athens we shall never know. But the first International Olympic Games were held in Athens in 1896, as Coubertin hoped. There was no actual team from France or England. But some American college boys did come, a Hungarian team, and a German team for the gymnastic events. A few others wandered into Athens as tourists or loners, without national backing. Despite mediocre marks, the Games were a great success. But they were not wholly different from those successful 1870 Olympics of the modern Greeks. They were *international,* and that difference is crucial. And they did not officially offer money prizes, as before. But the events were much the same, and the site was the same Panathenaic Stadium in Athens. Indeed, many of the spectators were the same as those of 1870.

Most of the athletes—230 out of 311—were Greeks. Busy with other matters, Coubertin gave the Greeks little help in their preparations. Greeks provided the organization, the site—and all of the money. Coubertin could produce none. The expense of restoring the stadium (marble seats and all, as Zappas wished) had been immense. Since they already had a recent tradition of modern Olympic Games in that very stadium, it is no wonder that many Greeks saw these Games as another edition in their own continuing series, now expanded into an international athletic festival. Nor does it surprise that when Coubertin sought all the credit for the 1896 Games and the entire idea of an Olympic revival (asserting that he was "the sole author of the entire project"), the Greek press called him a "thief."

The Greeks tried hard before, during, and after the 1896 Games to keep future editions of the Olympics in Greece. The American athletes supported the Greek cause, for they and the Greeks had a reciprocal Olympic enthusiasm. That enthusiasm, with the attendance, is what made the Games a success. The Americans won the most first places; the Greeks won the most medals and the unofficial point count. Yet as "no-money" amateur Olympics touched their hallowed soil for the first time in

1896, the Greeks lost the Olympic Games themselves. Coubertin whisked the "official" Olympics away to Paris for 1900, never to return home again.

Coubertin's devotion to Greece was perhaps more theatrical than real. His heart is, in fact, entombed at Olympia, but he never cared much for the real Greece, ancient or modern. In 1896 he began to publish his own nonsense about the ancient Greek amateurs, idealized athletes who participated in an aristocratic monopoly founded on heredity and dedicated to sport for sport's sake.

> The young Greek [athlete] spent the eve before the contest in solitude and contemplation under the marble porticoes of the gymnasium at Olympia, situated a little off to the side, far from the temples and the noise. He was required to be irreproachable[24] personally *and by heredity,* without the slightest blemish either in his own life or *that of his ancestors. . . .* He received as recompense [for victory] a simple verdant branch—the symbol of *disinterestedness.* [25]

There is no history here, just pure fancy. Every sentence is full of errors. There was no gymnasium at Olympia at the time of which Coubertin speaks. There were no rules whatsoever about unblemished lives, let alone ancestors' unblemished lives and heredity (an athlete needed to be a free Greek, no more). There is no evidence that Greek athletes spent any time in solitude, or ever understood "disinterestedness." Coubertin's athlete is no ancient Greek at all.[26] But he is a model Victorian amateur, and these are the words the Whitneys and Gardners wished to hear. Soon the real Greeks, the modern Greeks, got embroiled in another war with Turkey. "So much for Greece," as the Baron said. Vikelas' term on the IOC ended that year.

Coubertin needed more IOC members, and Caspar Whitney found his place among the more refined elements. Refined indeed. Of Coubertin's last dozen appointees before Whitney, there were two barons, a duke, five counts, and the prince of Romania. But the 1900 Paris Olympics were a disaster; the athletes did not even know they were competing in something called "Olympics," and the facilities were deplorable. The 1904 Olympics in St. Louis were a failure as well. European athletes did not come. But there were competitions among pygmies, savages, and Indians. Coubertin did not even bother to attend.

The Greeks held by far the best Olympics to that date in 1906, calling them the "Second International Olympic Games." For it was easy to discount the 1900 and 1904 affairs. The 1906 Greek Olympics had truly international competition, the marks were outstanding, and attendance excellent. No one doubts their success. But Coubertin managed to write them off as "unofficial" and made plans for Olympics in England for 1908. The 1908 London Games were not much good either. Coubertin's expected "Anglo-Saxon Olympics" were nearly ruined as the Americans and the English tossed around charges of cheating and so on as if our Revolutionary War had never ended.

Into this milieu stepped E. N. Gardiner, another classical scholar of the second rank. Seldom has the work of one man so dominated a scholarly field. E. N. Gardiner's scholarship became *the* scholarship on Greek athletics. It is now spread throughout every book, handbook, article, almost every reference to our subject. Where he is not quoted directly, his sentences appear ghostlike, unattributed, barely paraphrased.

Gardiner made no pretense of disinterested research. His stated aim in his 1910 book on ancient athletics was to mold public opinion on contemporary athletic controversies.[27] His first chapter is laced throughout with attacks on the "evils" of professionalism, English or Greek; it teems with encomia of the Victorian amateur ideology. His historical analogies are incredibly inapt. Greek athletics, he suggests, like English athletics, began in the universities and public (i.e., private) schools. (There were no such things, of course, in early Greece.) Gardiner generally uses the 1866 definition of "amateur." The archaic Greek athletes were all "genuine amateurs," "men of position," drawn from the aristocracy. But they knew the 1880 AAA "no money" rule, as well.

The early fifth century, Pindar's time, was a high point: "the well-born youths and princes for whom Pindar sang were actuated by no mercenary motives, but by the pure love of physical effort and of competition which is natural to all healthy youth." But soon Greek athletics began to "decline" and to "degenerate." Before the end of the fifth century, Gardiner says, the "excessive prominence given to bodily excellence and athletic success" had produced specialization and professionalism. "Sport became more and more the monopoly of a class"—the lower class.[28]

Remarkable here is the notion that bodily excellence and success can become negative characteristics. To be good in athletics is good. To be very good in athletics is bad. This antiathletic bias leaps out on Gardiner's next page, where he turns away from the "object lesson" of ancient Greece and lectures his audience directly, like the chorus in a parabasis of Aristophanes:

> Sport has too often become an end in itself. The hero-worship of the athlete tempts men to devote to selfish amusement the best years of their lives, and to neglect the *true interests* of themselves and of their *country.* The evil is worse with us, because our games have no value as military training. . . . Still more grievous than this waste of time

and energy is the absorbing interest taken by the public in the athletic performances of others.[29]

Our foremost scholar on Greek athletics is telling us that to take athletics seriously—as the Greeks certainly did—is "evil." It is a "waste of time and energy." Antiathleticism was always at the heart of the amateur movement, and strongest in academe. Gardiner's sentences hark straight back to Mahaffy, who warned us that there were "more serious" rivalries than athletics, "higher pursuits"—namely, as Mahaffy said, war and the service of one's country.

The true author of amateurism was the British public school. It inculcated in its privileged pupils a rigid, often inhumane code of ethics.[30] Exalting nationalism over individual worth, the public school code was essentially warlike, for its goal was to prepare Victorian aristocrats for the defense of the British Empire. All else was secondary to that aim. Mingling the catch-words of amateur athletics with militarism, its ideology openly glorified war as it denigrated athletics to mere servant status—namely, as military training. What happened "on the playing fields of Eton" had value, at best, only as it affected "the battle of Waterloo." The adage, often attributed to the Duke of Wellington (died 1852), actually dates from 1889. The true date makes far better sense.

At worst, athletics in amateur ideology were a frivolous indulgence of man's baser, more brutish and physical side—something that exuberant young boys get out of their systems before settling down to serious pursuits, such as managing family affairs or entering government service, preferably in the military. Athletics should never absorb the interest of grown men, and athletic excellence should never be placed on a par with excellence in other fields. The antiathletic attitude of his amateur associates always nettled Coubertin, whose Gallic idealism told him that an athlete should hope to be the best. With penetrating insight, Coubertin identified the mediaeval origins of amateurism's antiathletic bias:

> The pedagogues are always restrained to teach *measure;* it is their instinct . . .—a systematic opposition coming from their contempt for physical exercise. It is the reaction of the early days of Christianity that always remains; it is the unconscious hatred of the flesh.[31]

Here Coubertin is a most accurate historian. Even Gardiner's objection to the public's interest "in the athletic performance of others" descends in a straight line from Tertullian, who warned his fellow Christians to stay away from all the games.[32]

But there were, Gardiner confessed, worse things than athletics. Professional athletes were far worse, and Gardiner set his face against all athletic money, ancient or modern: "When money enters into sport, corruption is sure to follow." "Professionalism," he said, "is the death of all true sport." Gardiner saw no distinction between money honestly won and bribes taken to throw a contest. It was all "evil," a word appearing on almost every other page in Gardiner's books.

Yet there was one thing worse than a professional athlete: namely, a *working-class* professional athlete. With typical chronological sleight-of-hand, Gardiner recounts the sins of creeping Greek professionalism in the period of decline. The two ancient Greek cities of Italy, Croton and Sybaris, Gardiner sadly reports, offered cash prizes to athletes. "The increase of rich prizes was soon to put the poor man on a level with the rich. . . . For this Sybaris and Croton were largely responsible. They thought to encourage athletics by offering large money prizes. In reality they killed the spirit of the sport." But "these evils did not yet exist in the sixth century."[33]

Gardiner's social argument here is very clear. Social equality in athletics is "evil." But his historical argument is downright false; like other arguments for the Greek athletic decline, it must violently misdate the evidence. For the stories about Sybaris and Croton which illustrate the decline—the "evils which did not yet exist in the sixth century"—actually refer to *sixth-century* Sybaris and Croton. This topsy-turvy methodology is in fact the basis of most modern athletic scholarship. Mahaffy, Percy Gardner, Paul Shorey, E. N. Gardiner, every one of them consistently misdates Greek evidence by centuries—anything to make it yield the necessary thesis: the thesis of a pristine period of pure aristocratic amateurism, that brief bloom before the working class brought on degeneration.

Soon after Gardiner's 1910 book was well digested by its many readers, James Thorpe set out for the 1912 Stockholm Olympics. When his medals were taken away and his name expunged from the record, his teammate and fellow competitor, Avery Brundage, moved up from sixth in the pentathlon to fifth. In the decathlon Brundage had finished sixteenth.[34] With Thorpe disqualified he moved up to fifteenth, which place he claimed until he died. Brundage soon began to climb the administrative ladder of the Olympics as well. A member of the United States Olympic Committee in 1924, he became president in 1929 and led our team to Los Angeles in 1932—and to Berlin in 1936, when his declining to condemn Hitler helped to get him appointed to the IOC.

After the war, in 1948, the Olympics resumed in London. People clamored again for Thorpe to get his medals back. Brundage explained once more. We moderns could not break so hallowed a tradition as amateurism, even if we wished it. Liberalism of the rules spells ruin. Look at the Greeks, Brundage said:

The ancient Olympic Games . . . were strictly amateur . . . and for many centuries, as long as they continued amateur, they grew in importance and significance. . . . Gradually, however, abuses and excesses developed. . . . What was originally fun, recreation, a diversion, and a pastime became a business. . . . The Games degenerated, lost their purity and high idealism, and were finally abolished. . . . sport must be for sport's sake.[35]

Brundage obviously availed himself well of the ammunition provided by the classical scholars. I do not bother to cite chapter and verse. Finally, Brundage even attributed "the decline and fall of the Greek Empire" to professionalism in athletics: "When they lost their idealism, became materialistic, and could not even play for fun, the Greek hegemony vanished." They took athletics seriously, and the nation crumbled.

Brundage, often called "the last of the amateurs," was forced to retire in 1972, sixty years after Stockholm. He seemed of another age. And he was. Three years later he died. One Olympiad after his death, the IOC quietly liberalized the Olympic eligibility rules. It has already removed the word "amateur"—although it still, to this very day, excludes "professionals." Two Olympiads after Brundage's death, in fall 1982, the IOC restored James Thorpe's victories to the Olympic record book. And in 1983 the Olympic officials returned Thorpe's medals, or rather replicas of them, to the great athlete—or rather to his survivors. Thorpe himself died decades ago, a medalless, penniless alcoholic in a California trailer home.

If the Olympics survive the boycotts, Los Angeles in 1984, and Seoul, Korea, in 1988, I suspect that all vestiges of amateurism will disappear from the rules. Amateurism would now seem, in the modern world, almost a dead issue. Sarajevo, however, along with the Gault and Nehemiah court cases, proves that we must studiously devise a means to bury it. And we should take time out to examine historically how it affected the lives of Thorpe, Paavo Nurmi, Lee Calhoun, Brian Oldfield, Mildred Didriksen, Bill Toomey, and countless other superior athletes who lost their amateur standing and the right to compete in the Olympics—sacrificed to a false Greek god.

And the irony is this: as modern athletics shake off the very real yoke of amateurism, the ancient Greeks, whom it never fit at all, are now stuck with it. The myth of Greek amateurism now permeates all studies of classical sport, even the most scholarly reference works. A decade ago no classicist had ever even questioned it. But the Dutch scholar H. W. Pleket recently denied that the Greeks ever knew Brundage-style amateurism, the no-money-of-any-kind-1880-rule kind of amateurism.[36]

Pleket observes almost in wonder that *all* ancient athletes of *all* periods accepted whatever prizes and money they could win. Yet he questions only the outer surface of the Greek amateur myth. He does not peer back into that myth's almost hidden origins in the nineteenth-century elitist movement. Pleket still believes that every archaic Greek athlete, through Pindar's time, was an aristocrat. Even Koroibos "the cook"—which Pleket manages to convert from an occupational title to a priestly one—was obviously, Pleket says, from "a prominent family." It never occurs to Pleket to question the main premise: namely, the assumption that all archaic Greek athletes were wealthy aristocrats of noble birth.

Subconsciously reverting to the original 1866 amateur/professional distinction, Pleket argues that archaic athletes, such as Milo and Theogenes cannot really be professional athletes, for they were aristocratic nobles, born to so much wealth that they did not need the large sums of money which they won. The real professionals, he says, come later, from the lower classes. I pass over the semantic sleight-of-hand here. For Pleket never questioned the handbooks which told him that such athletes as Theogenes and Milo were wealthy nobles. The handbooks have no ancient evidence for that belief. It is merely a conceit, started by a man who could not tell the difference between the parallel bars and a horse race.

Notes

1. Some of the material in this paper appears in another form in my book, *The Olympic Myth of Greek Amateur Athletics* (Chicago, 1984).

2. (Pierre de Coubertin), "Encore l'affaire Thorpe," *Revue Olympique* (April 1913) 58–59; quotation on p. 59. Translations are mine.

3. Long Island race: Jennie Holliman *American Sports (1795–1835)* (Philadelphia , 1975) 152–54. Scottish games: Gerald Redmond, *The Caledonian Games in Nineteenth-Century America* (Cranbury, N.J., 1971) esp. 15–41. England: Peter Bailey, *Leisure and Class in Victorian England* (London, 1978) passim.

4. H. F. Wilkinson, *The Athletic Almanack* (1868) quoted (more fully) in Bailey (supra n. 3) 131.

5. Caspar Whitney, *A Sporting Pilgrimage* (New York, 1895) 163.

6. A letter printed in the July 1872 *Sporting Gazette,* quoted in Bailey (supra n. 3) 136.

7. *Times* (London), 1880, quoted in Bailey (supra n. 3) 135.

8. John Lucas and Ronald Smith, *Saga of American Sport* (Philadelphia, 1978) 156.

9. Ibid. 157.

10. Whitney (supra n. 5) 166–67 (emphases added). For the other phrases see 287f., 280f., 285f., and 166.

11. John Ketseas, "A Restatement," *Bulletin du Comité International Olympique* 83 (1963) 5 (Zappas' letter is quoted often in Greek sources). The best source for the modern Greek Olympic revival begun by Zappas is I. Chrysafis, *Oi synchronoi diethneis Olympiakoi agones* (Athens, 1930). There is no trustworthy report on these Games outside the Greek language. Several French and American authors have indeed published brief remarks on the "Zappas Olympics" (G. Bourdon, J. Grombach, R. Mandell, J. Mac-Aloon). But their reports are wholly wrong—so factually inaccurate that their accounts bear no relation to the Games which actually took place (see Young [supra n. 1] 39–42). My own account here is founded on Chrysafis, on Athenian newspapers of the pertinent dates (1859–1889), and on a few other nineteenth-century Greek documents.

12. Quoted in Chrysafis (supra n. 11) 84–85 (the translations of Chrysafis' text are mine).

13. John P. Mahaffy, "The Olympic Games at Athens in 1875," *Macmillan's Magazine* 32 (1875) 324–27.

14. John P. Mahaffy, "Old Greek Athletics," *Macmillan's Magazine* 36 (1879) 61–69.

15. John P. Mahaffy, *Old Greek Education* (London and New York, 1881) 29–32.

16. Percy Gardner, "Olympia," in *New Chapters in Greek History* (London, 1892), (a chapter reprinted from an earlier journal article). Ancient Greeks as English Victorian amateurs: Richard Jenkyns, *The Victorians and Ancient Greece* (Oxford, 1980) 217, 221.

17. Gardner (supra n. 16) 266–67.

18. Ibid. 299–304.

19. Pierre de Coubertin, *Mémoires olympiques* (Lausanne, 1931) 50.

20. Generally, Coubertin himself was not a racist. But he apparently courted racists when he thought they would help his cause. When Coubertin wrote these words, Caspar Whitney was president of the United States Olympic Committee. Whitney was openly racist, claiming that "the negro" could never "compare favorably" with the white race in athletics (Whitney [supra n. 5] 164). At this time Coubertin desperately wanted the cooperation of Whitney's United States Olympic Committee for the impending Olympic Games (his "Anglo-Saxon Olympiad") to be held in London in 1908.

21. Pierre de Coubertin, "Why I Revived the Olympic Games," *Fortnightly Review* 90 (1908) 110–15 (115).

22. Thirty-seven years after the Congress Coubertin felt free to be candid: "Amateurism! Always amateurism. . . . Today I can venture a confession. I was never deeply interested in this question. I used it as a screen [*paravent*] to convoke the Congress that was to re-establish the Olympic Games. Seeing the importance which people in the sporting world accorded it, I displayed the requisite zeal. But it was zeal without real conviction." *Mémoires olympiques* (supra n. 19) 102.

23. Paul Shorey, "Can We Revive the Olympic Games?" *Forum* 19 (1895) 313–23.

24. Compare Coubertin's later argument—and its phraseology—in his case against James Thorpe (quoted at the beginning of this chapter). When Coubertin rejected Thorpe on the supposedly ancient principle of "irreproachability," he cited no ancient source (there is none). He was citing no one but himself.

25. Pierre de Coubertin, "La préface des jeux olympiques," *Cosmopolis* 2 (1896) 146–59; quotation on p. 153; emphases added.

26. Coubertin's expressed model for the ancient Greek athlete here was, of all things, the mediaeval knight.

27. E. Norman Gardiner, *Greek Athletic Sports and Festivals* (London, 1910); stated aim: vii.

28. Ibid.; "well-born youths" of Pindar: 110; "excessive prominence" and "monopoly of a class": 4.

29. Ibid. 6; emphases added.

30. The militaristic public school code, specifically designed for a special social class and national purpose of the last century, is now thoroughly repudiated in Britain. Ironically, its ideology and catch-phrases linger on in the International Olympic Movement, founded by Coubertin "in the cause of Peace," as a universal institution for the twentieth century.

31. Coubertin (supra n. 25) 154.

32. Tertullian *De Spect.*, chap. 3 and passim.

33. Gardiner (supra n. 27) 81–82. The phrases in my previous paragraph are gathered from pp. 6, 134 ibid., and E. N. Gardiner, *Athletics of the Ancient World* (Oxford, 1930; repr. Chicago, 1980) 99, 103.

34. "Realizing that he was far behind in points, Brundage dropped out rather than run the 1500-meter race, which he hated" (Allen Guttmann, *The Games Must Go On* [New York, 1984] 26). Postscript: No one in the Los Angeles stadium on August 5, 1984, will ever forget, in contrast, the Olympic marathon finish of Switzerland's Gabriela Andersen-Schiess.

35. Avery Brundage, "Why the Olympic Games?" in *Report of the United States Olympic Committee: Games of the XIVth Olympiad; London, England, 1948* (n.p., n.d.) 21–26.

36. H. W. Pleket, "Games, Prizes, Athletes and Ideology," *Arena* (now *Stadion*) 1 (1976) 49–89; and "Zur Soziologie des antiken Sports," *Mededelingen van het Nederlands Instituut te Rome,* n.s. 36 (1974) 56–87.

Part Three

Olympia and the Olympic Games

Alfred Mallwitz

Cult and Competition Locations at Olympia

6

The topic "Cult and Competition Locations at Olympia" reminds us that in antiquity the Olympic Games were a component of a sacred festival and not only an exhibition of athletic performances, as they are today.[1] That it was always so, in fact, in each of the 293 Olympiads until the year 394 A.D. is shown by the repetition of the festival for Zeus every four years. The ceremonies did evolve over the years; for example, the festival was originally limited to one day and in the early fifth century expanded to five. But always the focus was on the sacrifice at the great altar (fig. 6.1), where, in good times, perhaps more than one hundred cattle (i.e., a hecatomb) were slaughtered and their thighs burned to ashes.

Although there is clearly a connection between cult and games, the nature of that connection remains a puzzle. The arrangement of the sanctuary plainly shows one peculiarity: the complete separation of the area of cult and the area of the Games (fig. 6.3). In the west is the Altis, the center of the sanctuary, with its great altar to Zeus. Next to it is the Pelopion. To the north are the Temple of Hera and the Metroon, and on the slope of Mount Kronos is the row of treasuries. To the south is the large Temple of Zeus, surrounded by votive offerings and victory monuments. Finally, to the east, is the Echo Colonnade, one hundred meters long, defining the boundary between the sanctuary and the stadium. Of course, this is the plan from approximately the fourth century B.C., and in many ways it does not correspond to earlier plans.

Were areas of cult and competition always so separate? And if so, do the two really belong together from the beginning? Or was the cult the older of the two, and the *agon* added later? Could not, however, the *agon* be a remnant of an earlier cult, such as that of Pelops, which had been carried over into the worship of Zeus? This latter hypothesis has won considerable favor.[2] It is stated as an almost proven fact in a book on the history

Fig. 6.1.
The north of the sanctuary. Photo from the model E.
Mallwitz.

of the Olympic Games, where we read, "It is certain, however, that originally Pelops was venerated in Olympia," and also, "In historic times, after the Doric migration, not Pelops but Zeus is the Lord of Olympia."[3] According to these statements, the Games began in Mycenaean times.

I do not want to go into the theories behind these assertions, because I believe they only cloud our view of the real problems of the early Greek sanctuary. The case for an altogether Greek origin of Olympia can no longer rely on Furtwängler's conclusions from the findings of the first major excavations of 1875–1881.[4] He claimed that none of the finds could be dated before the eighth century. This was vehemently denied by Dörpfeld, although without adequate evidence.[5] His later excavations in the Altis led to the surprising discovery that there was, after all, prehistoric material in the sanctuary: apsidal houses (fig. 6.2) with pottery and implements from the first half of the second millennium.

On the other hand, when Buschor and Schweitzer examined the finds and the excavations, they determined that "a clear stratum indicating the transition from prehistoric to Greek culture was not found." In particular, they remarked, "not a single fragment of Mycenaean ware was found among the large mass of sherds."[6] This was in 1922.

It was not until near the end of his excavations in the years 1928–1929 that Dörpfeld thought he had found the missing Mycenaean link. In a curved row of stones far below the Pelopion, there seemed to be the remains of a Mycenaean tumulus, which he called Pelopion I (fig. 6.4).[7] He did not, however, have even the smallest Mycenaean sherd to back up his theory. In order to form a judgment on Dörpfeld's Pelopion I, let us go back and examine the history of our excavations.

The first archaeologists to uncover the center of the sanctuary, in the excavations of 1875–1881, hit upon a black stratum at great depth in the northern part of the Altis (fig. 6.2). It covered the area from the Pelopion into the west stylobate and the opisthodomos of the Temple of Hera, and a little farther still toward to the west. Eastward it stretched from the Temple of Hera to the Metroon and a little farther south. The hatched area on figure 6.2 indicates its approximate extent. Thousands of Geometric votive offerings were found in this black stratum.[8] Among the small bronzes were primarily horses, but also cattle and other animals, such as birds, deer, and even beetles.[9] There were not quite so many terracottas, and among them only a few feminine figures.[10] Another type of votive offering is also important: the two-horse chariot in both clay and bronze.[11]

Notably, not one of these finds was undamaged. This would not be unexpected of fragile terracottas, but it does cause one to take note with respect to the much sturdier bronzes. Even the larger, more elaborate, and especially sturdy tripod cauldrons were in a damaged condition,[12] as if they had been divided into their separate parts. In addition to ring-handles and their corresponding figural ornament, the excavators found

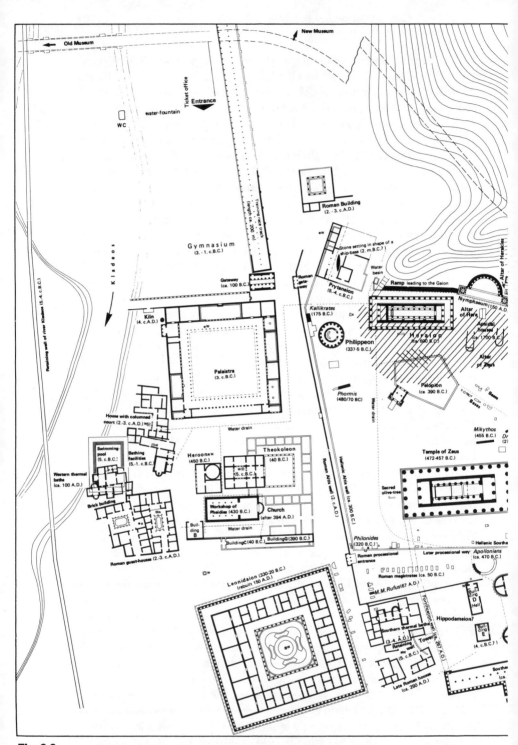

Fig. 6.2.
The sanctuary of Olympia

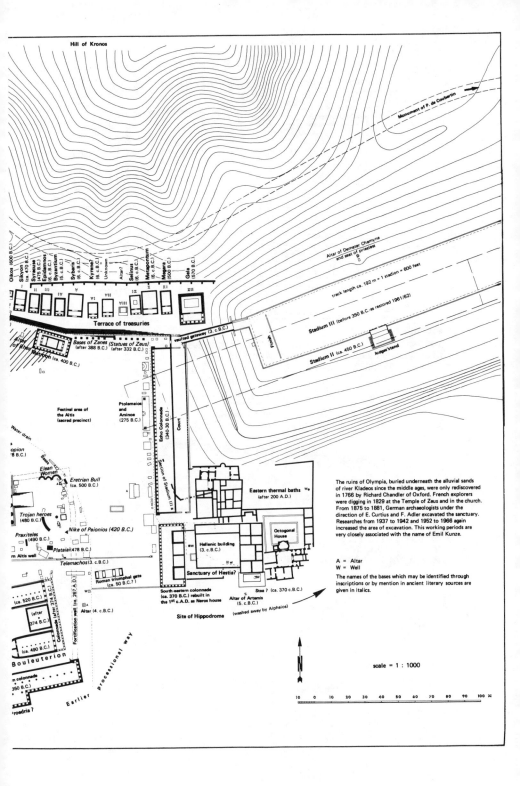

Hill of Kronos

Monument of P. de Coubertin

Oikos (600 B.C.)
Sikyon (ca. 470 B.C.)
Syracuse (475 B.C.)
Epidamnos (6. c.B.C.)
Byzantium (5. c.B.C.)
Sybaris (6. c.B.C.)
Kyrene (6. c.B.C.)
Unknown
Altar?
Selinus (6. c.B.C.)
Metapontum (6. c.B.C.)
Megara (500 B.C.)
Gela (570 B.C.)

Altar of Demeter Chamyne
and seat of priestess

track length ca. 192 m = 1 stadion = 600 feet

Terrace of treasuries

Stadium III (before 350 B.C.-as restored 1961/62)

vaulted gateway (3. c.B.C.)

Finish

Bases of Zanes (Statues of Zeus)
(after 388 B.C.)   (after 332 B.C.)

Stadium II (ca. 450 B.C.)

Judges' stand

Metroon (ca. 400 B.C.)

Festival area of
the Altis
(sacred precinct)

Ptolemaios
and
Arsinoe
(275 B.C.)

Echo-Colonnade
(340-30 B.C.)

Court

Water drain

...opion
...8 B.C.)

Elean
Women

Eretrian Bull
(ca. 500 B.C.)

Trojan heroes
(480 B.C.)

Praxiteles
(490 B.C.)

Nike of Paionios (420 B.C.)

Plataia (478 B.C.)

Telemachos (3. c.B.C.)

Altis wall

Roman triumphal gate
(ca. 50 B.C.?)

South-eastern colonnade
(ca. 370 B.C.) rebuilt in
the 1st c.A.D. as Neros house

ca. 520 B.C.)

(after
374 B.C.)

ca. 490 B.C.)

Bouleuterion

colonnade
350 B.C.)

roedria ?

Earlier

Processional way

Fortification wall (ca. 267 A.D.)

Altar (4. c.B.C.)

Sanctuary of Hestia?

Eastern thermal baths
(after 200 A.D.)

Octogonal
House

Hellenic building
(3. c.B.C.)

Stoe ? (ca. 370 c.B.C.)

Altar of Artemis
(5. c.B.C.)

Site of Hippodrome

(washed away by Alpheios)

The ruins of Olympia, buried underneath the alluvial sands
of river Kladeos since the middle ages, were only rediscovered
in 1766 by Richard Chandler of Oxford. French explorers
were digging in 1829 at the Temple of Zeus and in the church.
From 1875 to 1881, German archaeologists under the
direction of E. Curtius and F. Adler excavated the sanctuary.
Researches from 1937 to 1942 and 1952 to 1966 again
increased the area of excavation. This working periods are
very closely associated with the name of Emil Kunze.

A = Altar
W = Well

The names of the bases which may be identified through
inscriptions or by mention in ancient literary sources are
given in italics.

N

scale = 1 : 1000

10   0   10   20   30   40   50   60   70   80   90   100 M

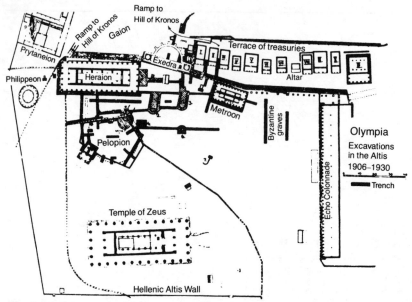

Fig. 6.3.
The excavations from W. Dörpfeld. From Mitteilungen des
Deutschen Archäologischen Instituts, Athenische
Abteilung, 92 (1977) 15, Abb. 3.

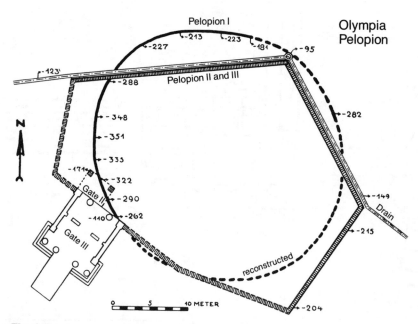

Fig. 6.4.
Pelopion I and II after W. Dörpfeld. Wilhelm Dörpfeld,
Alt-Olympia (Berlin, 1935) Vol. 1, p. 121, fig. 24.

cauldron legs, most of which had been forcibly broken into pieces. Since all of these finds lie in a stratum colored black with ash and charcoal and heaped with bones, the area must be a dump from one or several altars, a dump into which older, broken votive offerings were thrown as well.

The dispersal of this dump is therefore later than the bronzes found in it. I would like to discuss this point further. The density of the finds indicates that the center of the stratum was in a layer of stones between the Heraion and the Pelopion. These stones have been called an altar, perhaps even correctly.[13] In regard to this Furtwängler says: "Masses of primitive votive animals were found around the altar. Each stroke of the hoe brought forth several; in one week 700 bronze animals were collected here, and a great many terracotta animals as well."[14]

How is this stratum to be dated? Furtwängler writes: "One can distinguish two dark black strata of ashes here (that is, at the altar). The lower one, about twenty centimeters thick, lay next to the Pelopion about one meter under the water channel. . . . It contained an especially large amount of terracotta votives. Approximately thirty to forty-five centimeters higher, set apart by a layer of yellow sand, lay the second dark black stratum."[15] This sounds unambiguous, but is weakened by the following addition: "The two strata often approach each other and in places run together."[16] So a clear separation was not always possible.

Still, later excavations make it likely that Furtwängler was correct. Dörpfeld had earlier distinguished two strata under the third treasury, of which only the top one contained votive animals.[17] The same conclusion resulted from investigations in 1977 under the Treasury of the Sikyonians, about ten meters west of Dörpfeld's trench.[18] Here, too, we encountered, above prehistoric levels, a stratum with Geometric pottery, probably from the late eighth century. Only a few prehistoric sherds were mixed into it, and it contained no other votives. Clearly distinguishable from this stratum was the one above it, with Geometric and Subgeometric pottery as well as the usual votive offerings in the form of bronze animals and pieces of terracottas. According to the pottery, this stratum should be dated to the first quarter of the seventh century.[19] Since the area we examined was of a modest size, I am content for the time being to leave the dating at the first half of the seventh century.

Two findings of the early excavators prove to us that this upper stratum is more or less identical to the dump which was spread out over the northern part of the Altis. Not far from the altar and the Pelopion they found, inside a Geometric conical helmet, a broken bowl with the depiction of a lion.[20] In the same stratum, within the opisthodomos of the Heraion, they found a completely preserved hydria.[21] Gauer dates the bowl to the second quarter of the seventh century and the hydria somewhat earlier.[22] Diehl considers the hydria still Geometric,[23] and according to Heilmeyer it belongs in the second quarter of the seventh century.[24]

Heilmeyer wanted to date the stratum itself to the end of the seventh century and refers to aryballoi and alabastra that date from not before but long after 650 B.C.[25] According to their excavators, these pots also came from deep strata. But the excavators do not specify the black stratum, as they do for the bowl and the hydria.

The architectural findings from the Heraion argue independently against such a late dating. As I was able to show some time ago, the Temple of Hera was built all at once, from foundations to roof, without predecessors such as Dörpfeld had assumed.[26] The joined slabs that he found beneath the temple in Trench H 31 belong to an earlier installation of unknown purpose.[27] However one explains these slabs, they are later than the black stratum, which did not cover them, and earlier than the temple, which was built about 600 and employed the slabs in its foundation. If these slabs were installed after the dispersal of the ash stratum and before the erection of the temple, then one would not want to date them at the end of the seventh century, immediately before the temple was begun, but rather earlier. The black stratum is probably contemporary with an equally extensive leveled area in the east, for which debris from sacrifices and discarded votive offerings were used. We have studied this area thoroughly and dated it to the first half of the seventh century.[28] I will return to it in connection with the contest places.

Incidentally, it must be remembered that it is in this period that we encounter the first limestone sculpture in Olympia: a lion crouched down, ready to leap,[29] and a lion's paw with a human foot.[30] From the same time we have the remains of two tile roofs, which have come to light only in the most recent excavations. A fragment of one of them lay in Well 118, which was filled in about 650.[31] All of this indicates important changes in the sanctuary in the first half of the seventh century. More about this later.

Let us first turn to the Pelopion. What has been preserved for us and can be reconstructed is from the early fourth century B.C. (fig. 6.1).[32] Judging from its position in the sanctuary and its architectural elaborateness, the Pelopion must have been an important cult place. According to Pausanias, an ashlar wall enclosed a temenos where trees grew and statues stood, but he does not describe it more closely. He does not mention a hill or a grave. Pindar, in his first *Olympian Ode,* speaks of the *tymbos* (tomb) of Pelops, but he could be using poetic license. The wall, which is polygonal in plan (fig. 6.1), and the information of Pausanias cannot alone confirm the existence of a grave mound.

As I have implied, the black stratum was found inside as well as outside the Pelopion. The conclusion follows that there was no cult of Pelops in this place at the time the black stratum was dispersed. Unless it lay originally elsewhere, the cult must have come later. The late classical temenos presumably had a simpler, archaic predecessor of which hardly more than two ashlars in front of the Propylon remain (fig. 6.5).[33]

While investigating in the Pelopion, Dörpfeld, convinced of the great age of the cult of Pelops, came upon the row of stones which I have already mentioned. From the northeast corner of the Propylon it ran to the north with a slight curve and at considerable depth (fig. 6.5).[34] Dörpfeld recognized it as the remains of the border of a tumulus. Short probe trenches laid out in a circular pattern in order to prove the existence of a tymbos one hundred feet in diameter were only partly successful.[35] But Pelopion I was found. The link between the Greek and Middle Helladic periods was established by way of the Mycenaean Pelopion!

In my book *Olympia und seine Bauten* (134ff.), I tried to show that his Pelopion I never existed. I will repeat my arguments only briefly here. The curved row of stones, at its depth of –2.66 to –3.51 meters below the stylobate of the Temple of Zeus, is remarkably deep in comparison to the older (i.e., Middle Helladic) House 5 under the northeast corner of the more recent Pelopion, whose top edge is at –1.50 meters (fig. 6.6). Also, Wall *a*, which curves away above House 5, is only at a depth of –1.30 meters.[36] These differences of elevation make Dörpfeld's reconstruction of Pelopion I untenable (fig. 6.7). For the hill[37] does not rise above Wall *a* (at –1.30 meters), although the wall as well as House 5 would have to have been covered over by the hill in so far as the northern curve of the tymbos really did pass near the corner of the Pelopion (fig. 6.6). Thus, the possibility of a grave mound one hundred feet in diameter collapses. Even a narrower shape, such as an ellipse (which has been considered)[38] does not resolve the dilemma, because Wall *a,* reaching far to the southwest, would prevent the formation of a visible hill for the same reasons.

Finally, Dörpfeld had to admit he did not notice an associated surface either inside or outside the row of stones, nor did he notice any trace of the slope of the mound.[39] Nor did he find any pottery to support his assertion. Since there is also no evidence for the two succeeding mounds of figure 6.7, which the black stratum had already made nonexistent anyway, I do not know what, except perhaps myth, speaks for a Pelopion I. That the black stratum was dispersed without regard for a cult place supposedly in existence since Mycenaean times can only be understood in one way: there was no such cult place. What this row of stones actually was is hard to tell. It seems to me, with Dörpfeld's section before my eyes,[40] to be merely a work of nature, and far older than the Middle Helladic houses.

From this we can draw the following conclusion. According to Furtwängler, no finds from the sanctuary are older than the Geometric period. Furthermore, the first excavations and those of Dörpfeld which followed, and the painstaking investigation of the terrace of the treasuries, uncovered not even a hint of a Mycenaean level at any point in the large area of the northern Altis.[41] Therefore, while there are still parts of the Altis which, one might object, admit of further exploration, at the present

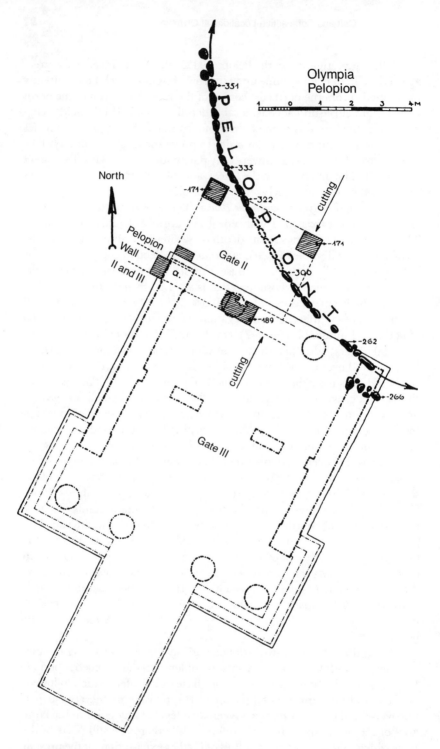

Fig. 6.5.
Pelopion Gate and the row of stones from Pelopion I.
Dörpfeld, p. 119, fig. 21.

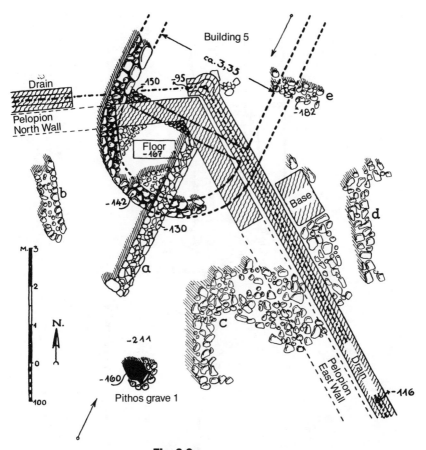

Fig. 6.6.
The Middle Helladic house 5 and Wall a beneath the northeast corner of Pelopion. Dörpfeld, *Alt-Olympia*, p. 76, fig. 3.

state of our knowledge it seems that there was no sanctuary, no place for
cult, in the Mycenaean era in the Altis. Heilmeyer's statement concerning
Geometric terracottas applies also to the whole sanctuary: "There is no
bridge in Olympia leading us back to Mycenaean times."[42] Thus, it
becomes unnecessary to go into all the theories deriving the Olympic
Games from the myth of Pelops.

It will be more fruitful to start with the idea that the cult of Zeus is the
first and oldest in this place. Insofar as Submycenaean needles and Protogeometric terracottas[43] can make a case, the cult is not older than the
tenth century B.C. Perhaps more extensive investigations of the lower
black stratum, which in any case is Geometric, will bring us a more exact
dating. For us the important point is that Olympia's sagas and myths
developed from Geometric times on, and not before.

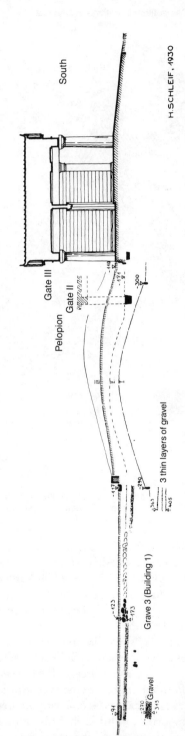

Fig. 6.7.
The reconstructed tumuli of Pelopion I/III. Dörpfeld, *Alt-Olympia*, Vol. 2, plate 5 (lower).

So the altar of Kronos on the top of the hill can only be decisively later, even though its priests were called *basilai,* or kings.[44] Kronos is the father of Zeus, and therefore he is worthy of veneration. Still more: in myth the two struggle for lordship; Zeus himself establishes contests among the gods. In these, Apollo defeats Hermes at the foot race and Ares at wrestling.[45] This story is meant to show that not men, but Zeus himself, greatest of the gods, established the Olympic Games. In antiquity, myth counted as a valid means of proof.

So it was that Rhea, the mother of Zeus, had her peripteral temple and cult in the Metroon. The purpose of her myth is quite transparent: to show that the *stadion* was the oldest and first *agon,* with its crowning of the victor by a wreath of olive branches. Rhea gave the child Zeus to the Kouretes of Mount Ida in Crete. Herakles was the eldest of these guardians of Zeus, and it was he who established the race and olive wreath for the victor.[46] According to Pindar, there could have been a kind of Idaean grotto in Olympia.[47] This feature Pausanias did not know and therefore left unmentioned. Perhaps Dörpfeld's identification of this grotto with the naïskos behind the Nymphaeum is correct.[48] The offering place in front of its entrance shows that it belongs among the oldest cult buildings in Olympia. The contemporary smaller round altar is built of the same buff lime marl as the walls of the oikos. It was later replaced by a somewhat larger round altar of shell limestone. This was succeeded, perhaps in the fourth century, by a rectangular altar oriented toward the east, and no longer bearing any relation to the oikos. Dörpfeld thought that this small building was covered over before the time of Pausanias. In view of the difference between the oikos' state of preservation and that of the treasuries, as well as the variance in elevations, this is probable.[49]

It has also been suggested that this construction is a double temple to Eileithyia and her son the serpent demon Sosipolis, but its small size alone makes this untenable.[50] Pausanias describes this cult at some length. It seems to belong to the older cults of Olympia, as does the cult of Aphrodite Ourania. The temple of Aphrodite Ourania, also on the slopes of Mount Kronos, was already in ruins when Pausanias saw it,[51] but sacrifices were still offered on its altars. Because these are cults of feminine deities, like Ge and Themis, who had altars on the Gaion,[52] the tendency has been to place their origins in great antiquity. We no longer see any reason to consider them so very ancient, although it seems that the cults on Mount Kronos, with the exception of Kronos' altar, belong among the early cults of Olympia.

Most of the more than seventy cults that Pausanias mentions have little or nothing to do with Zeus or the *agones.* Such a great number is typical of large sanctuaries and had increased steadily until the Roman Imperial period. The reasons for the addition of individual new altars can no longer be determined. Even Zeus had ten altars besides his great Altar,

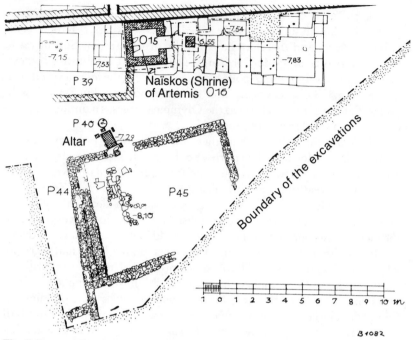

Fig. 6.8.
The sanctuary of Artemis in Olympia with the older (-7.29)
and the younger (-6.55) altar. After drawing by A. Mallwitz.

most of which must have stood close to the main one. We cannot discuss
them further here.[53]

It is regrettable that of all these altars only very few can be located.
Even the site of the great Altar of Zeus, of which not a stone remains in
situ, can only be approximated (fig. 6.2). Pausanias says that it lay the
same distance from the Pelopion as from the Heraion.[54] It is to be placed
south of the altar of Hera. Hera's altar lay on the eastern side of her temple
and Rhea's west of the Metroon. That of Herakles (the Cretan or the
Theban) must be the one west of the Treasury of the Sikyonians.[55] Finally,
the round altar on the grounds in front of the Bouleuterion belongs to
Zeus Horkios, to whom the Olympic oath was sworn.

An Artemis altar that Pausanias apparently saw toward the southeast
on his return from the hippodrome has become especially important for
us.[56] It is the only altar in Olympia whose sacrificial debris can be identified. The votives begin at the end of the sixth century. It was protected
from injury by wagons or animals by six curbstones, so it must have been
close to the road to the hippodrome (fig. 6.8). Among the votive offerings
were a kore of Sikyonian work and bronze and (one) gilded silver arm
bands,[57] in addition to a number of feminine protomes. The protomes

were later succeeded by Tanagra figurines and other statuettes, including a monkey with grapes.

The name of the goddess could not be surely determined from the kind of votives offered to her. Only the discovery of a later altar from the early Imperial period, farther north and at a higher elevation, furnished the name Artemis.[58] It was painted in red on the whitewashed sides of the blue-black limestone block that served as an altar. To this later altar belongs an oikos made of broken tile without mortar (Pausanias does not mention it). It probably once housed a small cult statue which earlier could have stood outside on the round base next to the older altar (fig. 6.8). To the left and right of the entrance to the oikos benches for offerings were built up. This leads us to conclude that in later times it was considered adequate to offer the goddess cakes, or perhaps fruit and grain.

None of the other cults have yet been identified. The round altar behind the Eretrian bull, surrounded by much later bases, remains as nameless as another, which must have once stood near the great Zeus Altar but was not found in situ. It could well have belonged to Zeus Herkeios, Zeus Keraunios, Zeus Kataibates, or others, all of whom had altars near the great one. This triglyph altar is at least datable because its outward curving base seems to be made of a capital and its triglyph frieze is certainly constructed out of a column drum from the Temple of Zeus. After the great earthquake of 373 B.C., the east façade of the temple down to the stylobate was removed and replaced with one of harder shell limestone.[59] The altar was fashioned out of the rubble. Soon after 373 it was dedicated to a new cult.

Among these places of cult, some of which were very modest, the Pelopion doubtless stood out in a special, prominent position, even though the sacrifice offered to its hero was only the blood of a black ram slaughtered in a pit.[60] The great significance of this hero is shown not only in the still-recognizable architectural elaborateness of his shrine, but also in the fact that early in the fifth century the east pediment of the Temple of Zeus took as its theme the chariot race between Pelops and Oinomaos.[61] Moreover, the *Odes* of Pindar witness to Pelops' importance at the same time.

If we decide that great antiquity of cult is not the explanation for Pelops' importance, we are led into another field of speculation. For discussion of this theme, one could ask if it must be true that the Eleans, migrating from Aetolia, necessarily brought Zeus to Olympia.[62] For the sanctuary lies in Pisa, and Pisa was a refuge for the older, Achaean population.[63] Now, the Achaeans were related to the Arcadians, and the shrine of Zeus Lykaios in the center of Arcadia was certainly not founded by Dorians passing through. Zeus could have already been venerated in a sanctuary by the Pisatans before the Eleans seized control of it. The following little-noticed statement of Ephorus also indicates this: "and the

Aetolians drove out the Epeians and took possession of the land; and they also assumed the superintendence, then in the hands of Achaeans, of the temple at Olympia" (translated by Horace L. Jones).[64] This can only mean the sanctuary, which previously belonged to the earlier inhabitants of Elis. And could it not be just these Achaenas who began the cult of Pelops in Geometric or later times?

The other question remaining to be discussed is whether the Games belonged to the cult from the beginning or were added later. We have already noticed the great distance between the Altar of Zeus and the stadium. Moreover, the Echo Colonnade, built in late Classical times, blocked entirely the view of the stadium from the sanctuary. It was not always so. Earlier explorations indicated that the Echo Colonnade and Stadium III with its western embankment were part of the same building program, which is why Stadium III was dated around 340 B.C.[65] But the original setting of the stadium was different. Before the colonnade was built, the back slope of the western embankment dropped toward the Altis and was held up by a terraced wall similar to the western part of the retaining wall for the treasuries.[66] A part of this wall is preserved under the foundation of the rear wall of the colonnade (fig. 6.9). So it is clear that the Echo Colonnade is the later building and the stadium older. Several things indicate that the stadium is part of the Early Classical building program to which the Temple of Zeus also belongs.[67] In any case the stadium is considerably earlier than the colonnade.[68] The slope falling toward the Altis (fig. 6.2) is, then, to be seen as the *theatron* that Xenophon mentions in connection with the battle between the Eleans and the Arcadians when they fought in the Altis during the one hundred and fourth Olympiad (364 B.C.).[69] According to Xenophon, the theatron was connected to a sanctuary of Hestia, which is still recognizable in the southeastern buildings and their courtyard.

This Classical Stadium III had a much more modest predecessor whose track was about eight meters narrower and whose finish line was about seventy-four meters further to the west than the later one (fig. 6.2).[70] Traces of it were found beneath the Echo Colonnade. To make room for the western embankment, which Stadium II lacked, Stadium III was located about seventy-five meters further east. Stadium II was open to the Altis; sanctuary and athletic field were not radically separated from each other. This stadium used to be considered Early Classical, but now it seems to be from the late sixth century. Its track evidently followed the course of a predecessor from the mid-sixth century that has left no traces, except for a few remains of a lower southern embankment,[71] since Track I was removed when the somewhat deeper track of Stadium II was laid.

This discovery was recognized and published by Kunze and Schleif. Countering it was Drees' conception, which placed the archaic Stadium I far to the west.[72] This plan proved especially attractive to other writers, though it lacked any sort of evidence. Not even a still older stadium—let

Fig. 6.9.
The rear wall of the Echo Colonnade crossing the retaining wall of the western embankment III.

us call it the "Urstadium"—is likely to have been so far west, because it would have come too close to the Metroon. The euthynteria of the Metroon, corresponding more or less to the ground level in that area, lies a good four meters higher than Track II, whose elevation can have differed only slightly from that of Track I.[73] One can reconstruct large areas of the early terrain, and it is clear that no stadium could have come as close to the Altar of Zeus as Drees' Track I would have.[74] There was not only a relatively steep incline from north to south, but also one from west to east.[75] The latter incline began to level off only where the Echo Colonnade later was. Thus, Kunze's conclusion that Tracks I and II followed nearly the same course is by far the more likely.

The plan of Drees gives us occasion to consider briefly the hippodrome, of which no trace has been found. No compelling reconstruction has yet been proposed,[76] although Pausanias discusses at great length this horse-racing track and its complicated starting mechanism in the form of a ship's prow. Drees' scheme completely contradicts the topography of Olympia and the information of Pausanias, who specifically states: "Passing out of and over the stadium at the point where the umpires [Hellanodikai] sit, you come to the place set apart for the horse-races and to the starting-place for the horses."[77] The starting place was evidently closed off on the west by the Stoa of Agnaptos. That means that the ship's prow, which was 400 feet or about 120 meters long, would have to be moved at least 200 meters east from where Drees put it, ending up about where he placed the finish line. The course of Drees' racetrack is also certainly wrong, because we are told that the side with the embankment for the spectators—that is, the southern side of the track—was no longer than the other. Because the northern side is bounded by a low hill, the racetrack must have extended out further, been closer to the edge of the hill to the north, and must have generally been longer. To visualize this let us look at the terrain east of the sanctuary more closely (fig. 6.10). The end of the hippodrome must have lain on the edge of the group of hills where Pausanias mentions the sanctuary of Demeter Chamyne.[78] Drees' reconstruction of the starting mechanism itself is surely wrong as well: the staggered arrangement of the boxes does not explain why the chariots started in a series from back to front.[79] In any case, there is little hope of finding anything of the hippodrome, as the mediaeval Alpheios probably destroyed it almost completely.

Let us return to the stadium, for which there are indications from as far back as the mid-sixth century. No one will doubt that the Games are older than this, even if one mistrusts the victor list of Hippias of Elis, which begins the reckoning of Olympic victors in 776 B.C.[80] We cannot go into the problematic aspects of this list here except to say that those who doubt its reliability concerning the earliest Games and the date 776 are probably right.[81]

The date is not made more secure by Heilmeyer's efforts to bring the development of Geometric statuettes into harmony with it.[82] The unspoken assumption of this attempt is that the cult of Zeus and the Games constituted a unit from the beginning. Actually, the thousands of artifacts from the ash strata in the north do not give us any information about the Games at all, not even the two-horse chariots, which would contradict the Olympic victor list at a decisive point: the list begins with the simple *stadion;* chariot races were not introduced until 680, in the twenty-fifth Olympiad, and then with four horses, not two.[83]

While the stone of Bybon and a broken jumping weight with an indecipherable inscription[84] were found inside the Pelopion at a deep level, we have absolutely no reliable evidence in the ash stratum itself for the Games. In the eastern part of the sanctuary this is not the case. There, quite aside from the stadium grounds, wells give witness to earlier contests.

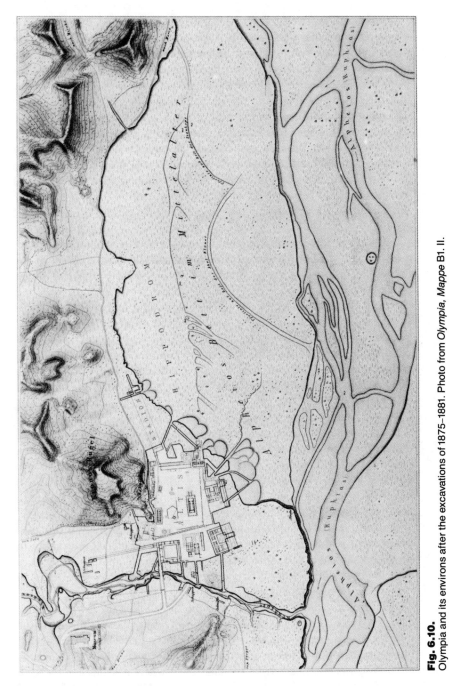

Fig. 6.10.
Olympia and its environs after the excavations of 1875–1881. Photo from *Olympia, Mappe* B1. II.

In all, about two hundred wells have been uncovered.[85] The forty-three in the northern embankment are outnumbered by four times that many south of the stadium. It is the location and dating of the wells which interest us the most. Although the northern part of the sanctuary has not been adequately examined, the excavations in the west and south show that there is no other area in Olympia with as many wells as the east.[86] This concentration is not accidental, nor can it be entirely explained by the nature of the soil. It is the proximity of the wells to the contest place that is decisive; they served as the source of water for the participants and spectators of the Games. The wells were nearly all simple, unreinforced earthen shafts, consequently usable for only a short time.[87] Additional evidence indicating the close connection of the wells to the Games is their fill, including the common pottery necessary for eating, drinking, and cooking.

On the northern embankment the most recent wells are from the second quarter of the fifth century; in the south, from the middle of the fourth.[88] The explanation for this is simple: in the early Classical period the slope of the Kronos hill was made into a spectator's embankment and could no longer be used for wells.[89] After the mid-fourth century, open stone channels supplied the sanctuary with water, and the digging of wells was no longer necessary.

Gauer's table of the common pottery from the wells of the northern embankment and the southeast[90] shows particularly clearly the connection between the festival of Zeus and the wells, although it does not include the post-1976 finds.[91] We can see the popularity of the Games increasing from one quarter of a century to the next by the growing number of wells. Although such statistics can easily be misleading, it is not by coincidence that in the early seventh century there were three wells and in the first quarter of the fifth century there were twenty-one. Around and shortly after the Persian Wars is the time when work on the Temple of Zeus was begun and the synoecism of Elis and probably the large expansion of Stadium III took place. This quarter-century is rightly seen as the heyday of the sanctuary. The subsequent decline from that high point is reflected in our table, which shows the number of wells decreasing. Remarkably, in the second quarter of the fifth century there were only half as many wells as in the first. This oddity is only partly explained by the construction of the northern embankment.[92]

The earliest limit for the date of the wells is the turn of the eighth century. Even though excavations since Gauer's have increased the number of early wells from three to nine, none from the Geometric period has yet been found. One might try to find early wells elsewhere, but the attempt seems pointless within the sanctuary, where it seems to have been forbidden to dig wells. Those in the east stop within the Echo Colonnade. Likewise, the wells in the south and west, stone-lined or unfortified, are all outside the Altis. And in the north, still not adequately explored for this purpose, so far only one well has been found, in the west in front of the Prytaneion. Even the Prytaneion had no well of its own inside, though it required a great amount of water to serve guests and victors. Why the Altis was kept free of wells when it would have needed a considerable quantity of water for a multitude of uses remains obscure. Therefore we cannot eliminate the possibility that there are Geometric wells in the north still to be found. It is unlikely, however, that there will be many of them, because the earliest contests certainly did not take place there.

Let us work with the idea that the Urstadium at all times lay in the east. The morphology of the terrain makes this the most plausible hypothesis, but that is not our only evidence. As the comprehensive plan shows, wells are lacking in the area of the running track and the southern embankment (fig. 6.11). This is not the chance result of a poorly managed excavation. For the track I can stand witness, because it was under my supervision in 1961–1962 that its entire surface was excavated.[93] We went down a minimum of half a meter in order to lay a concrete slab to expedite drainage to the south. It is utterly impossible that we could have missed any wells, whose fill always differs so obviously in color and consistency from the surrounding undisturbed earth. The southern embankment was excavated after 1938 at a time when one did not yet recognize wells as such, but called them *bothroi*. Since, however, the excavators dug all the way down to virgin soil, it would have been hard to overlook any wells.[94] The position of the wells, then, indicates that the oldest setting for the contests, the Urstadium, must have lain where Stadium I and its successors have left traces since the mid-sixth century.

So we see that the center of cult and the setting of the Games were already as far apart at the beginning of the seventh century as they were later. If the Games originated well before this date, even as early as 776, the year suggested by Hippias' list of Olympic victors, the spatial separation would hardly have changed. As already mentioned with regard to Drees' Stadium I, the terrain does not allow for any change. The still-considerable distance of one hundred meters leads us to ask if cult and Games were established at the same time or if cult is not the older of the two.

Let us leave behind all the traditions, especially the questionable victor list, and restrict ourselves to conclusions that can be drawn from archaeological findings. Then we cannot doubt that in Olympia the Games did not begin until about 700, but that the cult is considerably older, as shown by the finds dating back to the Protogeometric period.

Those who still insist that the Games began earlier must interpret the well statistics as indicating only an increase in the popularity of the Games. This view would agree well with the victor list. According to it, the pentathlon and wrestling were added to the three older contests in

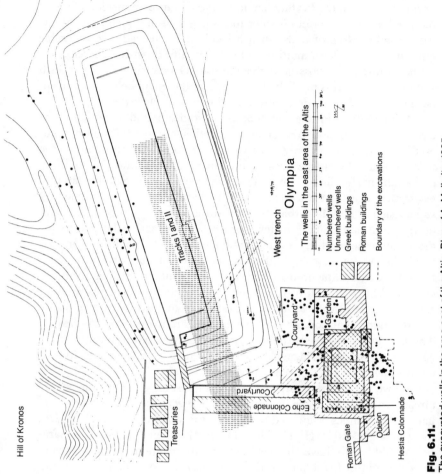

Fig. 6.11.
The excavated wells in the area east of the Altis. Plan of A. Mallwitz; 1985.
Courtesy of Deutsches Archaeologisches Institut.

Hill of Kronos

Treasuries

Tracks I and II

West trench

Olympia
The wells in the east area of the Altis

• Numbered wells
· Unnumbered wells

Greek buildings

Roman buildings

--- Boundary of the excavations

Courtyard

Garden

Courtyard

Echo Colonnade

Roman Gate

Odeion

Hestia Colonnade

708, during the eighteenth Olympiad; in 688, during the twenty-third Olympiad, boxing was added; and in 680, during the twenty-fifth Olympiad, the most fascinating of all the contests began, the four-horse chariot race. On the other hand, this late introduction of chariot racing is one of the arguments used against the veracity of the victor list, especially with reference to the much older votives of two-horse chariots. Still, we cannot dismiss the traditional order of the establishment of the various contests, all the more since the evidence from the wells gives credence to them.

Yet there is no reason to accept the supposition of the Olympic chronology that from 776 on the Games occurred every four years. Considering the importance which Olympia enjoyed already in the Geometric period, in view of the wealth of votives from that time, it is improbable that for the sixty-eight years before the pentathlon and wrestling were added there were only three types of foot race.[95] The interval between the early Olympiads must have been shorter, probably only one year. It is unlikely that the change to a quadrennial cycle was exclusively of a religious nature. There could have been a prosaic reason as well. For example, the organization of a track meet is relatively uncomplicated, whereas that of a chariot race is much more difficult and elaborate. Horses and chariots have to be brought to Olympia from great distances and then returned to their homes. It is hard to believe that many would be willing to do that every year. A longer time span between races would create better conditions and probably also greater incentive. With this in mind it seems possible that the change from yearly to quadrennial games occurred after the chariot race was introduced in the twenty-fifth Olympiad.

If this is true, then the beginning of the Games and the victor list lay not ninety-six years before (that is, in 776 B.C.), but only twenty-four. This brings us to the year 704, a date in better harmony with the beginning of the wells at Olympia. Now, I am not trying to present these calculations as certainties; they indicate only a possibility which does not go beyond the archaeological data.

We can summarize our discussion on this topic in the following way: the installation of the wells that bear witness to the Games predates the destruction of early votive gifts and the dispersal of the altar debris by only an inconsequentially short period of time. Both occurred in the first half of the seventh century. Therefore one could see a common cause for both.

In this connection I must add that the dispersal of sacrificial debris seems to be by no means limited to the region of the altar. Also in the east there was a natural depression, perhaps a type of *revma*, where altar debris had been dumped. This depression begins in the southern part of the Echo Colonnade and was used a few years before for Wells 98, 99, 100, and 101, which are all from the early seventh century. The depression stretches to the east across the courtyard of the Eastern Baths. It must have been a prominent aspect of the terrain for a long time and certainly even determined the placement of the Urstadium, built to the north of it. The later Stadia II and III had their drainage ditches directed into the depression.[96] It later served as the northern boundary of the buildings lying farther south. The sanctuary of Hestia with its colonnade, the earlier so-called Southeastern Building, and to the east the so-called Hellenic Building,[97] perhaps only slightly later, all avoid the depression in the same way. The House of Nero retains nearly all the same boundaries as its two predecessors. Not until the third century A.D. is the depression built over by the Eastern Baths where its northern extent cuts into the southern embankment of the stadium. Still, probably because the fill of the depression always remained unsuitable for building upon, the area was used for the courtyard. The actual rooms of the baths were built on better land to the south.[98] We have two meters' depth of sacrificial debris here to thank for a series of beautiful bronzes, including imported pieces: shields and bridle attachments from Italy, and from the east a Phrygian bowl and a shield from a northern Syrian workshop.

The debris shows that clean-up efforts extended over a large area and bears witness to the thorough, even radical, nature of the clearing-away. We are led to ask if the change in the sanctuary indicated by the quantity of debris can be attributed to events that have been preserved in the literary tradition for the first half of the seventh century. I am thinking of Pheidon, king or tyrant of Argos. According to Herodotus and Ephorus, he invaded Olympia and gave control of the Olympic Games, which the Eleans had previously held, to the Pisatans.[99] One would like to attribute the introduction of four-horse chariot races to Pheidon. The present view that Pheidon reorganized the Games not in the eighth Olympiad, as Pausanias states, but rather in the twenty-eighth of 668 B.C. fits this hypothesis.[100] This date also corresponds with both the report of Julius Africanus that the Pisatans controlled Olympia from the thirtieth to the fifty-second Olympiad (i.e., from 660 on) and the dating of the black stratum in the north of the Altis. One cannot resist the temptation to link Pheidon's invasion, the takeover of Olympia by the Pisatans, and the destruction stratum in a meaningful way.

The black stratum is hardly to be conceived of as the result of the desolation of battle. It is better understood as a rearrangement of the earlier altar area, which then gives us a comprehensible justification for the ash stratum. It would not have been a matter only of replacing the Altar of Zeus, but rather of satisfying new religious requirements, such as the veneration of Hera and Pelops would demand. Of course, Hera did not receive her temple and altar until the end of the seventh century.[101] Still, the installation with the jointed slabs was already in position when Hera's temple was built, and could have had something to do with her cult. A more fundamental change is indicated by the oldest limestone sculpture found nearby. That Pheidon brought the cult of Hera to Olympia has already been suggested and taken by itself is easily comprehensible, considering the great veneration which Hera enjoyed in Argos. It is more difficult to find an explanation for the cult of Pelops.

The myth of Pelops was at home in the Eastern Peloponnese, including the Argolid.[102] Furthermore, and unlike the myth of Herakles, it concerned a figure of the Achaean mythic cycle that could very well have been recognized by the Pisatans from antiquity.[103] But that would probably be insufficient reason to bring to Olympia this mythical figure. Rather, one would like to understand Pelops as an antagonist to Herakles in a mythological and political sense, against the background of the rivalry between Elis and Pisa. Indeed, Herakles emerges in the foundation legend of Olympia much more clearly, corresponding to the dominance of Elis and its claim to control Olympia.[104] Pelops' advantage, so to speak, seems to consist only in his greater "age."[105] Yet here also we must let these intimations be, acknowledging the thoroughly hypothetical character of my suggestions.

If we can understand the new arrangement of the place of cult in this way, then the new position of the great Altar of Zeus is more comprehensible. It was, so to speak, moved out of the middle of the ash stratum to its eastern edge. The altar faced east onto a broad free area which divided the place of sacrifice from the place of the Games. Here the participants at the festival congregated in order to attend the sacrifice at the altar while looking westward. At this early time they had only to turn to the east in order to see the place of the Games. The basic arrangement of space in the Altis did not undergo any more changes. The open area for the gathering of participants was only slightly diminished, by the Metroon at the edge of the treasuries' terrace wall, for example, or by the line of honorary monuments in front of the Echo Colonnade. The latter itself is to be understood as a substitute for the lost slope of the western embankment, the theatron. The advantage of it was to offer shade during the hot season when the Olympics took place.

In conclusion, let me only mention that according to the picture of the early sanctuary which I have developed here, the multitude of dedications of bronze and terracotta statues ceases at about the time that the athletic contests become a part of the cult.[106] This change, which needs to be further explored, has a somehow congenial aspect. It tempts us to explain the introduction of the *agon* in terms of the relationship that people of that time had with their gods, and not as a mechanical continuation of funeral games from dimmest antiquity, games whose original purpose was so ancient that with the change from hero to god it was forgotten.[107]

Notes

1. This contribution is to be regarded as an attempt to square new results of recent excavations with the contradictory literary tradition of Olympia. It is obvious that this theme could not be discussed here at full length. Most of it is only intimated and demands a comprehensive discussion, which I hope to give in *OlBer* XI (in preparation). Thus, my annotations give only selected references.

2. First uttered by A. Körte, "Die Entstehung der Olympionikenlisten," *Hermes* 39 (1904) 227; further, L. Ziehen, s.v. Olympia, *RE* 17.2 (1937) 2521; 18.1 (1939) 1, 70; H.-V. Herrmann, "Pelops in Olympia," in *Stele: Tomos eis mnemen tou Nikolaou Kontoleontos* (Athens, 1980) 59–74.

3. H. Bengtson, *Die olympischen Spiele in der Antike* (Zurich, 1972) 7.

4. A. Furtwängler, *Die Bronzefunde aus Olympia und deren kunstgeschichtliche Bedeutung, Abh Berl* (1879) 104 = J. Sieveking and L. Curtius, eds., *Kleine Schriften* (Munich, 1912) vol. 1, 339.

5. W. Dörpfeld, "Das Alter des Heiligtums von Olympia," *AM* 31 (1906) 205–218; in greater detail and collected: idem, *Alt-Olympia: Untersuchungen und Ausgrabungen,* 2 vols. (Berlin, 1935), hereafter cited as *AO.*

6. E. Buschor and B. Schweitzer, "Einzelfunde in Olympia 1922," *AM* 47 (1922) 48.

7. Dörpfeld, *AO* (supra n. 5) 118ff., fig. 24, here fig. 6.4

8. A. Furtwängler, *Olympia IV: Die Bronzen und die übrigen Kleinfunde* (Berlin, 1890) 28, pls. 10–34.

9. Ibid. 28ff., pls. 10–14; W. D. Heilmeyer, *Frühe Olympische Bronzefiguren: Die Tiervotive, OlForsch* XII (1979)

10. Furtwängler (supra n. 8) 43ff., pl. 17; W. D. Heilmeyer, *Frühe Olympische Tonfiguren, OlForsch* VII (1972) passim.

11. Furtwängler (supra n. 8) 39ff., pls. 15–17; W. D. Heilmeyer, "Wagenvotive," *OlBer* X (1966–1976) 59ff.

12. Furtwängler (supra n. 8) 72ff., pls. 27–33; F. Willemsen, *Dreifusskessel von Olympia, OlForsch* III (1957); M. Maass, *Die Geometrischen Dreifüsse von Olympia, OlForsch* X (1978) e.g., pls. 1, 3, 5.

13. Although there was found a hand-made jug in a bigger pithos (Furtwängler [supra n. 8] 198, pls. 69, 1203), later correctly recognized by Dörpfeld as a Middle Helladic grave of a child (*AO* [supra n. 5] 96, figs. 18, 19). This contradictory finding remained without explanation; see A. Mallwitz, *Olympia und seine Bauten* (Munich, 1972) (hereafter cited as Mallwitz, *Olympia*) 87.

14. Furtwängler (supra n. 8) 2.

15. Ibid.

16. Ibid.

17. *AO* (supra n. 5) pl. 8.

18. This research was carried out by Jürgen Schilbach in connection with the *anastilosis* of the western part of the terrace wall. The *anastilosis* is published in K. Herrmann, A. Mallwitz, and H. van de Löcht, "Bericht über die Restaurierungsarbeiten in Olympia," *AA* (1980) 361ff.

19. Cf. J. Schilbach, "Untersuchung der Schatzhausterrasse südlich des Schatzhauses der Sikyonier in Olympia," *AA* (1984) 225–36.

20. Furtwängler (supra n. 8) 200, pls. 69, 1296; W. Gauer, *Die Tongefässe aus den Brunnen unterm Stadion-Nordwall und im Südost-gebiet, OlForsch* VIII (1975) pls. 32, 3.

21. Fürtwangler (supra n. 8) pls. 69, 1287.

22. W. Gauer, (supra n. 20) 168.

23. E. Diehl, *Die Hydria: Formgeschichte und Verwendung im Kult des Altertums* (Mainz, 1964) 52.

24. Heilmeyer (supra n. 10) 4.

25. Ibid. 5; idem (supra n. 9) 20.

26. A. Mallwitz, "Das Heraion von Olympia und seine Vorgänger," *JdI* 81 (1966) 310–76.

27. *AO* (supra n. 5) pl. 13. Newly debated by me in (supra n. 26) 340f.

28. To be published by Schilbach in *OlBer* XI.

29. G. Treu, *Olympia* III: *Die Bildwerke in Stein und Thon* (Berlin, 1894–1897) 26, pls. 5, 1.2; A. Mallwitz and H.-V. Herrmann, eds., *Die Funde aus Olympia* (Berlin, 1980) pl. 93.

30. W. Dörpfeld, *AM* 31 (1906) 210, suppl., Mallwitz, *Olympia* 88, figs. 75, 76.

31. To be discussed in greater detail in *OlBer* XI.

32. F. Adler, W. Dörpfeld, et al., *Olympia* II: *Die Baudenkmaler* (Berlin, 1892–1896) 56, 73, pl. 42; Mallwitz, *Olympia* (supra n. 13) 133ff.

33. *AO* (supra n. 5) 118, fig. 21, here fig. 6.5.

34. Ibid. 119f.

35. Ibid. 120, figs. 23, 24.

36. Ibid. 76, fig. 3, here fig. 6.6.

37. Ibid. 77, fig. 4, pl. 5 below, here fig. 6.7.

38. Herrmann (supra n. 2) 67.

39. *AO* (supra n. 5) 121.

40. Ibid. 80, fig. 6.

41. This does not mean that no Mycenaean sherds have been found in Olympia (see H.-V. Herrmann, "Zur ältesten Geschichte von Olympia," *AM* 77 [1962] 13ff.). But they all come from alluvial strata and not from a Mycenaean level.

42. Heilmeyer (supra n. 10) 8.

43. H. Philipp, *Bronzeschmuck aus Olympia, OlForsch* XIII (1981) 34, pl. 1.1; 26, pls. 1, 2; Heilmeyer, (supra n. 10) 11, pls. 2, 3.

44. Pausanias 6.20.1; see *AO* (supra n. 5) 63ff.; Herrmann (supra n. 41) 3, 26ff.; R. Hampe, Review of E. Kunze et al., *VII Bericht über die Ausgrabungen in Olympia* (Berlin, 1961), *Gymnasium* 72 (1965) 79ff.

45. Pausanias 5.7.10.

46. Pausanias 5.7.6–7.

47. Pindar *Ol.* 5.17f.

48. *AO* (supra n. 5) 106ff., pl. 7. Against it: R. Hampe, " 'Idaeische Grotte' in Olympia?" in G. E. Mylonas, ed., *Studies Presented to David Moore Robinson,* vol. I (St. Louis, 1951) 335ff., and Herrmann (supra n. 41) 8, 10, n. 29.

49. Mallwitz, *Olympia* (supra n. 13) 155ff.

50. Affirmative, Herrmann (supra n. 41) 6f., fig. 1.

51. Pausanias 6.20.6ff.

52 Pausanias 5.14.10.

53 All cults are mentioned by L. Ziehen, s.v. Olympia (Kulte), *RE* 18.1 (supra n. 2) 48–71.

54. Pausanias 5.13.8.

55. Pausanias 5.14.9.

56. Pausanias 5.5.6.

57. Philipp (supra n. 43) 242ff., pl. 54.16.

58. E. Kunze, *AD Chronika* 18 (1963) 107f., pl. 142a, b; Mallwitz, *Olympia* (supra n. 13) 200ff., figs. 160, 167.

59. A. Mallwitz, "Neue Forschungen in Olympia (Theater und Hestiaheiligtum in der Altis)," *Gymnasium* 88 (1981) 108ff.

60. Pausanias 5.13.2.

61. See Herrmann in Mallwitz and Herrmann (supra n. 29) 161ff.; P. Grunauer, "Zur Ostansicht des Zeustempels," *OlBer* X (1966–76) 256ff.

62. Still E. Curtius (*Olympia* I [Berlin, 1897] 16ff.) and Dörpfeld (*AO* [supra n. 5] 69) are of the opinion that the sanctuary of Zeus goes back to Mycenaean times—that is, that Zeus is an Achaean deity. E. N. Gardiner, *Olympia: Its History and Remains* (Oxford, 1925) 48, saw certain relations between Olympia and Dodona. H.-V. Herrmann, *Olympia: Heiligtum und Wettkampfstätte* (Munich, 1972) 36; idem, "Olympia und seine Spiele im Wandel der Zeiten," *Gymnasium* 80 (1973) 180, and many other authors regard Zeus as a Dorian deity who came to Olympia with the Aetolians = Dorians.

63. See Herrmann, *Olympia* (supra n. 62) 43, n. 135, with bibliography.

64. Strabo 8.357 = *FGrHist* 70.115.

65. E. Kunze and H. Schleif, "Ost-Altismauer und Echohalle," *OlBer* II (1937–1938) 45ff.; "Das Stadion," ibid. III (1938–1939) 17ff.; V (1941–1942, 1952) 25ff.

66. W. Koenigs, "Stadion III und Echohalle," *OlBer* X (1966–1976) 353ff., fig. 112, pls. 39, 40.

67. To this result led the recent excavations in the southeast area of the sanctuary. More about this subject in *OlBer* XI.

68. Mallwitz, "Das Stadion," *OlBer* VIII (1958–1962) 59f.

69. Mallwitz (supra n. 59) 98ff.

70. E. Kunze, "Das Stadion," *OlBer* V (1941–1942, 1952) 12ff., pls. 5, 6.

71. E. Kunze and H. Schleif, "Das Stadion," *OlBer* II (1937–1938) 5ff., 20ff.; III (1938–1939) 5ff., 19ff.; V (1941–1942, 1952) 11f., pl. 2.

72. L. Drees, *Olympia: Götter, Künstler und Athleten* (Stuttgart, 1967) fly-leaf.

73. According to *OlBer* V (1941–1942, 1952) pl. 2, the difference between Tracks I and II (−4.00) must be less than 50 centimeters, and probably not more than 20 centimeters (−3.80).

74. The difference between the assumed level of Track I (−3.80) and the euthynteria of the Metroon (+ 1.07) amounts to nearly five meters!

75. This incline can be recognized by the declivity from the Metroon to the northwest corner of the Echo Colonnade (−325 euthynteria), which was necessary to get a plain level for the colonnade.

76. See H. Hitzig and H. Blümner, eds., *Pausaniae Graeciae descriptio* (Leipzig, 1896; repr. Hildesheim, Zurich, New York, 1984) vol. 2, pl. 6.

77. Pausanias 6.20.10.

78. Pausanias 6.21.1. For the situation see E. Curtius and F. Adler, *Olympia und Umgegend* (Berlin, 1882) 30, pl. 2, where the stadium and the hippodrome are drawn in.

79. H. Wiegartz has recently published a new and more plausible proposal: "Zur Startanlage im Hippodrom von Olympia," *Boreas* 7 (1984) 41–78.

80. J. P. Mahaffy, "On the Authenticity of the Olympic Register," *JHS* 2 (1881) 164ff., was the first scholar who uttered doubts about the chronology of the first Olympiad; see Körte (supra n. 2) 224ff. with better arguments.

81. This is emphasized again in Herrmann, *Olympia* (supra n. 62) 13, n. 14, and at full length in "Olympia und Seine Spiele" (supra n. 62) 173ff. Differently: A. Hönle, *Olympia in der Politik der griechischen Staatenwelt* (Bebenhauen, 1972) 6ff. In this connection we should discuss here the Truce of Iphitos, but it is a subject which goes beyond the limits of this paper.

82. Heilmeyer (supra n. 10) 90; idem (supra n. 9) 20ff. H.-V. Herrmann, *Bonn-Jbb* 182 (1982) 614, rejects Heilmeyer's arguments.

83. Like the two-horse chariots, the tripod cauldrons were sometimes regarded as victor prizes, as they were in Homer. But the quantity of miniature tripods, most of them very simply fabricated (see Maass [supra

n. 12] 117ff., pls. 63–69), contradicts this theory. For a different opinion, Herrmann, *Olympia* (supra n. 62) 77.

84. W. Dittenberger and K. Purgold, *Olympia V: Die Inschriften* (Berlin, 1896) 717, 720.

85. This number includes about thirty wells which were found before 1953. Most of them are only mentioned in the field notebook. Eight of them are published by E. Kunze, *OlBer* VII (1956–1958) 118ff.

86. The excavations in the southwest (area of the Leonidaion) brought to light no wells except one in the center of the Leonidaion. On the other hand more than fifteen wells were found in the area of the workshop of Pheidias: A. Mallwitz and W. Shiering *Die Werkstatt des Pheidias in Olympia, OlForsch* V (1964) 139ff., fig. 2, pl. 4.6.

87. Wells 18 and 26 in the northern embankment, Wells 2, 8, 84, 105, and the one without number in A 15 (*OlBer* X [1966–1976] pl. 1) are masonry wells.

88. Except the Hellenistic and Roman wells in A 15 (see n. 87), nos. 2 and 84.

89. Mallwitz (supra n. 68) 25ff.

90. Gauer (supra n. 20) 243.

91. The number of wells in the southeast area increased with the last excavations (1978–1980) from 97 to 129.

92. It must be remembered that only a part, perhaps the smaller part, of all wells which were dug in ancient times in Olympia have been found. Many wells must be situated farther south and east, where the mediaeval Alpheios destroyed the southern embankment of the stadium and the whole Hippodrome; see figure 6.11.

93. E. Kunze, *AD Chronika* 17 (1961–1962) 111, plan 2.

94. See *OlBer* V (1941–1942 and 1952) pl. 5.6.

95. Herrmann, "Olympia und seine Spiele" (supra n. 62) 174, points out the improbable time span of fifty-two years between the introduction of the first and the second *agon* of foot races.

96. See *OlBer* X (1966–1976) figs. 34, 36a.

97. Mallwitz, *Olympia* (supra n. 13) 205, fig. 165.

98. Ibid. 208, fig. 168.

99. Herodotus 6.127; Strabo 8.358 = *FGrHist* 70.118.

100. H. Bengtson, *Griechische Geschichte* (Munich, 1960) 75 n. 3.

101. W. B. Dinsmoor and H. E. Searls, "The Date of the Olympia Heraion," *AJA* 49 (1945) 68; Mallwitz (supra n. 26) 328; Herrmann, *Olympia* (supra n. 62) 94 n. 373.

102. Herrmann, *Olympia* (supra n. 62) 40, fig. 14; idem, "Olympia und Seine Spiele" (supra n. 62) 173.

103. Herrmann, *Olympia* (supra n. 62) 41.

104. Gardiner (supra n. 62) 61.

105. Pelops could also be understood as the originator of the most important event, the chariot race.

106. At the same time there is an increase in the Tropaea—that is, the offerings of armor and weapons to Zeus as a tenth of the booty. But it is not a sudden change in the offering customs. The late eighth and the early seventh century may be considered as a transitional period resulting in a thorough change, comparable to those of the second half of the fifth century, when the offerings of armor ceased.

107. Of course, what I have presented here can only be seen as a suggestion whose purpose is to stimulate new research in Olympia.

Hugh M. Lee

The "First" Olympic Games of 776 B.C.

7

This chapter will focus on two points: the year 776 B.C. and the program of that original Olympic festival. With respect to the latter, I shall also discuss the question of the evolution of the Olympic program.

The Games traditionally began in 776 B.C., when Koroibos of Elis won the only event, the stade.[1] Pausanias, one of our sources for this account, adds that a second running event, the *diaulos*, was added in the fourteenth Olympiad, namely 724 B.C. Subsequently, over the ensuing decades and centuries, the other contests were introduced.[2] Yet both the date of 776 and the limited program of the early Games have been subject to doubt. Let us first treat the matter of the program.

Gardiner rejects as "improbable" the Pausanian account that for thirteen Olympiads the stade was the only contest, and he adds that the first Olympiad must have included at least all the events mentioned by Pindar when he describes the mythical founding of the Games in heroic times by Herakles of Thebes.[3] These Games included the stade, discus, javelin, boxing, wrestling, and chariot race for four horses. More recently, Herrmann has also suggested the presence of contests other than the foot race, adding that these only gradually became consecrated and so a part of the official program.[4] And indeed, at first glance, it does seem unlikely that spectators and athletes would endure the length and expense of a trip to Olympic Games which consisted of a foot race and lasted no more than thirty seconds.[5]

The archaeological evidence also appears to favor the existence of a fuller program in 776. Boxers and charioteers are known centuries earlier from Minoan and Mycenaean art.[6] Chariots also appear in Linear B.[7] At Olympia itself, bronze statuettes of charioteers, dated to the eighth century, have been found. These are much earlier than 680 B.C., the date furnished by Pausanias as the year in which chariot racing became a part of the Olympic Games. The figurines apparently do not represent athletes, but rather the local aristocrats, who chose to present themselves in an equestrian manner, as befitted their class.[8] Nonetheless, this chosen mode of representation suggests the possibility that men so interested in being depicted as charioteers also had an interest in racing.

The excavations at Olympia have also brought to light numerous tripods.[9] They begin after 1000 B.C. and continue for three hundred years to the seventh century. Many were found in the area of the stadium and were placed outdoors. Just as victor statues filled the Altis in later times, so, too, the tripods must have adorned the site in Geometric times. It is difficult to imagine that none of the tripods were connected to athletics, and far more likely that at least some of them had something to do with sports.[10] Homer mentions tripods as prizes, both in the chariot race at the funeral games for Patroclus and also at a chariot race in games of King Augeias at Elis, forty miles from Olympia.[11] On Greek vases of the sixth century, we observe tripods as prizes for chariot racing, boxing, and other events.[12] On an eighth-century tripod leg from Olympia, we see two figures with raised fists struggling over a tripod. This could be an early depiction of a boxing contest, with the tripod as the prize.[13] The tripod leg antedates the inception of boxing in the Olympic Games of 688 B.C.

What possible connections could tripods have with athletics? First, they could have been Olympic prizes. Phlegon of Tralles tells us that it was not until the seventh Olympiad (752 B.C.) that olive wreaths were awarded.[14] Similarly, at the first Pythian festival involving athletes, prizes were awarded, to be replaced by laurel wreaths at the second.[15] Second, they could have been prizes in non-Olympic games. Finally, they could have been votive dedications in thanksgiving for a victory, whether the contest involved a tripod for a prize or not.

In the Homeric poems we find mention of running, boxing, wrestling, the javelin, discus, jumping, and the chariot race.[16] Whether one believes that the poems reflect practices of the Heroic period, the Late Geometric period, or some time in between, the presence of but a single event, the stade, at the Olympics of 776 and the meager program of foot races until late in the century seem inconsistent with the literary evidence.[17]

Yet the idea of a very simple first Olympics gradually evolving into something larger does have arguments in its favor. In the first place, no obvious reason comes to mind why anyone should invent so elaborate a series of dates for the evolution of the program.[18] Nor do the scattered sources for Olympic victors contradict Pausanias by giving us the names of winners in Olympiads earlier than that in which a given event was allegedly introduced.

Then there is the matter of the year 776, generally regarded by both ancients and moderns as the date of the first Olympiad. But here it is important to recall another tradition from antiquity, preserved in Phlegon of Tralles (floruit second century A.D.) and Eusebius (c. 260–340 A.D.), telling us that Koroibos, winner of the stade in 776, was not the first victor but the first *recorded* victor. Previously there had been twenty-seven Olympiads.[19] Koroibos' fame, and indeed the date 776, thus appear to be due in some degree to historical accident. Writing at this time was still new to the Greek world, and Koroibos happened to win at precisely the time when someone decided to employ this invention to record the name of the victor.[20] His twenty-seven predecessors were not so fortunate. Or it could also be that for at least some of the earlier winners writing was available, but no one deemed the victories and Games significant enough to be recorded. Whatever the case, the existence of Olympiads before 776 suggests the possibility that the Games then were not famous.[21]

Furthermore, to judge from the victor lists that have survived, the early Olympics were more of a regional festival than the Panhellenic celebration they later became.[22] Koroibos himself came from nearby Elis, a city which administered the Games for most of Olympic history. For the first hundred years, the victors come mainly from the Peloponnese. Not until 720 do we encounter the first non-Peloponnesian winner, and he hails from Megara on the Isthmos.[23]

To the above indications of small-scale Games, we may perhaps add the silence of Homer, who mentions nothing of Olympic Games, although he does allude to the games of Augeias at Elis. If we date the composition of the Homeric poems to the late eighth or early seventh centuries, his silence about well-known Panhellenic contests at Olympia may seem puzzling. but if the Games were not yet famous, there was no compulsion to mention them.

We thus face a dilemma, pitting on the one hand Pausanias' original humble Olympics against archaeological and literary evidence suggesting the practice of Olympic sports long before they were supposedly introduced. How do we resolve the contradiction? For a start, let me emphasize two guidelines. First, we must resist the temptation of imposing the later prestige of the Olympics upon its incipient stages. Second, we must maintain a distinction between Olympic Games—namely, a contest or contests at the festival of Olympian Zeus—and other contests held at or near Olympia. In other words, we should not assume that any evidence of athletics found at Olympia must pertain to the Olympic Games.

It is relevant here to discuss the relation of athletics to the worship of gods. Athletic contests are not an obvious way to honor a deity. Sports serve many functions; they provide recreation and exercise, an outlet for the competitive spirit, preparation for war, and entertainment for assembled masses. In a warrior society such as Homer describes, where men pride themselves on the *arete* of their bodies, athletics have a special place. At funeral games, the athletic contests are an especially appropriate way both to honor the dead and to entertain the assembled. If there is any connection between rituals and sports, it would more obviously seem to lie in the honoring of heroes, not gods.

But if any athletic event does have relevance to divine worship, that event is running. For example, we hear of runners bearing grapes in a festival called the Oschophoria.[24] At Brauron during the festival of Artemis, girls of various ages ran—though they did not necessarily race.[25] In religious festivals, torch races were popular, individuals or teams of runners striving to be the first to carry a lighted torch to the altar and thus earn the honor of setting it ablaze. At Olympia itself there existed a foot race in honor of Hera, featuring stade contests for girls.[26] The foot used to measure the stade seems to be the same as the foot used to measure the Temple of Hera, the girls thus running 200 Temple-of-Hera feet in their race, the men 200 Temple-of-Zeus feet in theirs.[27] The races are related in distance to the appropriate deity and run for the god. Thus, an archaic bronze statuette of a runner, inscribed "I belong to Zeus" (τὸ δί--Ϝος ἰμί) and found at Olympia, may indicate more than a thanksgiving.[28]

Many festivals of gods have nothing to do with athletics. And even if they include a run or race of some kind, it does not follow that athletics is the primary or a major focus of the religious occasion. Perhaps something like the following occurred at Olympia. As part of the festival of Zeus, a run in honor of the god takes place, whether the motive is primarily religious (to pay homage to the deity), more secular (to entertain the assembled), or a combination of the two. The fundamentally religious nature of the festival results, however, in the stade's being the only event for fifty years—longer if we accept the existence of twenty-seven Olympiads before 776. Over a period of time, the athletic side of the race becomes more prominent, creating pressure to add a second race, a double-stade, in 724, then a third, and finally nonrunning events. In time the athletic nature of the festival becomes pre-eminent, receiving a significant boost in this direction through the introduction in 680 B.C. of the most spectacular of all events, the four-horse chariot race. This unique combination of religious festival and athletic spectacle becomes so popular by the early sixth century that similar games are established at Delphi, Nemea, and the Isthmos.[29]

In sum, Pausanias' idea of a full-scale Olympic festival having developed gradually from a single event is plausible. We need not assume that the first Games contained more than the stade, as Gardiner proposed, nor need we resort to Herrmann's hypothesis that other events were held but were not sacred and so not listed. Gardiner in particular makes the mistake of imposing upon the early Games the fame and prestige befitting the Olympics which had evolved over a period of time.

Nor should we confuse games at or near Olympia with Olympic Games. This distinction allows us a way to account for the tripods and figurines found at the site and pointing to some kind of athletic activity. If we wish to press the evidence from mythology and literature, we can speculate about games of King Augeias at Elis or funeral games for Pelops or Oinomaos. But these would not be Olympic Games, games in honor of Zeus. So powerful a hold do the Olympic Games have over us that we tend to equate all athletic activity at or near Olympia with the Games. From historical hindsight, the association is tempting and may seem obvious, but it may not have been so in 776 B.C. or thereabouts. There is nothing to prevent games being held at Elis or Pisa or at Olympia itself which were not Olympic Games. Nor do dedications at Olympia necessarily have to be connected with Olympic Games; nothing a priori excludes the possibility that they refer to other contests.[30]

One further matter remains: the possibility that the date of 776 may be not too late but too early for the first Olympics. The excavations at Olympia have brought to light about two hundred wells in the vicinity of the stadium.[31] These wells were a source of water for the athletes and spectators, and their appearance and subsequent increase in number testify to the attraction of the Games, an attraction which grew over time. The earliest wells are dated to about 700 B.C. To account for this date, and the ensuing increase in the number of the wells, Alfred Mallwitz, the director of the German excavations at Olympia, has suggested that the Games began in 704 and were then held annually until the introduction of the chariot race in 680, whence the Games became quadrennial, the participants, according to Mallwitz, being reluctant to make the considerable effort of sending chariot, team, and athlete on a yearly basis.[32] Thus, Mallwitz preserves 680 B.C. as the twenty-fifth Olympiad, and the first Games, if held as proposed in 704, neatly correspond to the appearance of the wells.

The sponsors of the chariot entries were, however, wealthy men. Nor did reluctance concerning the effort of dispatching the horses, chariot, and rider prevent the establishment of the *periodos* of Panhellenic contests a little over a century later. With the *periodos* there were six Panhellenic chariot contests over a four-year period. The proposal of yearly Olympic contests also raises a problem. Gardiner has explained the custom of the *penteteris* from the halving of an eight-year cycle, the eight years being a Great Year which brought into harmony the solar years with the lunar months.[33] The inconveniently long cycle of each Great Year would then lead to the holding of a festival at its midpoint, thus leading to a festival every four years, at the inception of a cycle and then halfway through it.[34] There is also no evidence for yearly Games. On the other hand, the dates of the early wells and their growing number fit the hypothesis that the earliest Games were humble but were gaining in popularity at the turn from the eighth to the seventh century, as the expanding program suggests.

Very knotty problems continue to surround the early Olympic Games—matters such as the reliability of the earlier sections of Hippias' victor list or the relation of Pelops to Olympia.[35] Without new evidence these controversial matters will not be settled conclusively. In the meantime it is worthwhile to explore whether or not Pausanias' account of an evolving program is plausible. As I have endeavored to show, I believe that the account is indeed credible, especially if we heed the two guidelines that we not impose the spectacular athletic nature of the later festivals upon the earlier ones, and that we refrain from equating contests at or near Olympia with Olympic Games. It is indeed possible that the first festivals contained a single, brief foot race of some local youths who ran for Zeus but also for fun and for competition. And the first of these Olympic races may well have occurred before 776, too insignificant for anyone to have recorded.

Notes

1. Pausanias (5.8.1–5) claims that the first Olympiad was actually a refounding of games held in Heroic times. This chapter is not concerned with these alleged Olympics of the Heroic age, interesting as the question may be. For a recent discussion of the matter, see A. E. Raubitschek, "The Agonistic Spirit in Greek Culture," *Ancient World* 7 (1983) 3–7.

2. See Pausanias 5.8.6–11. The events and the years, all B.C., in which they were introduced (Olympiad in parentheses) are as follows: 776 (1st) stade; 724 (14th) *diaulos;* 720 (15th) *dolichos;* 708 (18th) pentathlon and wrestling; 688 (23rd) boxing; 680 (25th) four-horse chariot race; 648 (33rd) pankration and horse race; 632 (37th) boys' stade and wrestling; 628 (38th) boys' pentathlon, immediately discontinued; 616 (41st) boys' boxing; 520 (65th) armed race; 500 (70th) mule-cart race; 496 (71st) race for mares, which, together with the mule-cart race, was discontinued in 444; 408 (93rd) two-horse chariot race; 396 (96th) heralds' and trumpeters' contests; 384 (99th) four-colt chariot race; 268 (128th) two-colt chariot race; 256 (131st) colts' race; 200 (145th) boys' pankration. By the third quarter of the sixth century, the Games had acquired their principal athletic components.

3. Pindar *Ol.* 10.64–74. E. N. Gardiner, *Greek Athletic Sports and Festivals* (London, 1910) (hereafter cited as *GASF*) 52; idem, *Athletics of the Ancient World* (Oxford, 1930) (hereafter *AAW*) 35; and *Olympia: Its History and Remains* (Oxford, 1925) (hereafter *Olympia*) 87–88.

4. H.-V. Herrmann, *Olympia: Heiligtum und Wettkampfstätte* (Munich, 1972) 80–81.

5. The stade at Olympia in the Late Classical (fourth-century B.C.) stadium now visible at the site measures 192.28 meters. The world record for the 200-meter dash is 19.72 seconds, and that was run around a turn. Even with preliminary heats, the competition would not have lasted long.

6. Boxers appear on the rhyton from Hagia Triada, and two boy boxers can be seen on a fresco from Thera; for illustrations see N. Yalouris, ed., *The Olympic Games Through the Ages* (Athens, 1976) pls. 5–6, reprinted without a section on the modern Olympics as *The Eternal Olympics* (New Rochelle, N.Y., 1979). Chariots appear on a stele from Grave Circle A at Mycenae,

which may contain a representation of a chariot race; on a seal ring from shaft-grave IV in Grave Circle A; and on a fresco from Pylos. For illustrations see R. Higgins, *Minoan and Mycenaean Art* (London, 1967) figs. 99, 84, and 110 respectively. A chariot appears on a fresco from Pylos; see J. Chadwick, *The Mycenaean World* (Cambridge, 1976) 165, fig. 69.

7. For the chariot ideogram, see Chadwick (supra n. 6) 28. Chariots are mentioned in tablets found at both Pylos and Knossos. See Chadwick's discussion (supra n. 6) 164–71. The chariots may principally have been employed in hunting or warfare, the one depicted on the stele from Grave Circle A perhaps being an exception. It is a reasonable conjecture, however, that societies which used chariots also raced them. In *Il.* 23 we observe that the Achaeans race their war chariots at the funeral games for Patroclus.

8. The interpretation of the charioteer figures must take into account the numerous contemporary animal figurines. See W. Heilmeyer, *OlForsch* VII (1972) 38–40, esp. 40; and A. Mallwitz, *Olympia und seine Bauten* (Munich, 1972) 42; also, more recently, Heilmeyer, *OlForsch* XII (1979) 23.

9. See M. Maass, *OlForsch* X (1978); also idem, "Die geometrischen Dreifüsse von Olympia," *AntK* 24 (1981) 6–20.

10. Herrmann (supra n. 4), 78–79, believes that the tripods can be related to athletics. For a contrary view, see M. Maass, *OlForsch* X (1978) 4; also Mallwitz (supra n. 8) 43–46. The latter admits that tripods elsewhere are used as prizes, but denies this use to the Olympia vessels. He cites as one problem the fact that the number of tripods far exceeds the possible number of Olympic victors. However, it is not necessary that all the tripods have something to do with athletics; some may and some may not. And of those that do, it does not follow that they must celebrate an Olympic victory. As I point out later in this chapter, nothing a priori excludes the possibility of someone's winning in a non-Olympic contest and then making a dedication at Olympia.

11. *Il.* 23.264, 11.700.

12. Some examples with the source of an illustration include: a chariot race on the François vase in the Museo Archaeologico, Florence, and one on a Panathenaic amphora in the British Museum (B 144); an athlete of unidentified sport on a Panathenaic amphora in the National Museum, Copenhagen; and an armed race on an amphora in Munich. For illustrations, see respectively Yalouris, *Olympic Games* (supra n. 6) figs. 7, 9, 11, and 140, and L. Drees, *Olympia: Gods, Artists, and Athletes* (New York and Washington, D.C., 1968) color plate 9. Herrmann (supra n. 4) fig. 46 also contains a picture of the last. Boxers and tripods also appear in eighth- and seventh-century art; for a list see K. Fittschen, *Untersuchungen zum Beginn der Sagendarstellungen bei den Griechen* (Berlin, 1969) 28–30. In addition, a sixth-century black-figure amphora in the Villa Giulia gives us an athlete holding in his hands what appear to be boxing thongs; behind him another man carries a tripod.

13. Herrmann (supra n. 4), 78–79 and fig. 16b, c, believes the scene is athletic, and he reiterates this view in "Olympia und seine Spiele im Wandel der Zeiten," *Gymnasium* 80 (1973) 176. See also Fittschen (supra n. 12) 30–32, esp. 32. For the interpretation that the scene involves Apollo and Herakles fighting over the Delphic tripod, see Maass (supra n. 9) 36.

14. For Phlegon, see *FGrHist* II.257, pp. 1161–62. Again I emphasize that at least some of the tripods may have had an athletic connection.

15. Pausanias 10.7.5.

16. See *Il.* 2.773–75 and 23.627–38; also *Od.* 8.103, 8.120–30, 8.206, and 4.625–27.

17. That is, if the Olympic sports (namely, the events which later made up the program) were known and practiced, it would seem strange that in the most prestigious of Games there was only one event. The argument becomes even stronger if the sports had been known for centuries.

18. Gardiner, *GASF* (supra n. 3) 52, does give an explanation: "Probably the compiler dated the introduction of each new event from the first occasion on which he found a mention of it." Gardiner's concern is with the earlier part of the evolution of the program; he does accept the later. His explanation seems to me no more or less fanciful or credible than Pausanias.'

    I do not follow Pausanias in all respects, and reject his assertion (5.8.5) that new events were added as they were remembered from the alleged Olympics of heroic times. The idea of athletics and competition in the Heroic Age is, I believe, plausible enough; but that there were *Olympic* Games is another matter. Here I share Strabo's caution (8.3.30–33 C 353–58).

19. For Phlegon, see *FGrHist* II.257, p. 1160. For Eusebius, see *Chron.* col. 194. Eusebius cites as his source one Aristodemos of Elis, and also mentions a tradition, attributed to Callimachus, that there were thirteen Olympiads before Koroibos; this could mean four-year Olympiads, but the number is so close to being half of the twenty-seven Olympiads mentioned by Phlegon and Aristodemos that it makes one think of the eight-year cycle of the earliest Games suggested by Gardiner (infra n. 34).

20. For a discussion of the introduction of writing into the Greek world, see M. Guarducci, *Epigrafia Greca* I (Rome, 1967) 70–73.

21. The more Olympiads before 776, the more likely it is that some of the tripods found at Olympia may have been prizes.

22. For a convenient discussion of the Olympic victors, see L. Moretti, *Olympionikai: I vincitori negli antichi agoni Olimpici,* MemLinc ser. 8, vol. 8.2 (Rome, 1957), supplemented in *Klio* 52 (1970) 295–303.

23. This was the runner Orsippos or Orhippos, who may have originated the custom of nude competition at Olympia (Pausanias 1.44.1)

24. See the recent discussion of E. Kadletz, "The Race and Procession of the Athenian *Oscophoroi,*" *GRBS* (1980) 363–71, with further bibliography.

25. See L. Kahil, "Autour de l'Artemis attique," *AntK* 8 (1965) 20–33 and pl. 7–10, and "L'Artemis de Brauron: rites et mystère," *AntK* 20 (1977) 86–98 and pls. 18–21.

26. Pausanias 5.16.2–8.

27. See D. Romano, "The Ancient Stadium: Athletes and Arete," *Ancient World* 7 (1983) 9–16, esp. 13–14.

28. See R. Hampe and U. Jantzen, *OlBer* I (1937) 77–832 and pls. 23–24; also, Romano's comments (supra n. 27) 15.

29. If the Olympics did incorporate an earlier set of games, it is tempting to associate those contests above all with Pelops. Pausanias (5.13.1) calls him (not Herakles) the chief hero at Olympia, just as Zeus is the most honored god, and monuments in his honor were much in evidence, especially the Pelopion and the sculpture on the east pediment of the Temple of Zeus. We see that only the chariot race was introduced in 680, rather than a number of contests; and indeed, it is the chariot race which is associated with the myth. The mythical race took place in Pisa, and the Pisatans were the Achaean inhabitants of the region in the Mycenaean period before the Aetolians returned to Elis (Pausanias 5.3.1–6). For Pisa and Pelops, see Gardiner, *Olympia* (supra n. 3) 53–57, and Herrmann (supra n. 4) 37–48, 73–74, who in the latter passage sees in the geometric figurines of man and horse on the tripods a reference to Pelops. Mallwitz, however, points out *contra* Dörpfeld that there is no archaeological evidence to support a Mycenaean Pelopion; see Mallwitz (supra n. 8) 133–37. See also Herrmann (supra n. 13) 178–80, for further discussion.

30. The Persian helmet in the Olympia museum (inv. B 5100), a monument of the Athenian military victory in 490 BC, makes the point. One might expect that it would have been dedicated in Athens, perhaps to Athena, yet it turns up all the way across the Peloponnese in the sanctuary of Zeus. See E. Kunze, *OlBer* VII (1961) 129 ff.; Herrmann (supra n. 13) 11 and note 430; Mallwitz (supra n. 8) 32 ff.; and Mallwitz and Herrmann, *Die Funde aus Olympia* (Athens, 1980) 96.

31. See E. Kunze, *OlBer* II (1937–1938) 22, and *OlBer* VIII (1967) 4ff.; also W. Gauer, *OlForsch* VIII (1975).

32. I am deeply grateful to Alfred Mallwitz, who most kindly and graciously permitted me to see a copy of his paper after the symposium on The Archaeology of the Olympics at UCLA in April 1984.

33. The festival was also scheduled to coincide with the full moon. See Pindar *Ol.* 3.19, in the Oxford text by H. Maehler (Oxford, 1971); and also the scholiast's comments in A. B. Drachmann, *Scholia Vetera in Pindari Carmina* I (Leipzig, 1903) *ad Ol.* 3.33 b–c, 3.35 a–f.

34. See Gardiner, *Olympia* (supra n. 3) 68–72; also *GASF* (supra n. 3) 62–63, for other octennial festivals. The connection of an octoeteris to Olympia is, however, a matter of dispute. See most recently Stephen G. Miller, "The Date of Olympic Festivals," *AM* 90 218–20, (1975) with further bibliography.

35. I do not wish to underplay the very substantial difficulties surrounding Hippias' victor list. See Herrmann's note (supra n. 4) 216 n. 14, for a summary of the problems; also N. B. Crowther, "Studies in Greek Athletics, 1," *CW* 78 (1985) 520.

Part Four

Beyond Olympia (1)

The Other Panhellenic Games

Joseph Fontenrose

The Cult of Apollo and the Games at Delphi

8

The cult of Apollo probably came to Delphi in the Hellenic Dark Age and not earlier than 1000 B.C. Most authorities now agree with Wilamowitz and Nilsson that Apollo was Anatolian in origin.[1] His name does not appear in Linear B documents, an indication, though certainly not conclusive, that Apollo was unknown on the Greek peninsula in the second millennium B.C. It seems likely that the cult of Apollo reached Delphi between 1000 and 800, where he was known as Apollo Pythios, deriving his by-name from *Pytho,* the original name of the site.

Although there was a small settlement at Pytho in Mycenaean times, it then had no fame or wealth; it was probably unknown or nearly so beyond its Parnassian neighborhood. Certainly no Oracle had been established there before the tenth century at the earliest; indeed, there was no oracular establishment anywhere before 1000 B.C. There is also no evidence that there was any kind of sanctuary on the site of the Pythian Apollo's later temples before the eighth century, when the Oracle probably began its operations.[2] It is likely that the earliest temple was a wooden structure; the first stone temple was built in the seventh century but destroyed by fire in 548/7 (that is, the interior woodwork caught fire). This was replaced before 500 by the so-called Alkmeonid temple, which was destroyed by earthquake or slides in 373. The foundations now visible are those of the third temple, completed except for embellishments in 305 (fig. 8.1).[3]

The rites of ancient Greek religion were mainly sacrificial; sacrifices, accompanied by song and instrumental music, sometimes dance, were made under the open sky upon the altar, which was usually east of the temple, opposite the entrance, though never exactly on the temple axis. At Delphi from the second quarter of the fifth century B.C., sacrifices were

Fig. 8.1.
Temple of Apollo Pythios, front

made on the large altar before the temple dedicated by the people of Chios.

Only exceptionally were devotional services held inside a temple. It was the main function of a temple to house the god's image and the valuable votive offerings that city states and individuals made. But at Panhellenic shrines such as Apollo's at Delphi and Zeus's at Olympia, so many and costly were the offerings that a single building could not hold them all. Hence, many cities built shelters for their own and their citizens' offerings, subtemples in effect, conventionally called treasuries. Notable at Delphi are the treasuries of Athens, Siphnos, Sicyon, Corinth, and Syracuse; they and the others fill much of the temenos (the enclosure of the sanctuary). It is a large temenos, also enclosing temples of other gods, votive monuments, a theater, a spring house, and a *lesche* (men's club).[4] The stadium, in which athletic contests took place, was not situated in the temenos, but higher up the slope, some distance to the northwest (fig. 8.2).

Every cult had its own customs and traditions, and so some temples had other uses. Delphi had an oracular establishment, and the oracular rites were conducted in the interior of Apollo's temple. The Pythia, Apollo's prophetess, sat on a tripod in the adyton, in which were also placed the omphalos (earth's navel stone), a golden image of Apollo, and the tomb of Dionysus; but the interior plan of the temple is unclear both

Fig. 8.2.
View of Delphi: temple in lower center, theater to right,
above temple; stadium in upper right corner; Bay of Itea,
upper center

from excavation finds and from ancient literature, and is much disputed
among those who have studied the temple ruins (see n. 3).

We also have little knowledge about what actually took place in an
oracular session. We know more about what did not take place. Contrary
to popular beliefs about the Delphic Oracle, still current among the read-
ing public, there were no chasm and no gasses or vapors underneath the
temple. The soil and rock of Delphi are limestone and schist, not volcanic.
Limestone certainly allows caves and chasms, but no trace of any such
phenomenon has been found there. In any case the whole notion of toxic or
mephitic gasses issuing from a vent beneath the tripod and affecting only
the Pythia is too absurd to be given further consideration.[5]

The Pythia did not succumb to a frenzy or trance, as in the popular
fantasy; she did not rave and did not babble unintelligible sounds which
the priests and attendants then reduced to articulate speech, usually in
verse. As far as we can tell, she always in her own voice spoke a clear
answer directly to the consultant. She no doubt felt what she considered to
be Apollo's inspiration and showed her feeling, but that is all that we have
a right to say.[6]

She did not speak ambiguous predictions or directions; she spoke
almost no predictions at all; in fact, there is no certain record of a predic-

tion in surviving documents. She spoke directions and sanctions, always clear. Xenophon (*Anab.* 3.1.5–8, 6.1.22) records a typical response and the two kinds of question usually asked. When in doubt whether to accompany his friend Proxenos on the younger Cyrus' expedition into Asia, he went on Socrates' advice to Delphi and put the question, "To what god should I sacrifice and pray in order to accomplish with best result the journey that I intend, to fare well on it, and to return in safety?" Apollo replied, "To Zeus the King." Socrates told him that he had not asked the right question; he should have asked whether it was better to go on the expedition or stay home. Both are in fact the usual formulas of questions asked at Greek oracles, as shown by authentic records of Delphic responses and most impressively by the numerous lead tablets of questions asked at Dodona. Consultants asked, "Is it better and preferable that I/we do *X*? (λῷον καὶ ἀμεῖνόν ἐστι . . . , a phrase using two comparative forms of the adjective ἀγαθόν "good"). In all recorded instances of this question, the answer was, "It is better to do *X*," that is, a sanction for the action or enterprise proposed. Or consultants asked, as in Xenophon's question, "To what god should I sacrifice in order to have success . . . ?"[7]

Such are the responses recorded in contemporary records, in inscriptions, and by contemporary historians and orators. Any other kind of response (except occasional commonplace statements) does not to our knowledge have contemporary attestation, except for two that are certainly not authentic.[8] Accurate predictions of the future in specific terms, ambiguous predictions, ambiguous commands and prohibitions of the kind found in Herodotus' history, are not genuine pronouncements of the Delphic Pythia. They have the same character as the responses of legend and folktale, such as those spoken to Oedipus, Orestes, Agamemnon, and Kadmos. Nothing like them was ever spoken at Delphi or Didyma or any other ancient oracular establishment, as far as reliable records show (there is almost no example of such an establishment in modern times).[9]

Besides receiving sacrifices and being honored with other customary rites of worship, Apollo Pythios and the other gods of Delphi were honored with periodic festivals. It almost seems that a Delphian could celebrate religious festivities all the year round if he had the time and inclination. Here we are concerned with the greatest of all Delphic festivals, the Pythia, in honor of Apollo Pythios, celebrated every four years in historical times. From the early sixth century on, the most renowned feature of the festival was the Pythian *agon*—that is, the Pythian Games— second oldest (586) of the four Panhellenic agonistic meetings, though not much older than the Isthmian (581) and Nemean (570) Games.

According to Pausanias, the most ancient contest for which prizes were given involved the singing of hymns to Apollo, and the first victor was Chrysothemis, son of the Cretan Karmanor, who purified Apollo after the god had killed the dread serpent Python. Hence Pausanias places the beginnings of the festival in the earliest days of the world. In fact the mythical precedent of the festival contests was taken to be Apollo's combat with Python (or with the she-dragon of the *Homeric Hymn to Apollo*), the primeval contest that each octennial or quadrennial agonistic festival commemorated.[10]

Just when the earliest Pythian contests were instituted and for what reason we cannot be sure. They probably do not precede the eighth century and were obviously intended to honor Apollo. The early festival was entirely religious in character, and the inclusion of contests, musical or athletic, was a frequent feature of Hellenic religious festivals. It may be that the Python myth was not associated with the Pythian festival as primeval precedent until around 600 B.C. It was perhaps in the early sixth century that it first found recognition in the festival program.

Before 586 the only Pythian contests were musical. The hymn to Apollo was sung to the accompaniment of the kithara (lyre), played by the singer; and it was said that Hesiod was not allowed to compete because he had not learned to play the kithara.[11] Apparently before the First Sacred War the only contests were kitharodic. Contests in singing to the flute *(aulodia)* and in flute playing without song *(auloi)* did not appear before the sixth century, if the history known to Pausanias can be trusted.

The early Pythian festival with kitharodic contests was celebrated every eight years (nine years in ancient Greek inclusive reckoning), but there is some evidence of yearly religious observances without contests in the odd years on the seventh of Bukatios (Athenian Anthesterion, February or March); and so the seventh of every month was sacred to Apollo. But in 586, after victory over Krisa in the First Sacred War, the Amphictions established the first festival in which athletes competed. For these contests they gave prizes of value such as golden tripods. Thereafter they celebrated the Pythia quadrennially, and in 582 made of them an *agon stephanites,* a crown contest, awarding each victor a crown of bay leaves, as victors in the Olympic Games received a crown of wild olive.[12] The Pythiad (year of Pythian Games) occurred halfway between Olympiads. Pausanias counted the festival of 586 as the first Pythiad, but other sources take the first Pythiad to be the crown contests of 582.

Before 600 Delphi was part of the city state of Krisa or Kirra (two forms of the same name: KRISA > KIRSA > KIRRA), and in ancient Greek literature Delphi is sometimes referred to by that name. The town of Krisa/Kirra was situated on that arm of the Gulf of Corinth called the Gulf of Krisa (now called Bay of Itea) about a mile from the modern port of Itea, approximately five miles from Delphi (more by road). Krisa, it appears, laid exorbitant tolls and charges upon pilgrims to Delphi. Complaints were made to the Amphictiony of Anthela, an organization of Greek states that protected and superintended the sanctuary of Demeter and Kore at Anthela near Thermopylae. The Amphictions went to war with Krisa, a conflict that lasted several years between 600 and 590. After the fall of Krisa in 590, they took Delphi under their protection too and initiated the city state of Delphi, which now had control of the port city.[13] Before 590 the Delphians or Krisaians managed the Pythian festival; thereafter the Amphictions controlled the Panhellenic festival.[14]

In the festival of 586, according to Pausanias, the Amphictions instituted all the athletic contests of the Olympic program except the four-horse chariot race (*tethrippos;* but they apparently did not yet have the two-horse chariot race either at this time); and they added the long foot race (*dolichos*) and the two-stade foot race (*diaulos*) for boys. In the athletic, or gymnic, program (*gymnikos agon,* as the Hellenes called it) of all agonistic festivals, there was, when complete, a full range of contests for men and another set of contests for boys; and sometimes also there were separate contests for youths (ephebes), the definition of whom apparently varied from city to city.[15]

In the same festival the Amphictions also instituted singing to the flute (*aulodia*) and flute playing without song (*auloi,* simply "flutes"). The Arcadian Echembrotos won the prize in flute song and the Argive Sakadas in flute playing. Sakadas was also victor in 582 and 578, Pausanias tells us, and apparently Echembrotos, too, in flute song; but after 578 the *aulodia* contest was discontinued, because songs to flute music were usually elegies and so too melancholy for the audience. Contests in flute music, however, continued, and Pindar's final *Pythian Ode* (12) celebrates the victory of an *auletes,* Midas of Agrigentum (490 B.C.), the only Pindaric ode for other than an athletic or equestrian victor. Before Plutarch's time tragic contests were added to the program in performing arts.[16]

Neither at Olympia nor at Delphi did the archaic celebrations have all the events of later periods. Pausanias records the addition of contests at Delphi from time to time. In the eighth Pythiad the Amphictions instituted a contest in kithara playing without song. The date is probably 554; for though Pausanias places the first Pythiad in 586, he probably took this and the following Pythiad dates from a record in which Pythiads were reckoned from the 582 celebration. In the twenty-third Pythiad (484), the Amphictions introduced the hoplite race, in which the competitors ran a stade in full armor. In the forty-eighth Pythiad (382) the two-horse chariot race (*synoris*) was instituted, and in the fifty-third (362) a race of four-horse chariots (*tethrippoi*) drawn by colts; the boys' pankration in the sixty-first (330); the colt race (*keles:* a race of colts with riders) in the sixty-second (326); and the two-colt chariot race in the sixty-ninth (298).

The full program of Pythian gymnic events was much the same as that of other Panhellenic festivals. There were four foot races: stade *(sta-*

dion), two-stade *(diaulos)*, long-distance *(dolichos,* which varied from about a mile to three miles in length; the Pythian length is unknown), and the hoplite race.

The equestrian events were three: *tethrippos dromos,* a four-horse chariot race; *synoris,* a two-horse chariot race; and *keles,* a race of horses with mounted riders. As we have seen, the Pythian Games eventually included a second series of races in which colts ran instead of full-grown horses.

In the Classical and Post-Classical periods the program of the Pythian Festival was arranged in the following sequence of rites and events. We should observe that the Hellenic day, like the Hebrew day and the Christian holiday, began at sunset; thus, what we would call the evening of Bukatios 6 was for them the eve of Bukatios 7.

Bukatios 7. On the eve, or perhaps in the preceding afternoon, a *trittys* sacrifice to Apollo and other gods of Delphi introduced the festival. This was a sacrifice of three victims, usually three different kinds of animal: for example, bull, ram, and goat.[17] There were probably other sacrifices made by cities and individuals on this day. All sacrifices were probably accompanied by song. The *trittys* sacrifice was perhaps followed by some representation of Apollo's combat with Python, possibly consisting only of a rendition of the Pythian nome (infra). During the day the sacred procession moved through the streets of the town.

Bukatios 8. The sacred banquet began in the evening and continued through the following day. This was in essence a communion meal in which the roasted meat of the victims was consumed by the participants. Apollo's portion (and that of other gods) was the fat, bones, and some cuts of the less choice meat.

Bukatios 9. The musical contests took place this day.

Bukatios 10. This was the day of gymnic contests.

Bukatios 11. This was the day of chariot and horse races, with which the festival ended.[18]

The contestants in the contest of flute-players played the Pythian nome, which was invented by the Argive flutist Sakadas, victor in flute playing in the first Pythiad. It represented Apollo's combat with Python in five parts and is differently described by Pollux, Strabo, and a Pindaric scholiast. Pollux's outline seems to describe the earliest form; but the Pythian nome underwent changes at different times. In Pollux's text the nome began with the *peira* (test), in which Apollo looked over the field of combat. This was followed by the *katakeleusmos,* Apollo's challenge to the dragon. In the *iambikon* Apollo fights and wounds the dragon; trumpet notes sound, and probably flute notes mimic the grinding of Python's teeth as the god's arrow pierces him. The *spondeion* represents Apollo's victory, and in the *katachoreusis* Apollo dances to celebrate his victory. In other descriptions some terms are changed, usually to a related form, and in some instances defined differently. For example, the Pindaric scholiast defines the *peira* as Apollo's first attempt at battle, and the *iambos* as his abuse addressed to Python. Strabo describes the version that Timosthenes, who lived under Ptolemy II, played. The first part is *anakrusis*, a prelude; the second is *ampeira*, first attempt at combat. The *katakeleusmos* is not the challenge, but the combat itself, followed by *iambos* and *daktylos* together as paeans of victory, representing abuse of the dragon in *iambos* and rejoicing in dactylic hymns. Finally, in *syringes* (pipes) Python's hissings are heard as he expires.[19]

For the Pythian Games, as for the Olympic, a truce *(ekecheiria)* was proclaimed, forbidding hostilities for the period of the games. Mommsen and others have taken this to mean a cessation of war between Greek states long enough to allow competitors and spectators from even distant cities to travel to and from Delphi in safety. Mommsen thought that three months would be needed—Apellaios, Bukatios, Boathoos—that is, the whole summer. This would mean every summer for the truces of the four Panhellenic agonistic festivals; but it is obvious from Thucydides and Xenophon that summer was the principal season in which Greek states waged war on one another. Probably Harris is right in supposing that the truce forbade hostilities at Delphi (or Olympia, etc.) between competitors and spectators who came from states at war with each other. Perhaps the truce also forbade operations of war in the neighborhood of Delphi or Olympia and on the approaches thereto. In any case Hellenes from all cities gathered every four years at Delphi in peace and harmony to celebrate the festival and to compete in the Games.[20]

The Delphic stadium was placed on the only possible site on the slope on which town and sanctuary were situated. As already said, it is higher than Apollo's temple, some distance to the northwest (fig. 8.3). Here at the base of the westward extension of the Phaidriades, the spectacular cliffs behind Delphi, is a wide area of adequate length for the stadium race. It required only some cutting of the rock on the north side and the building of a retaining wall on the south side, so that seats could be constructed there. The place was first prepared for contests around the middle of the fifth century; but the structure whose remains are still visible (fig. 8.3) was built in the second century A.D. under the auspices of Herodes Atticus.[21] Before the fifth-century stadium was built, the Pythian gymnic contests probably took place at Krisa.[22]

At the east end of the Delphic stadium as we now see it are stones marked with grooves for the runners' start. Behind that is an arch in three parts dating from the Roman Imperial period. On the north side are twelve rows of seats, the lower rows broken in the middle by a niche for the *prohedria,* special seats for the president and officials of the Games. Stairways divide these rows into twelve sections. There were six rows of seats in the semicircular west end and on the south side, but the south seats have disappeared.

Fig. 8.3.
Stadium at Delphi

On the retaining wall of the stadium there is inscribed a law forbidding the taking of wine from the stadium and providing penalties for violations. Anyone who took wine out had to propitiate the god for whom it was intended, offer sacrifice to him, and pay a fine of five drachmas, about a dollar in gold or silver under the gold standard, a fairly heavy fine in classical Hellas.[23] The inscription was cut in the fourth century B.C., but the law inscribed is probably much earlier. It shows that rites of worship were performed in the stadium in honor of several gods; the wine was intended for libations.

On Delphi's steep hillside it was impossible to find a level space large enough for chariot races. So from the beginning the hippodrome was situated on the level land near Krisa.[24]

The contests of kithara- and flute-players and singers may have taken place in the stadium before a theater was built, but they and dramatic contests may have been presented, with such wooden structures as were needed, on the site on which the later stone theater was built in the second century B.C. The stone theater that can now be seen in a fairly good state of preservation occupies the northwest corner of Apollo's temenos (fig. 8.4), whence one has a splendid view of the whole sanctuary and of the Pleistos Valley. It has thirty-three rows of seats, divided horizontally by a *diazoma* and vertically by stairways that divide the seats into seven sections.[25]

Fig. 8.4.
Theater at Delphi

Like every other Greek community, Delphi had a gymnasium. Not only was it available to all male citizens for recreation and bathing, but it also served athletes as a training ground. At Delphi the gymnasium was situated on the slope between the Castalian spring and the Temple of Athena Pronaia on the eastern side of the town. Its remains can be seen below the modern highway. This structure was built in the fourth century, but there was apparently an earlier gymnasium. It was on this site, says Pausanias, that the boar wounded the young Odysseus when he went hunting with his grandfather, Autolykos, and his uncles.[26] The Delphic gymnasium occupies two terraces (fig. 8.5). On the upper terrace were the *xystos,* a roofed colonnade, and beside it a *paradromis* under the open sky, each a *stadion* long. In these runners could exercise themselves; in rainy weather they kept dry by running in the *xystos.* On the lower terrace were a large round pool, a dressing room, and a palaestra, the wrestling room (fig. 8.5).[27] No doubt the gymnasium was too small for all the athletes who came to Delphi for the quadrennial festival; but in summer weather they could train in the stadium or on suitable stretches of level ground elsewhere.

Many famous athletes of the Hellenic world competed in the Pythian Games. The mighty wrestler Milo of Croton won a victory in boys' wrestling and six in men's wrestling at Delphi.[28] Phayllos of Croton—sprinter, jumper, wrestler, discus-thrower, and therefore a pentathlete—won twice in the pentathlon at Delphi and once in the *stadion* race.[29] Theogenes of

Fig. 8.5.
Gymnasium at Delphi

Thasos, boxer and pankratiast, whose fame rivaled Milo's, won the boxing crown three times in the Pythian Games.[30] Statues of Theogenes and Phayllos were set up in Apollo's temenos. Numerous victors' inscriptions have been found at Delphi, some in the victor's own words, others inscribed in honor of a victor. As at Olympia and elsewhere, statues of victors were made and placed in the god's temenos at either public or private expense. This practice increased greatly in Hellenistic and Roman times, so that in the third century A.D. Apollo's temenos must have been crowded with victors' statues; besides these there were all the statues of deities and of honored persons placed there.

There survives a group of marble sculptures that stood on a pedestal northeast of Apollo's temple at Delphi, a row of originally nine figures, eight of which represented six generations of a noble Thessalian family, known as the Daochos group. It was dedicated by the younger Daochos, a tetrarch of the Thessalians and member of the Amphictions. From left to right stood figures of Apollo; Aknonios, Aparos' son; Agias, Telemachos, and Agelaos, Aknonios' sons; the elder Daochos, Agias' son; the elder Sisyphos, Daochos' son; the younger Daochos, Sisyphos' son; the younger Sisyphos, Daochos II's son.[31]

The torso and other members of six figures survive, or perhaps of seven: the identification of a nude torso with Telemachos is uncertain; formerly the statue of Sisyphos II (fig. 8.6) was identified as Telemachos. Missing are Apollo and Daochos II. Almost intact is the Agias statue (fig.

Fig. 8.6.
The Younger Sisyphos, formerly identified as Telemachos

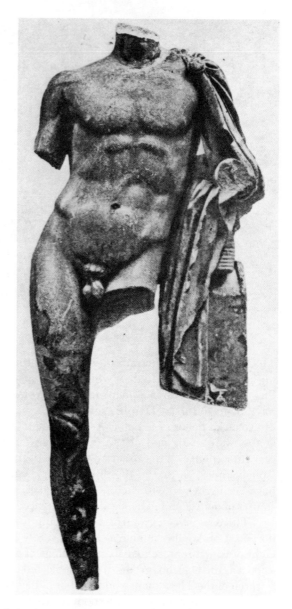

8.7). It is the finest work in the group, being a marble copy of Lysippos' bronze Agias, now lost, which stood in Pharsalos. Besides his torso, Agelaos has his head, right leg, and lower left leg.

These sculptures were made in the thirties of the fourth century B.C., when Daochos was old enough to be father of a young man; hence, his great-great-grandfather must have lived in the early fourth century or earlier. Since the three sons of Aknonios were athletes, their statues are

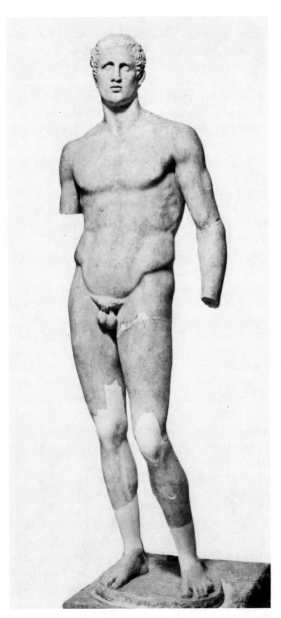

Fig. 8.7.
Agias

nude. Sisyphos II is also nude except that a cloak hangs from his right shoulder; he may have been an athlete too, but as yet without a victory; the inscription under his figure records none. Two figures wear a Thessalian cloak, another a Macedonian cloak.

Epigrams recording their victories were inscribed under the statues of the three athlete sons of Aknonios. Agias was the first Thessalian to win the pankration at Olympia, and he also won three Pythian, five Nemean, and five Isthmian victories. Although Lysippos could never have seen Agias, he portrays a pankratiast realistically, giving him a cauliflower ear. Telemachos, a wrestler, won Pythian victories on the same days as Agias did. Agelaos was a sprinter, a Pythian victor in a boys' race.[32]

Victors in the equestrian and musical contests also received honors and statues. The person honored for victories in chariot races was not the driver, but the man who owned the chariot and horses—a king or tyrant or rich man. Of Pindar's twelve *Pythian Odes,* seven are encomia of equestrian victors, six in chariot races (Hieron of Syracuse twice, Arkesilas of Kyrene twice, Xenokrates of Agrigentum, Megakles of Athens) and one in the horse race (*keles,* horse with mounted rider; the victor was Hieron of Syracuse). These are the first seven odes in the order named, except that the ode on Hieron's *keles* victory is third. Pindar has a good word for chariot-drivers too. In the fifth Pythian (26–39) he praises Karrotos, Arkesilas' charioteer, who won the victory crown for his patron, and did so without any damage to chariot or reins. Odes 8–11 honor (in the order named) Aristomenes of Aigina's victory in wrestling, Telesikrates of Kyrene's in the hoplite race, Hippokleas of Thessaly's in the two-stade race *(diaulos),* and Thrasydios of Thebes's in the boys' *stadion.* Finally, the twelfth Pythian, as already mentioned, honors Midas of Agrigentum for his victory in the flute-playing contest.

It is a charioteer who was the subject of the finest work of art found in the excavations of Delphi. That, I hardly need say, is the bronze charioteer, now visible in the Delphi Museum (fig. 8.8), one of very few surviving bronze sculptures from ancient Greece. It was found in 1896 buried in rubble behind the retaining wall north of Apollo's temple, probably covered in a slide, perhaps that of 373 B.C., which also destroyed the sixth-century temple. With it were found fragments of the sculptured chariot, reins, and horses' legs, and also an arm from the figure of a boy. The charioteer is complete except for his left arm. He is dressed in the ankle-length peplos that charioteers wore in the games and stands upright in the chariot-box, almost six feet tall, with the reins held loosely in his hand; for his victory is won and he is driving off from the finish line at a walking pace. The boy whose arm was found was perhaps one of two who walked in front leading the horses. No doubt the driver's patron stood beside him in the box as he drove triumphantly away, perhaps to receive the victor's crown from the magistrates of the Games; but nothing what-

Fig. 8.8.
Bronze charioteer

ever remains of that figure. The execution of the folds in the driver's peplos and of his hair are masterly (fig. 8.9), but the artist is unknown, although there have been several conjectures (e.g., Pythagoras of Rhegium).[33]

The fragmentary inscription on the base informs us that Polyzalos dedicated the sculpture. This Polyzalos was a son of Deinomenes of Syracuse. He was certainly not the charioteer and may not have been the patron victor. The sculpture and inscription are dated to the 470s or early 460s.[34]

At some point either athletic games for women were added to the Pythian program or women were allowed to compete in men's events. A Delphic inscription of about 50 A.D. records a dedication of statues of three sisters who had won victories in athletic contests. One of them,

Fig. 8.9.
Head of Bronze charioteer

Tryphosa, had won the *stadion* in the Pythian Games and also in the Isthmian, the first girl ever to win, so reads the inscription: this phrase may refer only to the Isthmian Games and would seem to indicate that she competed with boys. Her sister Hedea, we learn, had won a chariot race in the Isthmian Games. It is not surprising that some women were honored for victories in musical contests: these were probably open to women fairly early.[35]

The victor received a wreath of bay leaves (*stephanos,* "crown"), which he probably hung on the temple walls as an offering to Apollo. For Apollo, too, was poor, like his father, Zeus. Such was John Ruskin's conception of the Olympic prize: "no jewelled circlet flaming through Heaven . . . only some few leaves of wild olive, cool to the tired brow. . . . It should have been of gold, they thought, but Jupiter was poor; this was the best the god could give them." Plutarch also mentions palm leaves as prizes of Pythian victory; but probably these were only occasionally awarded to victors. In later times, it appears, Pythian victors also received apples as prizes. Several writers of the Roman period set Pythian apples beside Olympic wild olive, Isthmian pine, and Nemean celery;

and Delphic agonistic coins of the Imperial period show piles of round objects, which Robert interprets as the apples which victors received.[36]

Aristotle and his nephew, Kallisthenes, compiled a record *(pinax)* of all Pythian victors from the beginning and of all directors of the Games. The honors that the city of Delphi bestowed on them for this service are recorded in a Delphic inscription of about 335 B.C.[37] The city voted them praise and crowns, and ordered the comptrollers *(tamiai)* to have the record inscribed on stelai (stone slabs) in Apollo's temple.

In the Pythian Games the Amphictions themselves had the position of the Hellanodikai in the Olympic Games. According to a Pindaric scholiast, they were the agonothetes. This probably means that they appointed the agonothetes, the men who directed and judged the contests; for in the inscription on the three sister-victors, two men are named agonothetes of the Pythian Games in which Tryphosa had her victory.[38]

After 300 B.C. Pythian Games were established in other cities. An inscription of about 200 A.D. honors a victor in Pythia at Philippopolis, Tralles, and Hierapolis; and the Ionian cities celebrated Panionia Pythia, probably at Panionion. In 292 B.C. Demetrios Poliorketes, king of Macedonia, celebrated Pythian Games in Athens. At Delphi itself, after the defeat of the Gauls in 278, the Amphictions instituted a festival called Soteria, probably celebrated annually, in which the only contests were musical and dramatic. In 246/245 the Aetolian League, which then dominated Delphi, reorganized the Soteria as a quadrennial crown athletic festival in honor of Zeus the Savior and Apollo Pythios, to be isopythian in the musical, gymnic, and hippic contests. They were held in summer, probably in Bukatios, the month in which the Pythia were held, and in the Pythian year, so that in effect the Pythia and Soteria (which probably followed the Pythia) together constituted one prolonged athletic festival. An inscription mentions winter Soteria *(cheimerina Soteria),* celebrated annually, perhaps on the anniversary of the Gauls' defeat; it was confined to musical contests, and the victors were not crowned.[39] The winter Soteria in no way resembled the modern winter Olympics.

With the Soteria and the Ptolemaia at Alexandria, instituted a few years earlier, a new era begins in Greek athletic festivals. Cities began to convert their major local festivals, which usually included both musical and athletic contests, into Panhellenic crown festivals, *agones stephanitai,* isopythian, isolympian, and so forth. The Soteria were followed by the Asklepieia at Cos in about 242 and by the Leukophryenia at Magnesia-on-the-Meander in 207. Just before 200 Miletos instituted the Didymeia as a quadrennial crown festival, isopythian, in honor of Apollo Didymeus, who also had a great oracle. Thereafter Panhellenic games proliferated. There were the Hyakinthotrophia at Knidos, Asklepieia at Epidauros, Halieia at Rhodes. Under the Roman Empire victors' inscriptions list numerous athletic festivals. Perhaps not all of these were proclaimed crown games or isopythian or isolympian, but they had in effect become Panhellenic. The victors' inscriptions give evidence that athletes then traveled from one athletic festival to another, entering contests and seeking victors' crowns.[40]

Every city saw commercial advantages in a grand athletic festival every two or four years; such occasions were good for local business, since the festival would draw crowds of spectators and competitors from even distant cities, who would spend money in the host city for food, lodging, and local products. We might say that in the year 300 A.D. there was a bit too much of athletic sports and of agonistic festivals.

Notes

1. See U. von Wilamowitz-Moellendorf, "Apollon," *Hermes* 38 (1903) 575–86; M. P. Nilsson, *Geschichte der griechischen Religion* I³ (Munich, 1967) 559–84.

2. On early Delphi see P. Amandry, *La mantique Apollinienne à Delphes* (Paris, 1950) 204–11, 231–32; J. Fontenrose, *The Delphic Oracle* (Berkeley, Los Angeles, and London, 1978) 4–5 (other citations, ibid. 4 n. 3).

3. On the temples, especially the third, see F. Courby, *La terrasse du temple,* Fouilles de Delphes II, fasc. 1 (Paris, 1915); Emile Bourguet, *Les Ruines de Delphes* (Paris, 1914) 183–87; Frederik Poulsen, *Delphi,* trans. G. C. Richards (London, 1920) 143–57; Georges Roux, *Delphes: Son oracle et ses dieux* (Paris, 1976) 91–117.

4. See maps in J. Pouilloux and G. Roux, *Enigmes à Delphes* (Paris, 1963); Roux (supra n. 3) first end-map; Fontenrose (supra n. 2) 2–3, fig. 1.

5. See Fontenrose (supra n. 2) 197–203.

6. Ibid. 204–19.

7. Ibid. 42–44.

8. Ibid. H55–70.

9. Ibid. 228–32.

10. Pausanias 10.7.2. See J. Fontenrose, *Python* (Berkeley and Los Angeles, 1959) 15, 20, 456–58; A. Mommsen, *Delphika* (Leipzig, 1878) 168–73. Sources: Pausanias 10.6.5–7; Argumentum 3 of Pindar *Pyth.;* Ovid *Met.* 1.445–51.

11. Pausanias 10.7.3.

12. On the early history of the Pythian Games see Pausanias 10.7; Argumenta 1, 3, 4 of Pindar *Pyth.* Mommsen dated the first Amphictionic festival, when prizes of value were awarded, to 590, supposing that the quadrennial festivals began with the institution of crown games in 582 (supra n. 10) 153–54, 175, 178), although Pausanias 10.7.4 definitely places the first Amphictionic

festival in Olympiad 48.3 (586). *Pythía,* neuter plural, is the name of the Games; *Pythía,* feminine singular, is the name of the prophetess.

13. On the First Sacred War see Aischines *Or.* 3.107; Strabo 9.3.4, 418–19; G. Forrest, "The First Sacred War," *BCH* 80 (1956) 33–52; J. Fontenrose, *The Cult and Myth of Pyrros at Delphi,* University of California Publications in Classical Archaeology 4.3 (Berkeley and Los Angeles, 1960) 221–22.

14. See Mommsen (supra n. 10) 174.

15. See H. A. Harris, *Greek Athletes and Athletics* (London, 1964) 64–109.

16. Plutarch *Mor.* 674d.

17. *Corpus des inscriptions de Delphes (CID)* 10 = *IG* II², 1126, line 34; Mommsen (supra n. 10) 178–82.

18. See Mommsen (supra n. 10) 213–14. On the festival as a whole, see ibid. 149–214; Roux (supra n. 3) 171–74. According to Pliny (*NH* 35.9.58) a contest in painting was instituted in the mid-fifth century; in the first contest Timagoras defeated Panainos, Pheidias' brother. But nothing is said elsewhere about such a contest.

19. Pollux *Onom.* 4.84; Argumentum 1 of Pindar *Pyth.;* Strabo 9.3.10, 421–22. See Mommsen (supra n. 10) 193–94; Fontenrose (supra n. 10) 457–58.

20. Thucydides 5.1; *CID* 10 = *IG* II², 1126, line 48; Mommsen (supra n. 10) 163–65; Harris (supra n. 15) 155–56; Roux (supra n. 3) 172.

21. On the stadium see Pausanias 10.32.1; Bourguet (supra n. 3) 278–83; Poulsen (supra n. 3) 54; Harris (supra n. 15) 72, 142.

22. See Mommsen (supra n. 10) 202–203. But there is no certainty about gymnic contests at Kirra in the earliest Amphictionic festivals. The only support is Pindar's references to the *agon* at Kirra in *Pyth.* 10.15 and 11.12. But poets and other writers often referred to Delphi as Kirra/Krisa; *bathyleimon,* "with deep meadow," cannot be pressed very hard as indication of a site on the plain. It may be that the site of the fifth-century stadium was used earlier for foot races; a course could have been cleared, and spectators would sit on the hillside above.

23. *CID* 3 = *SEG* 1.209; P. Aupert, "Rapports sur les travaux de l'Ecole Française d'Athènes: Delphes 2. Stade," *BCH* 96 (1972) 895–99; 97 (1973) 526–27; 98 (1974) 783–84.

24. Pausanias 10.37.4; *CID* 10 = *IG* II², 1126, lines 35–36; Bourguet (supra n. 3) 278–80.

25. Pausanias 10.32.1; Bourguet (supra n. 3) 270–73; Poulsen (supra n. 3) 53–54; G. Daux, *Pausanias à Delphes* (Paris, 1936) 169–70.

26. Pausanias 10.8.8; Homer *Od.* 19.393–94, 428–58.

27. On the Delphic gymnasium see Pausanias 10.10.8; J. Jannoray and H. Ducoux, *Fouilles de Delphes* II: *Le gymnase* (Paris, 1953); Bourguet (supra n. 3) 294–302; Poulsen (supra n. 3) 50; Harris (supra n. 15) 144–48. On ancient gymnasia see Vitruvius *Arch.* 5.11.

28. Pausanias 6.14.5–8; Harris (supra n. 15) 110–13.

29. Pausanias 10.9.2; Harris (supra n. 15) 113–15.

30. Pausanias 6.11; *SIG*[3] = *IG* XII, 8; Harris (supra n. 15) 115–19; Fontenrose, "The Hero as Athlete," *CSCA* 1 (1968) 75–76.

31. *Fouilles de Delphes* IV, pls. 63–68; Bourguet (supra n. 3) 195–202; Poulsen (supra n. 3) 265–93; E. Will, "A propos de la base des Thessaliens à Delphes," *BCH* 62 (1938) 289–304, pls. xxx–xxxii; T. Dohrn, "Die Mamorstandbilder des Daochos Weihgeschenks in Delphi," *Antike Plastik* 8 (1968) 33–51, pls. 10–37; E. K. Tsirivakos, "Paratereseis epi tou mnemeiou tou Daochou," *ArchEph* (1972) 70–85, pls. 22–33; S. Lattimore, "The Chlamys of Daochos I," *AJA* 79 (1975) 87–88.

32. Inscriptions in *Fouilles de Delphes* III.4, 460.

33. *Fouilles de Delphes* IV, pls. 49–54; Bourguet (supra n. 3) 226–42; Poulsen (supra n. 3) 220–38.

34. Inscription in *Fouilles de Delphes* III.4, 452 = *SIG*[3] 351 = *SEG* 3.396; see Poulsen (supra n. 3) 222–23.

35. On the three sisters' victories, see *SIG*[3] 802; Harris (supra n. 15) 180. For women victors in musical contests see *Fouilles de Delphes* III.3, 249; *IG* IV, 682.

36. Palm leaves: Plutarch *Mor.* 724ab; Libanius *Laud.* 9.9. Apples: *IG* II[2], 3158; Lucian *Anach.* 9; *Anth. Pal.* 9.357; Maximus of Tyre 1.4, 34.8; Libanius *Laud.* 9.9; L. Robert, "Les boules dans les types monétaires agonistiques," *Hellenica* 7 (1949) 93–104; Roux (supra n. 3) 172–73.

37. *Fouilles de Delphes* III.1, 400.

38. See Heliodorus *Aith.* 4.1; schol. on Pindar *Pyth.* 4.68/116; Mommsen (supra n. 10) 166; Harris (supra n. 15) 150–51. For named agonothetes see *IG* IX, 2, line 44; *SIG*[3] 802; Plut. *Mor.* 674f. Sophocles *El.* 709–710 refers to *brabes/brabeis,* plural of *brabeus,* a judge or umpire, in reference to the chairot race of the Pythian Games, but probably employs the term to suit his verse, and not as the actual title of an official of the Games.

39. On Pythian Games elsewhere see *IG* II[2], 3169–70; Th. Wiegand, *Didyma* II: *Die Inschriften,* by A. Rehn, ed. R. Harder (Berlin, 1958) 252. On the Soteria see *Fouilles de Delphes* III.1, 481–83; III.2, 140, 141; III.3, 215; III.4, 356, 361, 362; *IG* II[2], 680; IX.2, line 187; G. Nachtergael, *Les Galates en Grèce et les Sôtêria de Delphes* (Brussels, 1977) 209–382, 401–95 (all inscriptions that concern the Soteria; 492–93, no. 80, for winter Soteria).

40. For the festivals mentioned see O. Kern, ed., *Die Inschriften von Magnesia am Meander* (Berlin, 1900) 16–87; *SEG* 12.368–84; *SIG*[3] 590; *Fouilles de Delphes* III.1, 308. Victors' inscriptions listing several festivals: e.g., *IG* II[2], 3169/70, XII.4, line 1102; *Greek Inscr. Brit. Mus.* 605, 611.

Stella G. Miller

Excavations at the Panhellenic Site of Nemea

Cults, Politics, and Games

9

A discussion of the archaeology of the Olympics and what we call the Olympic movement is really a discussion of Panhellenism. Panhellenism in antiquity involved all four periodic religious and athletic festival sites, not only Olympia, but also Delphi, Isthmia, and Nemea.[1] Although Isthmia and Nemea are less well known today than their sister sites, they once shared equally in the distinction of hosting a great festival to which the Greeks thronged. After all, the poet Pindar spread his talents evenly among the victors of all four festivals, and the super-athletes of antiquity were those who could claim victory in the full circuit.[2]

Olympia is, of course, not only the earliest but also the best-known of the sites, partly because of the long duration of the festival in antiquity, partly because of the wealth of literary testimonia concerning it, and, not least, because of the extraordinary nature of the material remains it has yielded. For all these reasons Olympia stands as the fundamental basis for study of Panhellenic games in antiquity and provides guidelines for excavation of other like sanctuaries.

Excavations at Nemea started in a serious way a decade ago, but even with a ten-year campaign just completed, there is still much to be learned about the site, topographically, historically, and archaeologically. Information concerning the results of these excavations has so far been appearing regularly in preliminary form.[3] The next phase of work at the site will be devoted to detailed study of the discoveries, which will then be presented in volumes to join those of Olympia, Delphi, and Isthmia. In view of these circumstances, the following discussion will attempt to collect and summarize certain aspects of the material discovered and indicate directions for future investigations, particularly as they concern cults, games, and politics at Nemea.

According to tradition, Nemea was the last festival to be elevated to Panhellenic status. This occurred in 573—that is, shortly after the installation of Delphi and Isthmia.[4] That these three sanctuaries were distinguished in this way and at this particular time was obviously an answer to certain needs and circumstances of the time, however poorly these are understood today.[5] Among the many questions which could be posed in this connection is why, after the beginning of the sixth century, there were no more Panhellenic festivals founded throughout the rest of antiquity, despite an abundance of local games, both pre-existing and newly founded.[6] Such questions can give rise to speculation but few, if any, firm conclusions. They are, moreover, matters which go beyond the scope of this chapter. However, it must be noted that the archæological evidence shows that activity at all three sites extended well back into at least the eighth century, several centuries before their founding as Panhellenic. At Isthmia, for example, the early Temple of Poseidon was apparently erected as early as the first half of the seventh century.[7] At Nemea the nature of this early activity is but poorly defined and exists so far only in scrappy remains, mainly ceramic together with a few bronze fragments. However, the concentration of sherds of eighth- and particularly seventh-century date in the immediate vicinity of the Temple of Zeus is suggestive.[8] Whatever else one concludes, it can be inferred from all of this that the festivals were established as Panhellenic on the basis of pre-existing local cults.

Nemea's history as a site thus extends back into the Geometric period. Several phases of very well documented prehistoric activity centered mainly on Tsoungiza, the hill to the west of the sanctuary, but such activity is attested also in scattered areas through the sanctuary itself.[9] The question of continuity from the Bronze Age through the Dark Age is one of widespread interest, a multifaceted and controversial subject.[10] In accord with the general pattern, however, the evidence from Nemea for continuity is negative: there is no Dark Age material which can be securely dated before about 800. It seems, in any case, likely that the age of revival in the eighth century will have seen the rise of a multitude of sanctuaries with circumstances differing among them.[11] Whatever else, the myths surrounding the founding of the individual game sites (the myth at Nemea concerns the death of the baby Opheltes) are not proof of the direct descent of the games from prehistoric times.

The story of Opheltes' death by a snake was the subject of several ancient plays, including the partially preserved *Hypsipyle* of Euripides.[12] The Nemean Games were instituted, it was said, to commemorate this event, and it is, of course, the counterpart to the story of Pelops at Olympia.[13] According to Pausanias, Opheltes' tomb, one of the noteworthy sites at Nemea, was surrounded by a kind of stone fencing.[14] This enclosure contained, besides the baby hero's own tomb and that of his father, also altars which are not otherwise described. The location of this shrine is unfortunately not closely defined; Pausanias, in his quite elliptical account of the remains, mentions it after noting the grove of cypresses around the temple, and it is not clear what degree of proximity may be implied.

Excavations at the site have revealed a hero shrine located toward the southwestern part of the sanctuary which is a good candidate for being the spot mentioned by Pausanias. Detailed study of the structure has yet to take place, but its general outlines are clear. Its shape is that of an unroofed, unevenly formed pentagon, reminiscent of the Pelopeion at Olympia.[15] The present structure can be dated to the third century, but it is built over at least two earlier phases which go back to the Archaic period. The walls of the existing structure consist of a foundation course and a series of orthostates with intermittent buttresses which it supports. Traces of what may be a porch were found along the north wall at the east end. Within the enclosure are a number of stones, of which one grouping looks much like a chamber. Could this be one of the tombs noted by Pausanias, that of Opheltes or of Lycurgus, his father? Recent probes have failed to yield the proof necessary to confirm the nature of the chamberlike structure, but the conclusion that it played a role in the worship enacted at the spot is virtually inescapable. Moreover, it is also clear from the abundant finds that it is a chthonic cult spot, lead curse tablets[16] and a caduceus or kerykeion indicative of Hermes Chthonios being among them.[17] Furthermore, the presence of two figurines, one seemingly of a female holding a smaller figure (Hypsipyle with Opheltes?)[18] and an unusual male child holding a mask at his face (Opheltes himself?)[19] is suggestive. The shrine's location at some little remove from the Temple of Zeus is perhaps odd if one considers Opheltes' apparent significance at Nemea, but it is difficult to know just how much veneration was actually accorded to the local hero. In any case, this shrine remains a very likely candidate for the "Ophelteion."

Although other gods were worshiped at Nemea,[20] it was Zeus, as at Olympia, who was the chief deity, and it is his temple which dominates both sanctuaries. In the case of Zeus at Nemea we know little from the written testimonia, but a considerable amount of information can be derived from the remains. The standing temple, dating to the fourth century, is well known both as a landmark and as a sacred structure which has through intensive study become widely known in architectural literature.[21] Its Archaic predecessor, lying directly beneath, is more shadowy. It appears to have been long, slender, and nonperipteral. Its roof, hipped at least at the back, was decorated with brilliantly colored ridge tiles and antefixes.[22] This temple, built apparently in the first half of the sixth century (i.e., around the time when Nemea became the site of a Panhellenic festival), was the victim of a violent destruction in the late fifth century.[23] It was replaced only after the middle of the fourth century by the existing temple with its triple architectural order.

The sequence of destruction and later reconstruction of the temples as well as the nature of the votive material can probably be attributed to historical events. The late fifth-century destruction which caused the early temple to disappear was part of a general devastation which severely damaged much, if not all, of the Sanctuary of Zeus. That it was brought about by human agents is clear from the quantities of weapons regularly discovered in the widespread destruction level.[24] From written sources it is known that Nemea was under the control of Kleonai when Pindar was writing odes in the 460s. However, Xenophon implies that Argos, which declared the Nemean truce in 338, was in control at that time. Whether the destruction of the sanctuary can be directly linked with a shift in power is not certain, but it remains a plausible hypothesis. Certainly in later times the Games were definitely under Argive control.[25]

Whoever the agents of the savagery at Nemea were, it was a shockingly aggressive event to have taken place in a Panhellenic sanctuary whose participating members were, at least theoretically, protected by sacred truces and which should have been inviolate. In point of fact, of course, the truth is rather different; indeed, there was well-attested violence surrounding the Delphic and Olympic Games as well.[26] The reasons behind these episodes (to the extent that we understand them) will have varied, but power struggles and basic human greed were surely among them. It must not be forgotten that although the host city will inevitably have had a multitude of responsibilities with regard to the Games, it will also have derived both immediate fame and actual economic gain from such activities.

In any case, we know with regard to the Panhellenic sites that there was indeed rivalry and occasional conflict over what city was to control (and reap benefits from controlling) the Games.[27] Archaeological evidence has repeatedly indicated an absence of activity following the general destruction at Nemea during roughly the first half of the fourth century. It seems a virtually inescapable conclusion that the Games were physically moved to Argos in that interval (as they were later) and were held there under her supervision for some decades.[28] After the middle of the fourth century, however, the Nemea sanctuary was revitalized: a major building program was undertaken which included the construction of the new temple, a new stadium, and various buildings around the sanctuary.[29]

It would appear that Argos retained control of the Games after this shift back to Nemea,[30] but historical considerations suggest that outside forces were at play. The subject is complex, and beyond the limits of the present chapter. It seems likely, however, that Macedonian power lay behind this activity. It was, after all, the Macedonians who, following the critical battle of Chaironeia in 338, held the power in Greece. It was the Macedonians who had an interest in retaining and renovating such traditional meeting places as the Panhellenic sites as a ready means of unifying control both physically and spiritually. It was also the Macedonians who had at this time the means to undertake such an extensive building program. Finally, it seems in keeping with the spirit of territorial settlement undertaken by the Macedonians that the Games at Nemea should have been physically returned to their traditional home.[31]

It is the sanctuary of this period in the later fourth century, dominated by the existing Temple of Zeus, which was essentially to endure throughout the Hellenistic period. However, in the next several centuries the Games continued to serve as something like a political football, shifting back and forth between Argos and Nemea until their definitive move to Argos, probably by the first century B.C.[32] Certainly by Pausanias' day the site had been long abandoned, as indicated by his comment: "In Nemea is a noteworthy temple of Nemean Zeus, but I found that the roof had fallen in and that there was no longer remaining any image" (2.15.2). It is hardly the picture of activity one might expect for a supposedly inviolate Panhellenic sanctuary.

Against this intermittently turbulent background, then, people gathered at Nemea, at least at intervals, to participate in the festivities of which the Games were, of course, a focal point and whose culmination was the crowning of victors with wild celery.[33] The various games at Nemea will have taken place in two basic locales, the hippodrome and the stadium. Excavations have so far failed to reveal the situation of the hippodrome, although scattered finds suggest horsy activity: parts of horse bits[34] and, most significantly, a fragmentary bronze plaque of around 500 B.C., recording the dedication of a race horse.[35] This last was discovered east of the Temple of Zeus, and although its find spot could be taken as suggesting the proximity of the hippodrome itself, it seems rather more likely that the plaque was simply presented at the temple as an offering to mark an equestrian victory. Speculation might suggest that the likeliest place for the hippodrome is the large flat area northwest of the temple, not far from the waters of the Nemea River. Preliminary investigations in that area, however, have so far failed to produce any traces of the racecourse with its appurtenances.[36]

The field events took place, of course, in the stadium, which from the second half of the fourth century was located on the hillside southeast of the sanctuary proper. Probes have revealed that there was no predecessor to the stadium on this spot and that the earlier stadium (obviously required by the nature of the festival) must be sought elsewhere.[37] Although it, like the hippodrome, has so far escaped detection, several hints point toward its location, perhaps in the region east of the Temple of Zeus, but in any case closer to the sanctuary itself.

Discovery of a starting block of early type reused as a threshold in Hellenistic times for the xenon some one hundred meters south of the temple is the primary evidence for the existence of an early racetrack in the general vicinity.[38] Additional excavation will be required to pinpoint its location, but a reasonable possibility remains the broad, flat area east of the temple where areas of deliberately laid claylike surfacing dating to the sixth century have been detected.[39] This, taken in conjunction with the discovery of an Archaic votive deposit containing a pentathlete's gear in the vicinity, indicates the desirability of further investigation here at some future date.[40]

Further excavations will also be required to determine the location of certain other athletic facilities which should exist in connection with the bath house belonging to the fourth-century building program.[41] The bath house itself, located to the southwest of the Temple of Zeus, contains three chambers of diminishing size. The smallest of these is sunken and tripartite in plan. At the center is a plunge pool fed by a water source which enters its south wall. On either side is a smaller area separated from the pool by a low partition wall. Each of these areas contains four bathtubs which have water piped in from outside. Near the bath one would expect to find a gymnasium and palaestra on analogy with the situation at other athletic centers.[42] A starting block, evidently of Hellenistic date, discovered lying (out of place) above the foundations of the bath on its western side,[43] suggests that these additional facilities are to be sought somewhere in the vicinity. So far, however, they remain elusive.

Archaeology is sometimes aptly described as the laboratory of history. It is concerned not only with buildings and monuments, but also with the people who were active there. The Panhellenic festivals were the setting for activities of many different sorts, and people both known and unknown participated in aspects of the celebrations. Future work—both the detailed study and publication of finds as well as further field investigations—will shed more light on the circumstances of their activities at Nemea.

Notes

1. The term "Panhellenic sanctuary" is sometimes used loosely to include other major festival centers, such as that at Delos (e.g., C. Rolley, "Les grands sanctuaires panhelléniques," in R. Hägg, ed., *The Greek Renaissance of the Eighth Century B.C.: Tradition and Innovation, Proceedings of the 2d International Symposium, Swedish Institute in Athens, 1981,* 4, 30 [1983] [hereafter cited as *The Greek Renaissance*] 109–114). I use it here specifically to refer to the four Panhellenic festival centers. For a good brief survey of the centers, see M. Andronikos, "Panhellenic Games," in N. Yalouris, ed., *The Eternal Olympics,* (New York, 1979) 66–73. Still standard,

if much out of date, is E. N. Gardiner, *Athletics of the Ancient World* (Oxford, 1930) 36–37.

2. See H. C. Montgomery, s.v. Περιοδονίκης, *RE* 37 (1937) 813–16. For victory lists see J. H. Krause, *Die Pythien, Nemeen und Isthmien* (Leipzig, 1841), much in need of updating, and L. Moretti, *Olympionikai: I vincitori negli antichi agoni Olympici* MemLinc ser. 8, vol. 8,2 (Rome, 1957) 53–198.

3. See excavation reports: "Excavations at Nemea, 1973–1974," *Hesperia* 44 (1975) 143–72; "Excavations at Nemea, 1975," *Hesperia* 45 (1976) 174–202; "Excavations at Nemea, 1976," *Hesperia* 46 (1977) 1–26; "Excavations at Nemea, 1977," *Hesperia* 47 (1978) 58–88; "Excavations at Nemea, 1978," *Hesperia* 48 (1979) 73–103; "Excavations at Nemea, 1979," *Hesperia* 49 (1980) 178–205; "Excavations at Nemea, 1980," *Hesperia* 50 (1981) 45–67; "Excavations at Nemea, 1981," *Hesperia* 51 (1982) 19–40; "Excavations at Nemea, 1982," *Hesperia* 52 (1983) 70–95; "Excavations at Nemea, 1983," *Hesperia* 53 (1984) 171–92.

   Specialized studies which have appeared so far include the following: B. H. Hill and C. K. Williams II, *The Temple of Zeus at Nemea* (Princeton, 1966); S. G. Miller, "New Problems at Nemea," Symposium, Olympia 1974, in U. Janzten, ed., *Neue Forschungen in griechischen Heiligtümern* (Tübingen, 1976) 63–75; idem, "The Pentathlon for Boys at Nemea," *CSCA* 8 (1976) 199–201; D. G. Romano, "An Early Stadium at Nemea," *Hesperia* 46 (1977) 27–31; S. G. Miller, "Turns and Lanes in the Ancient Stadium," *AJA* 84 (1980) 159–66; B. K. McLaughlin, "New Evidence on the Mechanics of Loom Weights," *AJA* 85 (1981) 79–81; S. G. Miller, "A Miniature Athena Promachos," in *Studies in Athenian Architecture, Sculpture, and Topography* (Festschrift H. A. Thompson), *Hesperia* Suppl. 20 (1982) 93–99; S. G. Miller, "Kleonai, the Nemean Games, and the Lamian War," ibid., 100–108; F. A. Cooper, S. G. Miller, S. G. Miller, and C. Smith, *The Temple of Zeus at Nemea: Perspectives and Prospects* (Athens, 1983); R. S. Stroud, "An Argive Decree from Nemea Concerning Aspendos," *Hesperia* 53 (1984) 193–216; S. G. Miller, "Poseidon at Nemea," in *Philia epe eis Georgion E. Mylonan,* I (Athens, 1986) 261–71; S. G. Miller, "Archaic Relief Wares from the Nemea Area," in *Philia epe eis Georgion E. Mylonan,* II (Athens, 1987). For prehistoric bibliography see also n. 9 infra.

4. See K. Hanell, s.v. Nemea, *RE* 32 (1935) 2322–27; cf. also *Hesperia* 46 (1977) 20.

5. It has been suggested that the Nemean Games (controlled by Kleonai but with Argive approval) were set up to challenge Kleisthenes and his Sikyonian festival; see G. L. Huxley, *Greek Epic Poetry* (Cambridge, Mass., 1969) 49–50; M. F. McGregor, "Cleisthenes of Sicyon and the Panhellenic Festivals," *TAPA* 72 (1941) 266–87, esp. 277–86.

6. On local games see Gardiner (supra n. 1) 37–42. For games patterned after the Nemean festival see Hanell (supra n. 4) 2327.

7. Cf. O. Broneer, *Isthmia I: The Temple of Poseidon* (Princeton, 1971) 3, 53–55.

8. Note especially a bronze Geometric horse (*Hesperia* 44 [1975] 171, pl. 41c), which, however, was found in silted fill in the fourth-century stadium. It had presumably washed in from the hillside above. Should a Geometric hilltop shrine be sought there? Zeus Apesantios was worshipped on Mount

Apesas at the northern end of the Nemea Valley according to Pausanias (2.15.3), and eighth- and seventh-century ceramic material abounds in an ashy deposit on its peak: cf. M. K. Langdon, *A Sanctuary of Zeus on Mount Hymettos, Hesperia* Suppl. 16 (1976) 107; and D. W. Rupp, "Reflections on the Development of Altars in the Eighth Century B.C.," in *The Greek Renaissance* (supra n. 1) 101–107, esp. 101–102. For Geometric pottery from the sanctuary at Nemea, see *Hesperia* 45 (1976) 178–80, pl. 31d; *Hesperia* 51 (1982) 23, pl. 9e, g, h; *Hesperia* 52 (1983) 74, pl. 19a. The character of this pottery fits in with the Argive tradition; cf. J. N. Coldstream, "The Meaning of the Regional Styles in the Eighth Century B.C.," in *The Greek Renaissance* (supra n. 1) 23.

For seventh-century material see especially a bronze griffin ear (*Hesperia* 47 [1978] 65, pl. 17c); for the type see H.-V. Herrmann, *OlForsch* XI. 2 (1979): *Die Kessel der orientalisierenden Zeit: Kesselprotomen und Stabdreifüsse*, passim. For seventh-century pottery see *Hesperia* 46 (1977) 16, pl. 9e; *Hesperia* 48 (1979) 82–83, cf. pl. 26b; *Hesperia* 49 (1980) 180–81; *Hesperia* 50 (1981) 54–55; *Hesperia* 51 (1982) 23; *Hesperia* 52 (1983) 74; Miller, "Archaic Relief Wares from the Nemea Area" (supra n. 3).

9. For prehistoric remains in the sanctuary see *Hesperia* 44 (1975) 167–69; *Hesperia* 47 (1978) 63–64; *Hesperia* 48 (1979) 82; *Hesperia* 49 (1980) 190, 197–98; *Hesperia* 52 (1983) 82, pl. 24c. For prehistoric activity on the hill of Tsoungiza see *Hesperia* 44 (1975) 150–52, pls. 34–35; *Hesperia* 45 (1976) 174–177, pl. 29; *Hesperia* 49 (1980) 203–205, pl. 52b–c; *Hesperia* 51 (1982) 37–40, pls. 17–18. See also C. W. Blegen, "Neolithic Remains at Nemea," *Hesperia* 44 (1975) 251–79; J. C. Wright, "Excavations at Tsoungiza (Archaia Nemea): 1981," *Hesperia* 51 (1982) 375–97. Full-scale excavation began on Tsoungiza under the direction of Mr. Wright in 1984.

10. The subject of continuity, also discussed in this volume by C. Renfrew and J. Puhvel, is much debated. I cite only a few recent treatments: Rolley (supra n. 1); J. N. Coldstream, *Geometric Greece* (London, 1977) esp. 327–32; A. Mallwitz, *Olympia und seine Bauten* (Munich, 1972) 77–82; A. M. Snodgrass, *The Dark Age of Greece* (Edinburgh, 1971) esp. 394–401. Espousing the opposite position—that continuity existed throughout the Dark Ages—are S. Hiller, "Mycenaean Traditions in Early Greek Cult Images," in *The Greek Renaissance* (supra n. 1) 91–99; H.-V. Herrmann, *Olympia: Heiligtum und Wettkampfstätte* (Munich, 1972) esp. 37–79.

11. Cf. T. Hadzisteliou Price, "Hero-cult and Homer," *Historia* 22 (1973) 129–44; J. N. Coldstream, "Hero-cults in the Age of Homer," *JHS* 96 (1976) 8–17; idem (supra n. 10) 341–56; A. M. Snodgrass, "Les origines du culte des héros dans la Grèce antique," in G. Gnoli and J.-P. Vernant, eds., *La mort, les morts dans les sociétés anciennes* (Cambridge, 1982) 107–119.

12. After his death Opheltes was also known as Archemoros, signifying recognition of the doomed expedition of the Seven Against Thebes. For Euripides' *Hypsipyle,* see G. W. Bond, ed., *Hypsipyle*[2] (Oxford, 1969). On the lost *Adrastos* tetralogy of Aeschylus, which dealt with the subject, see H. J. Mette, *Die Fragmente der Tragödien des Aischylos* (Berlin, 1959) 92–95. See also Apollodoros *Bibl.* 3.6.4, with commentary by J. G. Frazer, Loeb Classical Library (Cambridge, Mass., 1921). For the iconography of Opheltes-Archemoros, see G. Bermond Montanari, s.v. Archemoros, *EAA* I (1958) 543–44; E. Simon, "Archemoros," *AA* (1979) 31–45; E. Simon, s.v.

Archemoros, *LIMC* II.1(1984) 472–73; cf. also J. P. Small, *Studies Related to the Theban Cycle on Late Etruscan Urns,* Diss. Princeton (Rome, 1981) 137–38, and n. 44.

13. On Pelops see P. Orlandini, s.v. Pelope, *EAA* 6 (1965) 20–21; L. Lacroix, "La légende de Pélops et son iconographie," *BCH* 100 (1976) 327–41. On the Pelopeion see Mallwitz (supra n. 10) 133–37.

14. Pausanias 2.15.2–3: "Around the temple is a grove of cypress trees, and here it is, they say, that Opheltes was placed by his nurse in the grass and killed by the serpent. The Argives offer burnt sacrifices to Zeus in Nemea also, and elect a priest of Nemean Zeus; moreover they offer a prize for a race in armour at the winter celebration of the Nemean games. In this place is the grave of Opheltes; around it is a fence of stones, and within the enclosure are altars. There is also a mound of earth which is the tomb of Lycurgus, the father of Opheltes." Trans. W. H. S. Jones, Loeb Classical Library (Cambridge, Mass., 1978). For a discussion of the "fence of stones" see *Hesperia* 48 (1979) 84, but note that the wall there tentatively identified as the "fencing" of the Heroön was not subsequently verified; cf. also *Hesperia* 49 (1980) 181–82, 190. For cypress trees around the Temple of Zeus, see *Hesperia* 46 (1977) 11, 22.

15. On the Pelopeion see n. 13 supra. For excavation of the Nemean Heroön see *Hesperia* 49 (1980) 194–98; *Hesperia* 50 (1981) 60–65 (with plan, 60, fig. 6, and aerial photograph, pl. 11); *Hesperia* 53 (1984) 173–94. There was also an early attempt to identify the Tomb of Opheltes with a mound over the Early Christian basilica and xenon by G. Cousin and F. Durrbach, "Inscriptions de Nemée," *BCH* 9 (1885) 349, an identification repeated by W. H. D. Rouse, *Greek Votive Offerings* (Cambridge, 1902) 38.

16. On curse tablets see D. Jordan, "Two Inscribed Lead Tablets from a Well in the Athenian Kerameikos," *AM* 95 (1980) 225–39 with references, esp. 226–28; also D. C. Kurtz and J. Boardman, *Greek Burial Customs* (London, 1971) 217.

17. On Hermes Chthonios or Psychopompos, see H. Sichtermann, s.v. Hermes, *EAA* 4 (1961) 2–10, and S. Karusu, "ΕΡΜΗΣ ΨΥΧΟΠΟΜΠΟΣ," *AM* 76 (1961) 91–106. On hero cults and rituals connected with them, see P. Stengel, "Chthonischer und Totenkult," *Festschrift Paul Friedländer* (Leipzig, 1895) 414–32; idem, *Die griechischen Sakralaltertümer, Handbuch der klassischen Altertumswissenschaft,* v.3 (Munich, 1890) 67–101; Rouse (supra n. 15) 3–38; E. Rohde, *Psyche*[8] (London, 1950) esp. 115–55; L. R. Farnell, *Greek Hero Cults and Ideas of Immortality* (Oxford, 1921) 39–47.

18. *Hesperia* 49 (1980) 194, pl. 44e.

19. *Hesperia* 50 (1981) 65, pl. 25g. Cf. also a small bronze figurine discovered some distance away, which might represent the hero as well: *Hesperia* 49 (1980) 192, pl. 42 a–b.

20. Most prominent is the structure, tentatively identified as a temple, located some 140 meters north of the Temple of Zeus. Cf. *Hesperia* 51 (1982) 20–21 with plan, fig. 1, and photographs, pl. 7a–b.

21. Cf. publications by Hill and Williams (supra n. 3), and Cooper et al. (supra n. 3).

22. On the early temple see *Hesperia* 47 (1978) 63; *Hesperia* 49 (1980) 183–87; *Hesperia* 50 (1981) 51–55; *Hesperia* 52 (1983) 74–75. Important recent studies which have a bearing on the appearance of the early temple are by A. Mallwitz: "Walmdach und Tempel," *BonnJbb* 161 (1961) 125–40, and "Kritisches zur Architektur Griechenlands im 8. und 7. Jahrhundert," *AA* (1981) 599–642, with bibliography.

23. On the late fifth-century destruction, see *Hesperia* 46 (1977) 9–11, 21; *Hesperia* 47 (1978) 65, 82–83; *Hesperia* 48 (1979) 82; *Hesperia* 49 (1980) 186; *Hesperia* 50 (1981) 51; *Hesperia* 51 (1982) 22.

24. Ibid.

25. On the subject of control of the Games through their history, see D. W. Bradeen, "Inscriptions from Nemea," *Hesperia* 35 (1966) esp. 323–30. Cf. excavation reports in the following: *Hesperia* 45 (1976) 190, n. 28; *Hesperia* 46 (1977) 9–10, 22; *Hesperia* 47 (1978) 83; *Hesperia* 48 (1979) 79–81, 90, 93; *Hesperia* 49 (1980) 200–201; *Hesperia* 51 (1982) 28, 30, 35. Recent discussions include the following: P. Amandry, "Sur les concours argiens," *BCH* Suppl. 6 (1980) 245–47; M. Piérart and J.-P. Thalmann, "Nouvelles inscriptions argiennes (I)," *BCH* Suppl. 6 (1980) 267–69; M. Piérart, "Argos, Cléonai et le koinon des Arcadiens," *BCH* 106 (1982) 119–38; Miller, "Kleonai, the Nemean Games, and the Lamian War" (supra n. 3) 106–107; P. Amandry, "Le bouclier d'Argos." *BCH* 107 (1983) 627–34; K. Adshead, *Politics of the Archaic Peloponnese* (Avebury, 1986) 72–76. Cf. also Stroud (supra n. 3) esp. 214.

   A series of starting blocks have been recently discovered in the Argive Agora, but whether they have anything to do with the Nemean Games held at Argos remains to be seen. Cf. M. Piérart and J.-P. Thalmann, "Argos II— Agora: Zone du portique," *BCH* 102 (1978) 776, 778–79, figs. 7, 11–12; M. Piérart, "Argos II—Agora: zone ouest," *BCH* 105 (1981) 904–905, fig. 17.

26. Cf. at Olympia the battle of 364 between the Arcadians and the Eleans, fought in the Altis. See Mallwitz (supra n. 10) 98. On the Sacred Wars surrounding the Delphic festival see H. W. Parke and O. E. W. Wormell, *The Delphic Oracle* (Oxford, 1956) passim.

27. Cf. the legendary struggle between Elis and Pisa for control of the Olympic Games. See Mallwitz (supra n. 10) 79–80.

28. See references in n. 25 supra.

29. On the fourth-century building program see especially *Hesperia* 46 (1977) 21–22; *Hesperia* 48 (1979) 103.

30. Cf. discussion in *Hesperia* 48 (1979) 78–80.

31. On Macedonian connections with Nemea, see *Hesperia* 48 (1979) 103. Cf. also a summary of a talk by the author given at the joint meeting in 1981 of the Archaeological Institute of America and the American Philological Association, "The Macedonians at the Panhellenic Sanctuaries," *AJA* 86 (1982) 276–77.

32. See n. 25 supra.

33. On the crown of victory see O. Broneer, "The Isthmian Victory Crown," *AJA* 66 (1962) 259–63; also M. Blech, *Studien zum Kranz bei den Griechen* (Berlin and New York, 1982) 134–37; Adshead (supra n. 25) 76–82.

34. Cf. *Hesperia* 50 (1981) 64, pl. 23d.

35. Cf. *Hesperia* 53 (1984) 184, pl. 41d.

36. Pausanias (6.20.19) notes the presence above the turning point of the Nemean hippodrome of a red rock which flashes in the light and frightens the horses. It is not determinable whether Pausanias is referring to the hippodrome used in his day (which would have been at Argos) or the one at Nemea; the fact that he mentions the phenomenon in passing while discussing the hippodrome at Olympia makes the matter especially complicated.

37. *Hesperia* 49 (1980) 200–203.

38. Cf. Romano (supra n. 3); also *Hesperia* 52 (1983) 81–82, 93–95.

39. *Hesperia* 52 (1983) 81–82.

40. *Hesperia* 52 (1983) 78–80, pls. 22b and 23e.

41. The bath house was substantially uncovered in excavations of 1924 and 1926 by Carl Blegen and his associates. Cf. C. W. Blegen, "The American Excavation at Nemea, Season of 1924," *Art and Archaeology* 19 (1925) 176–79; idem, "Excavations at Nemea, 1926," *AJA* 31 (1927) 430–31, with photograph of bathtubs, fig. 8. For more recent investigations see *Hesperia* 52 (1983) 82–92. Publication of the building as a whole will take place in the future. On baths in general see R. Ginouvès, *Balaneutiké: Recherches sur le bain dans l'antiquité grecque, Bibliothèque des Écoles Françaises d'Athènes et de Rome* 200 (Paris, 1962). The Nemean tubs resemble those of Eretria and Priene (ibid. pl. 28, figs. 90 and 92, respectively).

42. Cf., at Olympia, Mallwitz (supra n. 10) 270–89; at Delphi, J. Jannoray, *Fouilles de Delphes* II: *Topographie et architecture—Le gymnase* (Paris 1953). In general see also Gardiner (supra n. 1) 72–85.

43. *Hesperia* 52 (1983) 93–95, fig. 7, pl. 28b.

Part Five

Behind the Scenes

Amenities and Nutrition

Stephen L. Glass

The Greek Gymnasium

Some Problems

10

Despite the long and frequently useful existence of what Rachel Sargent Robinson has optimistically called the *Sources for the History of Greek Athletics*,[1] one is continually struck by the inadequacy of those sources for just those points at which we are in the greatest need of enlightenment. The inescapable truth is that a large portion of such evidence as we have is disconnected, late, uncritical, relentlessly anecdotal, or usually all four at once. It is in the face of these odds that our use of such evidence is understandably, if amiably, capricious. Some of us have been moved to credit such as Pausanias when he names, say, Pelops as a founder of the early Olympics and assigns, thereby, a very great antiquity to the games.[2] As professional antiquarians, after all, we share an inherent and collective enthusiasm for the venerability which belief in the Greek heroes confers, and these Greek heroes, in a sense, are still our heroes. When the same source, however, reports the view that Apollo was a successful competitor at the very first Olympics,[3] we reject that information because, one supposes, gods are a more abstruse business, and the Greek gods are not, after all, our gods—all of this, at best, an equivocal historical process, as Finley pointed out some twenty years ago with his customary eloquent asperity.[4] In a similar way we are reluctant to employ vase-painting to increase our understanding of Greek architecture simply because we have Greek architecture on hand and can readily grasp, therefore, just how incomplete or swiftly allusive the details of architectural renderings on vases tend to be.[5] We are not so fortunate as to have any ancient Greek athletes about, however, so we are wont to look at representations of athletes on those same vases as if they were mimetically accurate renderings of competitors caught with nothing less than photographic verity.

We turn to the material evidence itself in the hope that the very solidity of some foundations will provide the kind of security which the literary

and even epigraphical sources do not. The results, however, seem dis-
quietingly analogous to those attending our examinations of the ancient
theater. That is to say, the monuments themselves tend to be rather later
than we would like, and the interpretation of their realities suffers from
rather excessive expectations engendered by modern experiences of the
kinds of events which took place within their precincts. Eugene Vander-
pool of the American School of Classical Studies at Athens regularly used
to warn fledgling archaeology students that the Theater of Dionysos in
Athens had been systematically murdered over the years by its friends—a
multinational force which never approached the excavations there without being certain in advance of what they would find. In similar fashion,
we still train in gymnasia, run, jump, and throw in stadia, and generally
participate in some of the same forms of competition as did the Greeks.
Even though that athletic tradition to which we see ourselves as heirs is
clearly a discontinuous one, such similarities as we seem to perceive lead
us, often unconsciously, to interpret our evidence otherwise. So it is that
as students of ancient athletics we are in need not only of some of the most
elemental kinds of information, but frequently of more detached ways of
interpreting that evidence.

We have, for example, the stadia at the four great Panhellenic sites,
carefully excavated and admirably published. And yet we are still unsure
of how ancient runners started, how they turned, how they finished, and
how the problems associated with such critical moments informed the tac-
tics of the races. The answers may not even be—indeed, are likely not to
be—the same at every site and every period.[6] Atkinson has warned
against the archaeologist's taking refuge in what he termed "a smug nescience." I hope I am not being smug when I confess a genuine disquiet at
the magnitude of my nescience in these matters.

Aside from the stadium and associated running facilities, the only
other important surviving architectural monument to the Greek penchant
for athletic activity is the gymnasium, with its close associate, the palaestra. When one turns to those, the specific objects of my attentions, the
difficulties seem both striking and disappointing, for, as again with the
theater, we have to deal with an institution so peculiarly, if not singularly,
Greek that we feel an unusually intense need to understand. One will
readily recall Pausanias' derisive observation that the city of Panopeus in
Phocis hardly deserved to be termed a *polis,* lacking, as it did, the basic
architectural requisites of a Greek city: government offices, gymnasium,
theater, agora, and public water works.[7] Similar remarks by such as
Aelius Aristides, Dio Chrysostomos, Philostratos, and Plutarch make it
clear that, in later antiquity at least, the gymnasium was regarded as a
distinctly Hellenic phenomenon.[8] By the periods of these writers, of
course, the gymnasium had become an institution whose functions
greatly exceeded its original physical training aspects.[9] The gymnasium

complex in full Hellenistic flower and thereafter was a public area, controlled by a corps of municipal officers and frequented regularly by men of all ages.[10] In such an atmosphere of training and relaxation—*exercitatio et delectatio,* as Cicero put it[11]—intellectual pursuits of ever-increasing variety took root and grew quickly, engendered and encouraged by regular attendance and easy concourse. Lectures, concerts, libraries, governmental offices—all found a ready gathered and receptive public in the gymnasia. One readily recalls that the not insubstantial fame of the Athenian gymnasia was due, in considerable measure, to the philosophers who made them their centers of activity. That is probably why Crassus found it necessary in the *De Oratore* to remind Catulus that "Gymnasia were invented many generations before philosophers began to babble in them."[12]

It also seems sadly clear that gymnasia were invented many generations before any of the gymnasia which are actually preserved to us. As this gap in material evidence interferes to no small degree with our understanding of the gymnasia we do have, I would like to turn my attention to one or two apposite and early problems.

I do not here concern myself with such speculative issues as the origins of Greek athletics. Our sociologists of play assure us that people everywhere have always sported, and if that be true, then it should be no surprise to us that the peoples of the Bronze Age Aegean did likewise. Though I personally am not willing to make the sizable leap of both faith and chronological continuum required to link the mysterious events of the Bronze Age with the Panhellenic programs of the Classical period, any solutions to such questions, I feel, would not be of much help to my dilemmas in any case. We are discussing the gymnasium—an area set aside for the practice of *gymnasia* (physical exercises)—and, though Greek tradition associated athletic competition with great antiquity, it tended to assign *gymnasia* a later place in time. The Greek heroic figures appear in literature already invested with athletic prowess, either participating in formal contests or striving against adversaries in rather technical athletic terms.[13] The Homeric tradition itself contains, with some exceptions, a remarkably full roster of classical competitive events.[14] One may scarcely quarrel, then, with the standard assertion that the Heroic and epic traditions, as we have them preserved, were fashioned for an audience not only familiar with but enthusiastic about athletic performances and techniques. Of formal physical training for such events, and especially for its own sake, we have conspicuously little, and nothing whatever of any individual or collective interest in training for other ends: to acquire, for example, the physical state of being *kalos* (beautiful)—despite the fact that, in Homer, this state is regularly associated with and contributes to *arete* (prowess).[15] If Marrou is correct in asserting that the old-time Athenian education was the Aristophanic sporting one,[16] and that a man both physically and morally attractive—*kalos kagathos* (beautiful and good)—was its desired end (the evidence is slimmer than Marrou makes it appear),[17] then it is to the gymnasium and its inherent ties to physical appearance, rather than competitive expertise exclusively, that one ought to look. Indeed, that difference may suggest why it is that Homer, who knows a great deal about athletics, knows nothing—or at least says nothing—about the gymnasium or *gymnasia*.

To the ancient world, the noun *gymnasion* and the verb *gymnazo* had obvious and inextricable assocations with *gymnos;* "naked." Isidorus puts it most succinctly: although remarking that the gymnasium was "a place for general excercise" *(generalis exercitionum locus)*,[18] it was more specifically so called "because young men work out in the nude" *(quod iuvenes nudi exercentur)*.[19] That the gymnasium and nudity (and, one might add, pederasty) were inherent concomitants and, at the same time, singularly Greek was the common tradition of classical antiquity.[20]

On this crucial point of athletic nudity, a certain consistency may be observed in the ancient accounts, which assert that this practice was a relatively late historical phenomenon evolved by the Greeks and abhorred by the barbarians. Thucydides remarks that it was not long before his time (οὐ πολλὰ ἔτη ἐπειδὴ) that athletic nudity was invented.[21] Plato says essentially the same thing, while Plutarch, oddly, offers the same information in a dialogue which he sets at the end of the first or the beginning of the second century A.D.[22] This anachronism in Plutarch, one might posit, derives from a careless inclusion of what must have been a well-worn and standard chronological observation.

Somewhat opposed to this tradition of later times is the famous etiological account of Orsippos (or Orhippos) of Megara, who, according to the scholiast to Thucydides I.6.5, was the first to run naked at Olympia. Pausanias, passing the grave of Orsippos, tells us essentially the same story.[23] A copy of the epitaph of Orsippos was discovered in 1769 and appears to be a Hadrianic copy.[24] Eustathius places the event in the fourteenth Olympiad,[25] as does Eusebius.[26] Dionysios of Halicarnassos gives the fifteenth Olympiad, telling us that it was not Orsippos who accomplished the great innovation, by accident or design, but Acanthus the Lacedaemonian.[27] Both Didymus[28] and the *Etymologicum Magnum*[29] date Orsippos to the thirty-second Olympiad. Clearly all of the various Olympic dates furnished for Orsippos' dramatic disrobing seem too early for either Plato or Thucydides to have remarked that athletic nudity was, relative to their own times, a recent development. One might suggest that the authors in question were indulging in rather loose chronological speculation, that the dates for Orsippos are uniformly too early, or that the custom originated by Orsippos was only gradually adopted by other athletes and met generally wide acceptance at a measurably later date. The evidence for Orsippos himself is so widespread and so varied that it is probably to be taken somewhat more seriously than the customary Just-So tales which the Greeks were wont to fashion to explain the origins of complex practices and social institutions. It also seems an inescapable conclusion that the gymnasium itself reflects this wide adoption of the custom of nudity in athletic performance and took its name from this singular practice. What is striking, of course, is that athletic nudity was the prevailing factor in the nomenclature—that the training center should have been widely called the nude place rather than, say, the running place, as it appears to have been in Crete.[30] This, if nothing else, suggests that the *kalos* portion of the *kalos kagathos* equation may have played a stronger role in early Greek physical training than the available evidence explicitly reveals. In any case, since the gymnasium, as I have noted, is a fixed concomitant or logical result of athletic nudity, and athletes both nude and protected by a codpiece can still be seen in mid-sixth-century vase-paintings,[31] Thucydides and Plato might have remarked, with equal justification, that it had not been long before their time that the gymnasium itself was built and frequented.

What we can say specifically of these early gymnasia, however, is difficult to establish with certainty, and any attempt at reconstruction must be made, as I have said, in the absence of any physical evidence earlier than the mid-fourth century B.C. Nor is there much in the way of apposite literary or epigraphical evidence which is itself contemporary with the early gymnasia to which we would like to have access.

There is no doubt that by the middle of the sixth century B.C., the four great Panhellenic festivals had substantial programs of athletic contests. Festivals of a more local nature, such as the Panathenaia, appear to have quickly followed suit. The sheer proliferation of athletic festivals and events would have necessitated some kinds of training and training grounds, though there is no reason to assert that the arduous Olympic training requirements of which Pausanias speaks were in force during the Archaic period.[32] Still, there were particular events—the field events, most certainly—which required, if not necessarily formal training, certainly considerable practice, and specialized kinds of facilities in which to perform them adequately and/or safely. Theognis may be the first to refer to such an area when he writes:

Happy the lover who *gymnazetai* and, returning home,
enjoys the whole day with a handsome youth.[33]

The interesting verb *gymnazetai* appears here for the first time. Ought we to translate it "spends time in the gymnasium" or "practices *gymnasia*"? Whichever the case, and each view has its adherents,[34] Theognis' lover has to return home after his gymnastic efforts, and one is entitled to ask from where, if not from some area which had been set aside for such activity, however formally designed such an area might have been. Is there, then, other evidence which might suggest that actual gymnastic establishments contemporary with Theognis did indeed exist?

The only gymnasia of the sixth century B.C. which are known to us by name are those ascribed to that period by tradition—the three famous establishments in Athens: the Academy, the Lykeion, and Kynosarges. Of these, only the Academy's location is specifically known—though strong cases can be made for the other two—but the remains of structures found in the Academy are of uncertain date and purpose.[35] Demosthenes says that Solon established severe penalties for thefts from all three gymnasia.[36] Aeschines, recalling similar types of legislation by early lawmakers, remarks that Solon or Drako commanded the *paidotribai* (trainers) to close the doors of the palaestrae before sunset and not to open them before sunrise because of the dangers of pederasty.[37] There is no way of knowing whether or not the palaestrae referred to here were part of, equivalent to, or independent of the three great gymnasia. The ancient figures of famous lawgivers, it is true, tended to attract legislation to themselves which was not properly theirs.[38] Still, there is some corroborative evidence that the three gymnasia in Athens, whatever their physical appurtenances, were indeed extant in the sixth century B.C. Hipparchos, the tyrant, is said to have constructed a wall around the Academy which was proverbial for its expense,[39] while Theopompos mentions that Peisistratos founded the Lykeion.[40] For Kynosarges there is no such unequivocal statement, although Themistocles' traditional association with it may argue for a relatively early date.[41] Certainly the tradition that the three great gymnasia belonged at least to the later years of the Archaic period was close enough to the truth to enjoy general credibility. Of their physical aspect we know little. If Solon did indeed pass a law relating to the closing of doors, and if Hipparchos did construct an expensive wall around the Academy, then the athletic areas were, at the very least, set off and reasonably independent architecturally. Aristophanes writes about running races below the sacred olives in the Academy,[42] and Plutarch tells us that Cimon was responsible for providing the Academy with a well-watered grove, running tracks, and shady walks[43]—perhaps those same walks which Cicero calls "justly famous" in the *De Finibus*.[44] Appian tells us that Sulla cut enough wood in the Academy to construct huge siege machines,[45] and Xenophon speaks of cavalry displays held there.[46] This evidence, taken together, would suggest that generally these early gymnasia were large, outdoor areas, equipped with at least rudimentary running facilities, and set off, and to some degree protected, by outside walls. Aristotle appears to support this general picture when he writes that a man is punished more severely for theft from a palaestra or agora than from a private house because the former are so open and thus vulnerable.[47] The interior appointments of the early establishments may have been more substantial than the picture I have drawn, if one is to believe the tale that Polykrates burned the palaestrae on Samos because the pederastic relationships they engendered threatened his tyranny.[48] For other sixth-century evidence, one may add the famous tests of Cleisthenes of Sicyon to find a suitable mate for his daughter Agariste. Herodotus says that he set up for the suitors *dromon kai palaistren*.[49] This could be and has been taken to mean either that he established a running track and palaestra[50] or simply that he made them compete in running and wrestling.[51] The young suitors, we are further told, were sent *es gymnasia*—that is, either to gymnasia[52] or to perform gymnastic exercises.[53] The question of a physical entity in either passage remains, then, uncertain, as, one supposes, does the historicity of the entire incident.

In any case, such spare evidence as does remain to us suggests that athletic areas—gymnasia and palaestrae—did exist in some defined form in the sixth century B.C. That such a date generally coincides with both nudity and athletics and a growing proliferation of athletic competition is surely no surprise.

Up to this point the terms "gymnasium" and "palaestra" have been employed almost interchangeably as two fused manifestations of the same architectural and social phenomenon. It will now be profitable to ask if we can discern those distinctions between the two that the very existence of the two terms would seem to suggest. The voluminous information on this particular problem was originally collected by Krause in 1841.[54] Yet Forbes's assertion in 1929 is still sound, if disconcerting, today: "the truth is that no categorical answer, applying to all countries and centuries, can possibly be given."[55] One should also bear in mind that though antiquity obviously distinguished between the two from time to time and place to place, no ancient source explicitly discusses that distinction. Still, there are certain conclusions which perhaps may be generally inferred.

The words themselves would seem to indicate that *gymnasion* is a general term and *palaestra* a specific one. It will be recalled that Isidorus refers to the *gymnasion* as a "place for general training," whereas he notes that *palaestra* refers specifically to wrestling, from which it takes its name etymologically.[56] What excavators have always termed the "palaestra" at Olympia, Pausanias calls a *peribolos* (enclosure), and remarks that therein the athletes have their wrestling workouts, or *palaistrai*.[57] It is clear from the context that he does not refer here to palaestrae in an architectural sense. Despite the generality of one term and the specificity of the other, it is difficult to assert historical priority for either. The lover of Theognis, one will recall, *gymnazetai*, but Solon, on the other hand, is said to have dealt with both palaestrae and gymnasia. But the uncertain question of priority aside, certain textbook distinctions are customarily made, and they are essentially these:

1. The gymnasium is a public complex; the palaestra a private one.

2. The palaestra is intended to serve *paides* (youths); the gymnasium is reserved for older groups.

3. The palaestra is a specialized and distinctive structure which is an integral part of any gymnasium but which can be an independent entity. A gymnasium cannot exist, however, without a palaestra.

It would be in order to examine each of these in turn.

That the gymnasium is invariably a public institution is virtually indisputable, and the evidence, from Solon's alleged attentions on down, is quite wide.[58] One may also recall that a gymnasiarch was inevitably a public official. There is also ample evidence of the private character of a palaestra. One may consider the palaestra in Plato's *Lysis,* several private palaestrae on Delos, and a fairly substantial list of others.[59] Nonetheless, there are some problems: it is perfectly clear that not all palaestrae were, in fact, private. First of all, several gymnasia of note certainly encompassed palaestrae somewhere within their limits. This is true of the Academy and Lykeion,[60] among others, and it is unlikely that we are speaking of public institutions with an amalgam of private sections within their precincts. Nor is it easy to devise some thesis to say that palaestrae in gymnasia were, perforce and by association, public whereas independent examples are private.[61] The palaestra of the period of independence on Delos was quite clearly controlled by the Hieropoioi and hence likely to have been public.[62] The city of Halicarnassos had the power, unilaterally, to usurp the *paidike palaistra* (youths' palaestra) while it was repairing its Phillipeion gymnasium.[63] The people of Corinth constructed the palaestra in the Timoleonteion.[64] It would appear, then, that although gymnasia seem to be unequivocally public, palaestrae may be either. A curious passage in pseudo-Xenophon is worth reciting here: "Some of the rich (in Athens) have private gymnasia, baths, and dressing rooms, but the public constructs for its own use many palaestrae, dressing rooms, and baths."[65] The two areas clearly have the same accoutrements but have reversed our common perception of public versus private control. Some editors have simply excised the offending passage from their readings,[66] others have traded "gymnasia" for "palaestrae" in the appropriate slots,[67] and still others have simply shaken their heads in aggrieved puzzlement.[68] Nonetheless, the author is clearly making a distinction here, and perhaps it is most economical to suggest that this is simply a tart reference to the reversal of the proper ordering of things—a view which would certainly be in keeping with the general tone of the entire work. The author must have perceived a public gymnasium and private palaestra as normal, and a gratuitous and excessively democratic change of status as something requiring the caustic commentary he offers.

The thesis that palaestrae were intended for *paides* only is one of long standing[69] but presents many difficulties. The first of these concerns the Greek words for the more common age groups: *paides, epheboi,* and *neoi.* It is obvious that the precise ages intended by these words varied from place to place and time to time. It is equally obvious that the words were not always used in their more technical senses, but employed in a far more general way to mean simply "youth," without any more confining strictures.[70] This alone makes such evidence as we have difficult to assess.

The earliest source which associates the palaestrae with *paides* concerns those laws of Solon which purportedly directed the *paidotribai* to observe specific opening and closing hours for their palaestrae in order to protect the *paides* from the amorous attentions of older men.[71] Perhaps, like the hypothetical private status of independent palaestrae, this is an old distinction of which we have lost almost all trace in later historical periods. For it is certain that *paides* were not the only group to frequent palaestrae. On Samos, there was in the third century B.C. an "elders' palaestra" *(gerontike palaistra),*[72] while at Halicarnassos is found the expression "youths' palaestra" *(paidike palaistra),*[73] a clear redundancy if palaestrae were inherently for the young. One may wonder, somewhat frivolously perhaps, if all of the suitors for the hand of Agariste, for whom Kleisthenes erected *kai dromon kai palaistren,*[74] were merely *paides.*

To argue the issue from the other direction, one may note that there were *paides apo gymnasion* (youths from gymnasia) at Oropos.[75] *Paidotribai* themselves, usually associated with palaestrae and obviously with *paides,* are found working in gymnasia, at least from the third century B.C. on.[76] Despite their seemingly unequivocal title, *paidotribai* also train *epheboi* and *neoi.*[77] Thus, again, it would appear that if palaestrae were ever exclusively or primarily for *paides,* as they may well have been at some early point, the distinction had largely disappeared by the time we can begin to associate written evidence with extant monuments.

That the palaestra and gymnasium should embody different planning concepts seems only reasonable from several points already raised. We have seen, for example, that the words *palaistra* and *gymnasion* themselves indicate an elemental and original diversity of purpose: the *palaistra* intended for a specific activity, and the *gymnasion* embracing a far more general enterprise. To bolster this further, we have also noted some specific references to the presence of palaestrae in gymnasia and to their independent existence as well. Since the two areas are thus distinguished, there is every reason to expect some distinction in appearance as well.

Vitruvius describes the palaestra *apud Graecos* (among the Greeks) in some detail: palaestrae, he notes, are essentially square or rectangular peristyles *(peristylia quadrata sive oblonga)* surounded by colonnaded aisles *(porticus),* behind which are to be found spacious recesses *(exedrae spatiosae)* with benches *(sedes),* and various specialized rooms with names to match:

an *ephebeum, coryceum, loutron, elaiothesium, conisterium,* and a series of Latinate bathing accoutrements far more Roman than Greek.[78] These rooms, not all of which are attested by Greek evidence, point up the distinctive quality of gymnastic establishments in that none of these rooms has to do by name with any of the standard competitive events. Vitruvius does not confuse the palaestra with the gymnasium, as has been asserted,[79] but clearly notes when his description leaves the bounds of the palaestra. However, it is interesting to realize that Vitruvius never uses the term *gymnasium,* most probably because the gymnasium is more of a precinct set aside for a general activity than a distinct architectural unit. Once outside the palaestra, the Vitruvian description is concerned with paths and walks *(semitae et ambulationes),* groves and plane trees *(silvae et plantanae),* a covered running track *(xystos)* and the open-air tracks *(paradromides).* The landscaping, not being a formal part of any Greek architectural entity, is described in Latin; the actual facilities, in Greek. In this light it is interesting to observe that the physical appurtenances of the Academy and the Lykeion, the two gymnasia about which we have the most abundant literary testimonia, are described most often in just those Vitruvian terms: walks, groves, and tracks. Of these early complexes virtually nothing is said in the ancient evidence about those more specialized rooms to which Vitruvius refers as parts of his Greek palaestra.[80] Indeed, the references to palaestrae of any kind in the Academy and Lykeion are very rare indeed.[81] But taken as a whole, the evidence would seem to reinforce what Vitruvius seems to imply: when one adds running tracks and shaded walks to the more particularized palaestra, one has, as a unit, a gymnasium. Surely certain earlier passages in Greek literature which speak, for example, of the establishment of *dromoi kai palaistrai*[82] recall a point at which the two entities were entirely separate and distinct. Seemingly free-floating *dromoi*—tracks without spectator facilities, as Romano defines them—are several and well known, if not always well understood.[83]

The only site where we are prepared to compare a full gymnasium with a palaestra, both relatively well preserved and specifically identified by the epigraphical evidence as "gymnasium" and "palaestra," is on Delos. The *peristoion* (peristyle)—as it is epigraphically termed—of the Delos gymnasium and the so-called "Palaestra of the Lake"[84] both consisted of peristyle courtyards with rooms distributed along certain of the aisles, as per the Vitruvian dictates. Although the accounts of the palaestra are not nearly so complete and systematic as those of the gymnasium, they still demonstrate certain features clearly in common: a peristyle with porticos *(stoai),* several *exedrai* (recesses), a *sphairisterion* (ball court), and a *loutron* (bath).[85] Some of these same terms are employed in the gymnasia at Pergamon and Delphi.[86] The gymnasium and palaestra on Delos, with all of their similarities, differ markedly in layout only in the presence of running facilities in the gymnasium: a stadium and covered running track. On Delos, then, we would appear to have confirmed the hypothesis presented by the literary evidence: that the essential difference between a gymnasium and a palaestra lies in the presence of running facilities in the gymnasium. I know of no certain extant gymnasia without such facilities, and positive examples such as those at Olympia, Delphi, Pergamon, Priene, and, of course, Delos will come swiftly to mind.[87] It is also interesting to note that much of the literary and all of the epigraphical evidence seems not to refer to a palaestra by that name when what we have come to recognize as a palaestra architecturally is actually part of a gymnasium. Note, for example, the gymnasia at Delphi, Delos, and Pergamon, where the peristyle court area is called simply *peristylos* or *peristoion*. One will recall that what we have always called the "palaestra" at Olympia Pausanias refers to as a *peribolos* (enclosure), perhaps regarding it informally as part of the gymnasium complex. This would seem to indicate that the palaestra in a gymnasium tended to lose that nominal identity which it possessed as an independent structure.

Structurally, then, a palaestra with facilities for running is a gymnasium. But even that description is something of an oversimplification in that these added facilities must have served not only runners but also those field events—discus and javelin—requiring more open space than a simple palaestra could provide. True, nothing like the fabled expanses of the Academy and Lykeion have yet been discovered, but then both of these gymnasia were regarded as exceptional in antiquity.

As I have tried to demonstrate, the evidence for sixth-century gymnasia and palaestrae does only slightly more than assure us of the existence of such establishments at such an early date. Fine distinctions of function, internal areas, and nomenclature belong largely to the Hellenistic period and beyond. Vitruvian structures, some of them quite anachronistic, have only the most general relationship to our preserved athletic complexes, which, like the evidence surrounding them, are mostly late. Between the fuller information of the Hellenistic period and the bare outlines of Solonian and Peisistratid Athens lies the fifth century, similarly bereft of material evidence but of obvious importance to the subject.

During the fifth century B.C., in fact, there appears to have been a marked proliferation of gymnasia and palaestrae, or at least the list of named examples which one could produce from the literary evidence becomes markedly longer.[88] On the individual aspects of these, however, our information is still woefully weak. Plato's *Lysis* and *Euthydemos* purport to tell us something of gymnastic complexes, but not in any systematic fashion. In the *Lysis,* Plato describes a palaestra newly constructed (νεωστὶ ῷκοδομημένη)) and encountered by Socrates, evidently for the first time, on the road from the Academy to the Lykeion by the Panops fountain and near a city gate.[89] Socrates, it is interesting to observe, asks his young friend Hippothales: "What is this place and how do you spend your time here?"[90] One wonders how seriously we are to take the questions. Is it possible that a palaestra could have been built in such a prominent location in what was, after all, not a very large town, and any citizen not know of it? Were palaestrae so numerous that it was difficult to keep track of them all as they went up? Were they so nondescript and sequestered from the outside that one enclosure looked rather much like another? Plato describes it in a way that suggests this last possibility: he calls it a "sort of enclosure: (περίβολον τέ τινα) which had to be entered through a closeable door and which effectively sealed off the activities within from outside gaze (εἰσέλθοντες δὲ κατελάβομεν . . . παῖδας).[91] Certainly Socrates does not know what the structure is and has to ask not only what it is but what it is for. Surely a correct answer to the first question would have furnished the answer to the second. But Hippothales responds, "It's a palaestra and we spend our time there in discussion." This exchange sounds suspiciously like a fifth-century question and a fourth-century response—the palaestra as athletic complex *cum* philosophical school. In any case, most of the boys were in the open-air court (ἐν τῇ αὐλῇ . . . ἔξω),[92] while some were in a corner of the dressing room, or what the Greeks termed the "undressing room" *(apodyterion)*.[93] The succeeding brief description makes it clear that the *apodyterion* was visible from the court and, thus, must have been one of the rooms surrounding it. Also, the room with its "corner" was probably part of a quadrilateral structure and was large enough to permit Socrates and a companion to retire to a quieter part of it. An undressing room must have been almost a sine qua non of any gymnastic establishment—though Vitruvius, curiously, fails to mention it—and it is not particularly surprising to see it mentioned in the *Onomasticon* of Pollux only as one of the many areas of exercise (χωρία τῆς ἀστήσεως).[94] Nothing more is said of the physical appurtenances of this unnamed palaestra, although one may assume that its proximity to the Panops fountain and its water supply was not merely fortuitous.

The *Euthydemos* supports the account of the *Lysis* and supplements it slightly. Socrates remarks that he was in the Lykeion alone in the *apodyterion* when two brothers, Euthydemos and Dionysodoros, came in with a small group of disciples and proceeded to walk about ἐν τῷ καταστέγῳ δρόμῳ (in the covered *dromos*).[95] They had completed two or three circuits (δύ᾽ ἤ τρεῖς δρόμους) when Kleinias entered with a group of admirers. Kleinias spied Socrates from the entrance and joined him. Dionysodoros and Euthydemos, after glancing over at Socrates and Kleinias from their sheltered *dromoi,* decided to join them.[96] Some of the basic similarities of this account with that of the *Lysis* are clear: Socrates ensconces himself in an *apodyterion* which is visible from the entrance.

This time, however, there is no express mention of a court. Instead, Euthydemos and Dionysodoros enter and walk about in a covered *dromos (katastegos dromos)*. Delorme argues that the two young men were strolling along a covered track,[97] but it is more likely that the covered dromos referred to here was the protected passage or aisles behind the colonnade of a peristyle court. Given the structure of the preserved gymnasia we have, it is difficult to reconstruct a gymnasium in which anyone on the running tracks (covered or otherwise) would have full view of any of the rooms in the palaestra area. Whether or not the colonnaded passages around a peristyle court could conceivably be termed *dromoi* is a pertinent question. Admittedly we are not often told what they were called; on Delos they were simply designated *stoai*.[98] The word *dromos* has strong associations with running, but from time to time was used to indicate any sort of passage.[99] Vitruvius suggests that the peristyle aisles are called *diaulos* by the Greeks because they have (or should have) a circuit of two stades in length.[100] It might be mentioned parenthetically that only Olympia has peristyle aisles of anywhere near half that dimension,[101] and falls, perforce, well short of two Olympic stades. Vitruvius' terminology, despite his claims, has no support in Greek literature or epigraphy. Still, it seems unlikely that he would have invented it out of whole cloth, and perhaps this suggests that to employ a running term such as *dromos* to describe the aisles around a gymnasium court is not so odd as may be initially supposed. The picture of a peristyle court with an *apodyterion* on one side visible from the entrance, into which one could see while making the circuit of the surrounding aisles, is entirely consistent with the basic layout of gymnastic establishments preserved in later periods. It is possible that one might add to these bits of information the Pausanian description of the *archaion gymnasion* (old gymnasium) at Elis.[102] Here a simple enclosure, called *xystos,* protected running tracks which were planted with plane trees. A separate track for competition was set apart from the practice facilities, though whether this means that the competition track doubled as the local stadium, as it did at Delos and Priene, is unclear. The simplicity of the arrangement commends it to an early date, but *archaion* carries no more precise strictures.[103]

Such, then, is the picture of these important athletic establishments—the gymnasium and palaestra—which can be drawn at a point reasonably close to their inception. It is admittedly brief and incomplete, but currently it is all that the evidence will permit. Still, the faint glimmerings of the Vitruvian complex and the Hellenistic gymnasia upon which the Vitruvian mandates are based are already visible in the sixth and fifth centuries B.C. The numerous threads I have left dangling do not, I fear, reach quite to the gymnasium at Delphi, our earliest preserved example, and the full picture of the gymnasium as an architectural reality necessarily picks up, as it seems to have begun, *in medias res*. One may hope that the as yet undiscovered gymnastic complex at Nemea may help to provide a more complete picture.

Notes

1. From her monograph of the same name: *Sources for the History of Greek Athletics in English Translation* (Cincinnati, Ohio, 1956).

2. Pausanias 5.8.2.

3. Pausanias 5.7.10

4. M. I. Finley, "The Trojan War," *JHS* 84 (1964) 1–2.

5. The admonitions of F. B. Tarbell in *AJA* 14 (1910) 428ff. and esp. 433 are still apposite.

6. Cf. the evidence amassed by D. G. Romano, *The Stadia of the Peloponnesos,* Diss. University of Pennsylvania, 1981, esp. 268ff.

7. Pausanias 10.4.1

8. Aelius Artistides *Or.* 14, p. 363 (Dindorf); Dio Chrysostomos 48.9; Philostratos *VS* 2.26; Plutarch *Adv. Colot.* 31 (1123 D–E); *Macc.* 2.4.9–16.

9. C. A. Forbes, *Greek Physical Education* (New York and London, 1929) 72.

10. Cf. M. P. Nilsson, *Die hellenistische Schule* (Munich, 1955) passim, but esp. 1–4.

11. Cicero *De Or.* 2.5.20–21.

12. Ibid.

13. One may mention such obvious examples as boxing (Polydeukes and Amykos), wrestling (Theseus and Kerkyon), the foot race (Atalanta and Melanion/Hippomenes), chariot racing (Pelops and Oinomaos), and the discus (Perseus and the death of Akrisios). Further, Prometheus (Philostratus, *Gymn.* 16) is credited with the invention of gymnastics and furnishing the information to Hermes. Herakles (schol. to Pindar *Pyth.* 9.214) shares the same distinction. Theseus is said to have introduced the art of wrestling, having learned it from Athena or from his charioteer, Phorbos (schol. to Pindar *Nem.* 5.89). The tradition of funeral games among the heroes is particularly persistent. L. Malten, "Leichenspiel und Totenkult," *RömMitt* 38–39 (1923–24) 300–340, lists thirty-three such accounts compiled from literary allusion and artistic tradition. The funeral games for Pelias on the chest of Kypselos (Pausanias 5.17.5–11) are especially representative of this genre.

14. The only notable omission from the list of classical events with which the Homeric poems are familiar is the pankration, although its combined elements, boxing and wrestling, are clearly present.

15. W. Donlan, "The Origin of Καλὸς κἀγαθός," *AJP* 94 (1973) 370.

16. H. I. Marrou, *A History of Education in Antiquity* (New York, 1956) 43–45.

17. To my knowledge the phrase never appears in a pedagogical context.

18. *Etym.* 15.2.30.

19. *Etym.* 8.6.17.

20. The references here are legion. Among them, cf. Plato *Rep.* 425c; Aeschines *In Tim.* 10; Thucydides 1.6.5; Plutarch *Quaest. Rom.* 40; idem, *Amat.* 750A–751A, 751F–752C. That the gymnasia and their associated pederastic practices were peculiarly Greek is attested by Herodotus 1.135; Plato *Symp.* 182b–c; Xenophon *Cyr.* 2.2.28; Cicero *Tusc.* 4.70. Cf. *Macc.* 2.4.10–15.

21. Thucydides 1.6.5.

22. Cf. supra n. 20.

23. Pausanias 1.44.1.

24. Cf. E. L. Hicks and G. F. Hill, *A Manual of Greek Historical Inscriptions*[2] (Oxford; 1901) 3–4 n. 1.

25. *Comm. ad Il.* 23.1.683.

26. *Chron.,* vol. 1, p. 195, ed. Schoene.

27. 7.72.3; cf. Pausanias 5.8.7.

28. *Comm. ad Il.* 23.1.683.

29. *Etym. Magn.* s.v. γυμνάσια.

30. *Suda,* s.v. δρόμοι; cf. Pausanias 3.14.6.

31. In E. N. Gardiner, *Greek Athletic Sports and Festivals* (London, 1910) figs. 123 and 128.

32. Pausanias 5.24.9.

33. *Eleg.* B, 11.1335–36.

34. J. Carrière takes it to mean "fréquente au gymnase" (*Theognis de Mégare* [Paris, 1949] p. 158), whereas J. Delorme dismisses this and translates instead "se livre à la gymnastique" (*Gymnasion* [Paris, 1960] 19 and n. 6), since he would prefer to see the physical gymnasium as a somewhat later development.

35. An excellent and objective summary of the work to date on the Academy can be found in *Megale Hellenike Egkulopaideia Sumpleroma* 22, (Athens, 1958) 340–44. The most trustworthy plan so far published is by A. A. Papagiannopoulos-Palaios in *Polemon* E (1952–1953) 74–78. The extremely early use of the site is attested (EH II–III) in *Ergon* (1956) 10–13.

36. *In Timoc.* 114.

37. *In Tim.* 10.

38. Cf. C. Hignett, *A History of the Athenian Constitution,* (Oxford, 1952) 89; Delorme (supra n. 34) 36–37. Aristotle displays the same justifiable skepticism: *Pol. 1273b ff.*

39. *Suda,* s.v. τὸ Ἱππάρχου τειχίον; other accounts credit him with an expensive wall παρὰ τὴν Πυθίαν; cf. Gregory of Cyprus 3.81; Apostolios 17.8.

40. *Ap.* Harpokration, s.v. Λύκειον. The same source also quotes Philochoros as crediting the Lykeion to Pericles. Pausanias (1.29.16) writes that Lycurgus built the gymnasium πρὸς τῷ Λυκείῳ, as does Plutarch (*Vit. X. Orat.* 841c–d). *IG* II², 457, 11, lines 65–69, seems to suggest that he embellished rather than founded the Lykeion.

41. Plutarch *Them.* 1.2.

42. *Nub.* 1005–1008; cf. Eupolis *ap.* Diog. Laert. 3.7.

43. Kim. 13.8.

44. *Fin.* 6.1.2.

45. *Mith.* 30.

46. *Hipparch.* 3.

47. *Pr.* 29.14.

48. Athenaeus 13.602d. He writes that the palaestra was ἀντιτειχίσματα to the citadels of Polykrates. Cf. Dionysius of Halicarnassus 7.9.3 for a similar threat to Aristodemos of Cumae. The pederastic associations of the Greek gymnasium constitute a problem far too complex and enigmatic for this paper to treat fairly within its allotted span. In general cf. the apposite remarks of K. J. Dover, *Greek Homosexuality* (Cambridge, 1978) passim, but esp. 54ff.

49. Herodotus 6.125.

50. So K. Schneider, *Die griechischen Gymnasien und Palaestren nach ihrer geschichtlichen Entwicklung,* Diss. Freiburg, 1908, 20–21.

51. So Godley in his Loeb translation.

52. So J. H. Krause, *Die Gymnastik und Agonistik der Hellenen* (Leipzig, 1841) I 109 followed implicitly by Delorme (supra n. 34) 264.

53. How and Wells, s.v.

54. Krause (supra n. 52) I 107ff. The problem, of course, has been reconsidered many times since, to little additional profit. Cf. *inter al.,* Schneider (supra n. 50) 28ff.; idem, s.v. palaistra, *RE* 18.2 (1942) 2472–73; J. Oehler, s.v. gymnasium, *RE* 7.2 (1912) 2009–2011; Gardiner (supra n. 3) 467ff.; Forbes (supra n. 9) 76ff.; Delorme (supra n. 34) 253ff.

55. Forbes (supra n. 9) 77.

56. *Etym.* 18.23–24: "Locus autem luctationis palaestra vocatur . . . palaestram ἀπὸ τῆς πάλης id est a luctatione." The difficulties posed by the more metaphorical uses of γυμνάσιον καὶ παλαίστραι, as evidenced by the phrase καί αὐτὴ πάλη, have been noted supra.

57. Pausanias 6.21.2.

58. Cf. *inter al.* Ps. Aristotle *Oec.* 2.1346b; Plutarch *Amat.* 755C; Pausanias 10.4.1; *SEG* IX, 4, 1, line 44. Solon, one will recall, passed laws regarding the Athenian gymnasia (supra). Whether or not he actually did is irrelevant here. That a public official should perform this function was obviously not considered an untoward assertion. Lycurgus worked on the Lykeion with public funds (supra n. 40). The city of Halicarnassus repaired one of its

gymnasia, the Phillipeion; cf. C. A. Forbes, *Neoi* (Middleton, Conn., 1933) 48–49. The gymnasiarch, too, was invariably a public official: ibid. 21ff., but esp. 22.

59. Cf. the list of private palaestrae in Krause (supra n. 52) I, 110. Cf. also Schneider (supra n. 50) 30–31.

60. E.g., at Olympia (Pausanias 5.15.8); at the Lykeion (Plutarch *Vit. X. Orat.* 841c–d); in the Academy (Hyperides, In *Dem.* fr. 6, col. xxvi, ed. Blass, p. 17); at Corinth (Plutarch *Tim.* 39.4); cf. Pollux *Onom.* 3.24.

61. This appears to be Forbes's implicit point in *Greek Physical Education* (supra n. 9) 80–82.

62. Cf. the definitive report by J. Delorme in *Explorations archéologique de Delos*, fasc. xxv: *Les Palestres* (Paris, 1961) 77–175.

63. Cf. supra n. 58.

64. Plutarch *Tim.* 39.4.

65. *Resp. Ath.* 2.10.

66. E. Rupprecht, "Die Schrift vom Staate der Athener," *Klio Beiheft* 44 (1939) 106–107.

67. Forbes (supra n. 9) 80.

68. E.g., H. Frisch, *The Constitution of the Athenians* (Copenhagen, 1942) 213 and 256–57.

69. Cf. Krause (supra n. 52) I, 117ff.; Schneider (supra n. 50) 71–72; idem, *RE* 18.2 (1942) 2491–92; Gardiner (supra n. 31) 469–70.

70. This problem is most clearly pointed up by C. A. Forbes (supra n. 58) and is somewhat analogous to that presented by Latin *adulescens.*

71. Aeschines *In Tim.* 10; cf. also Theophrastos *Char.* 7.5; Xenophon *Lac.* 2.1.

72. *BSA* 59 (1935) 476, lines 2–3.

73. Forbes (supra n. 58) 48–49.

74. Herodotus 6.126.

75. *IG* VII, 414, 11, lines 29–31. Cf. Antiphon 2.1ff., for *paides* in a gymnasium.

76. Cf. J. Juethner, s.v. Paidotribes, *RE* 18.2 (1942) 2389–96, esp. 2389–90.

77. Aristotle *Ath. Pol.* 42.3; Aeschines *In Ctes.* 246.

78. *De Arch.* 5.11.1ff.

79. So Schneider (supra n. 50) 64. Cf. F. Granger in the Loeb edition of Vitruvius, vol. 1, 306, n. 2.

80. Academy: Aelian *V H* 3.19 (περίπατος and κῆπος); Diogenes Laertius 3.20 (κηπίδιον); Apuleius *De dog. Plat.* 1.4 *(hortulus);* Aristophanes *Nub.* 1005 (ὑπὸ ταῖς μορίαις ἀποθρέξει); cf. schol. ibid. (ἐπεφύτευτο δὲ τῷ γυμνασίῳ δένδρα); Cicero *Fin.* 5.1 (non sine causa nobilitata spatia); Eupolis *ap.* Diogenes Laertius 3.7 (ἐν εὐσκίοις δρόμοισιν Ἑκαδήμου θεοῦ); Plutarch *Kim.* 13.8 (τὴν δ᾽ Ἀκαδήμειαν ἐξ ἀνύδρου καὶ αὐχμηρᾶς κατάρρυτον ἀποδείξας ἄλσος ἠσκημένον ὑπ᾽ αὐτοῦ δρόμοις καὶ συσ-

κίοις περίπατοις). Lykeion: Diogenes Laertius 5.11.51–52 (κῆπος and περίπατος); Theophrastos *Hist. Pl.* 1.7.1 (πλάτανος); Plato *Euthyd.* 272e–273a κατάστεγος δρόμος). Cf. also the Pausanian description of the old gymnasium at Elis (6.23.1).

81. To my knowledge there is only one: Hyperides *In Dem.* fr. 6, col. xxvi, ed. Blass (supra n. 60) 17. Similarly, there is only one for the Lykeion: Plutarch *Vit. X. Orat.* 841c–d.

82. Cf. Herodotus 6.126; Euripides *Andr.* 575ff.

83. Romano (supra n. 6) 244ff.

84. Cf. J. Audiat, "Le Gymnase de Delos et l'Inventaire de Kallistratos," *BCH* 54 (1930) 95–130. Cf. also *IG* XI, 2, 165, line 48.

85. Audiat (supra n. 84); Delorme (supra n. 62). I am not here concerned with the individual difficulties presented by some of the terms (e.g., σφαιριστήριον), nor with the problems involving their precise positions in the ground plans of the structures in which they are located epigraphically.

86. Cf. P. Schazmann, "Das Gymnasium," in *Altertümer von Pergamon* (Berlin, 1885–1937) vol. 6, and the evidence published in *AM,* particularly 29 (1904), 121–50; 32 (1907) 190–214; and 33 (1908) 328–57. For Delphi, of particular importance is the work of M. Homolle, "Le Gymnase de Delphes," *BCH* 23 (1899) 560–83, esp. 564ff. Surprisingly few changes of major importance were revealed by J. Jannoray's final publication of the gymnasium in 1953; "Le Gymnase," in *Fouilles de Delphes* II: *Topographie et architecture.*

87. Lacking any running facilities, the "gymnasium" at Epidauros might be an exception to this observation, were its identification more secure. No ancient author mentions the gymnasium, and only two inscriptions of uncertain date allude to its presence at the site (cf. *IG* IV, 1467, and A. Burford, *BSA* 61 (1966) 316–17). The identification still rests essentially on the summary report by P. Kabbadias, *To Hieron tou Asklepiou en Epidauro* (Athens, 1900) 143–48. J. Delorme, sensing the structural anomalies, iden-tified it as a palaestra ("Recherches au Gymnase d'Epidaure," *BCH* 70 [1946] 108), and stronger doubts were expressed by S. Glass, *Palaistra and Gymnasium in Greek Architecture,* Diss. University of Pennsylvania, 1967, 102ff. and 247ff.). A. Frickenhaus, "Griechische Banketthaüser," *JdI* 32 (1917) 131–33, noted that three of the rooms in the "gymnasium" could have been designed for dining. Keying on Frickenhaus' observations, R. A. Tomlinson dismissed the "gymnasium" at Epidauros entirely as an ath- letic complex, preferring to see it as an *estiatorion* analogous to one attested in the Asklepieion on Delos. Cf. "Two Buildings in Sanctuaries of Asklepios," *JHS* 89 (1969) 106ff. Although Tomlinson explicitly avoids the issue of gymnasium versus palaestra (ibid. 110 n. 25), it seems clear that prevailing opinion has, for some time now, rejected Kabbadias' original gymnasium. Tomlinson's new "gymnasium" set in the complex of rooms directly north of the stadium is not persuasive. See his *Epidauros* (London, 1983) 69.

88. E.g., the list in Schneider (supra n. 50) 30ff.

89. *Lys.* 204a, 203a. We do not know the precise location of this fountain. Cf. W. Judeich, *Topographie von Athen*[2] (Munich, 1931) 414–15.

90. *Lys.* 204a.

91. *Lys.* 203b, 206e.

92. *Lys.* 204a.

93. *Lys.* 206e. I would take ἔξω to mean open to the sky, as well as "outside" in relation to the *apodyterion.*

94. *Onom.* 9, 43; cf. Ps. Xen. *Resp. Ath.* 2.10.

95. *Euthyd.* 272e–273a.

96. *Euthyd.* 273b.

97. Delorme (supra n. 34) 55; cf. Schneider (supra n. 50) 63.

98. Cf. the Kallistratos inventory (supra n. 84) 11.122–23 and 133.

99. Cf. C. Wachsmuth, *Die Stadt Athen in Alterthum* (Leipzig, 1890) vol. 2, 279ff.

100. *De Arch.* 5.11.1.

101. The basic discussion is by Paul Graef and R. Borrman, in E. Curtius and F. Adler, eds., *Olympia, Ergebnisse der von der deutschen Reich veranstaltenen Ausgrabungen* (Berlin, 1890–1896) text II, 113ff., and plate vol. II, pls. LXXIII–LXXVIII. Cf. E. N. Gardiner, *Olympia: Its History and Remains* (Oxford, 1925) 289.

102. Pausanias 5.23.1ff.

103. So Schneider in *RE* 18.2 (1942) 2493, who believes it to be the oldest palaestra of which we have any record.

Jane M. Renfrew

Food for Athletes and Gods
A Classical Diet

11

The evidence for food at the ancient Olympic Games is based entirely on literary sources, and these are neither very detailed nor comprehensive, diet being mentioned casually in discussion on other topics. Nonetheless, it was thought to be of interest to collect this information together as it gives an interesting insight into the life at Olympia during the festival. The information can be considered under four main headings, covering the most important features of the recorded evidence. First, we consider the food for the Olympic athletes themselves, which, as we shall see, varied through the long time span of the original Olympic Games, and also according to the different types of sport undertaken; then the food of the gods—the sacrifices offered at the various altars in the sacred precincts at Olympia. Linked to this were the celebratory feasts associated with the Games, and finally the food of the spectators. It must be remembered that Olympia was situated in a fairly remote and underpopulated part of the Peloponnese and that, since there was no large permanent settlement there, everything in the way of food had to be brought in to support the whole festival when it occurred once every four years. When the festival was at the peak of its fame, spectators flocked there in their thousands: the stadium had a capacity of 40,000.

The Diet of the Athletes

Only one of the many manuals on physical training has survived from antiquity, and that is Philostratus' *Handbook for the Athletics Coach,* dating to the first quarter of the third century A.D. Of the early athletes he says (43):

The Old School did not even recognize such a thing as temperament but trained only physical strength. . . . Barley cakes served as their food and unleavened bread of unsifted wheat, and their meats were of the ox, the bull, the goat, and the roe, and they annointed themselves richly with oil from the wild olive and the oleaster. In this way they were free from illnesses when training and grew old slowly. Some of them used to compete for eight Olympiads [thirty-two years], and others for nine; they were excellent in hoplite service and used to fight in defense of the ramparts, not falling there either but meriting prizes and trophies. They regarded war as a training for gymnastics, gymnastics as a training for war.[1]

Then medical science began to take a hand in shaping the diet of the athletes, introducing (44):

the habit of sitting down before the period of exercising, gorged with food. . . . [Moreover] they brought in luxurious chefs and caterers by whom men were made into epicures and gluttons, treated to indigestible bread sprinkled with poppy seed; contrary to regulations they made use of fish as a food, discoursing on the nature of fish from their habitat in the sea, saying that those from swampy places are fat, that soft ones come from near cliffs, fleshy ones from the deep sea, the seaweed produced this one and other kinds of sea moss produced a tasteless kind. Still further, the doctors brought on the flesh of swine with wondrous tales about it, directing that herds of swine down by the sea should be considered injurious on account of the sea garlic which grows in abundance along the shore and the coast, and prohibiting the use of those near rivers because they may have fed on crabs. The only kind of pigs they recommended eating, while training, were those fattened on cornel berries or acorns.

Clearly different sports require different physiques: the runners need to be lightly built, with long legs, whereas the boxers need to be more solid and weighty: "A boxer derives some advantage from a belly, for it wards off blows from the face when it projects into the path of the opponent's thrust."[2] Thus, it is not surprising that the athletes whose diets have been recorded are those of prodigious strength. The most famous must be Milo of Croton in southern Italy. He had a long and distinguished career as a wrestler, beginning by winning the boys' event in 540 B.C. He went on to win the men's wrestling in five successive Olympiads from 536 to 520 B.C. He also was victorious once in the boys' and six times in the men's events at the Pythian Games at Delphi, and also won ten times in the Isthmian and nine times in the Nemean Games. Five times he was *peri-*

odonikes, or winner of the quadruple crown, a title given to the man who won at all four of the "crown" festivals in the same cycle.[3] He is reported to have had a normal daily diet of twenty pounds of wheat, the same weight of bread, and eighteen pints of wine. On one occasion at Olympia he put a four-year-old bull on his shoulders and carried it round the stadium, after which he cut it up and ate it all alone in a single day.[4]

The introduction of meat into the athlete's diet has been attributed to Pythagoras, the trainer and philosopher. One tradition claims that Eurymenes of Samos was the first meat-eating victor in a heavyweight event at Olympia.[5] Pausanias claims that Dromeus of Stymphalos, twice winner of the *dolichos* at Olympia about 480 B.C., was the first athlete to train on a meat diet.[6] Previously the main source of protein for the Olympic athletes was fresh feta cheese, "straight out of the basket," as Pausanias puts it.

The usual Greek diet consisted of a thick vegetable soup, bread, cheese, olives, and fruit. Fish was eaten both fresh and dried, but meat was a rare and luxurious commodity. In addition they had a variety of cakes made with honey. It is probable that the moralists' denunciations of the supposedly excessive diet of the athletes were partly the outcome of envy: Euripides called the athletes "the slaves of their jaws and the victims of their bellies." Plutarch ascribes to the coaches and trainers of his day the belief that intelligent conversation at meals spoils the food and gives the diners a headache![7]

The only other fragmentary references to the Olympic athletes' diet which I have been able to trace are the claim that Charmis of Sparta, victor in 668 B.C., trained on a diet of dried figs;[8] Xenophon's advice to men in training not to eat bread;[9] and the assertion that the Pythagoreans in the Italian instep area around Croton had a taboo against athletes' eating beans.[10]

The Food of the Gods:
Public and Private Sacrifices

The Olympic festival lasted for five days and was held to coincide with the second or third moon after the summer solstice every four years. The Games were held in honor of the god Zeus, and a visit to the games was also a pilgrimage to the sacred grove known as the Altis. At first simple altars were erected in the grove, and the offerings to Zeus—primitive terracotta and bronze figures of men and animals—were hung in the trees. From the sixth century B.C. on, the sacred grove was adorned with temples, treasuries, halls, elaborate altars, and hundreds of marble and bronze statues, mainly dedicated by victors to Zeus. Most remarkable of all was the huge (thirteen meters high) gold and ivory statue of Zeus by

Pheidias set within his magnificent temple—one of the seven wonders of the ancient world.

The chief sacrifice of the Games was the sacrifice of one hundred oxen on the Altar of Zeus in the morning of the middle day of the festival. The oxen were presented by the people of Elis, and they were sacrificed at the open-air altar. In Pausanias' time it consisted of a stone base on the top of which was a conical heap of ashes some seven meters high. Once the oxen had been slaughtered, their legs were carried to the top of the ash mound, and there they were burned in a fire of silver poplar branches. Zeus was believed to take sustenance from the smoke. Once burnt, the ashes were mixed with water from the River Alpheios close by and plastered onto the ash mound, which solidified and increased in height year by year.

The Prytaneion, which was the administrative center for the festival, also housed the sacred flame of Hestia, goddess of the hearth, which was kept burning night and day and provided a flame to light the fires on all the altars in the Altis. It was built about 470 B.C. Ash from the sacrifices made to Hestia was also added to the mound of the great Altar of Zeus.

On the evening of the second day of the Games, under the rising full moon, chthonian sacrifices of black rams were offered to Pelops in the Pelopeion. Pelops was worshipped more than other divine heroes at Olympia by the Eleans. The ram's neck was given to the woodman at the altar, but not the rest. The woodman's job was to provide both cities and individuals with white poplar for sacrifices at a fixed price.[11]

There were sixty-nine altars in the sacred enclosure of the Altis, and once a month the Eleans offered sacrifices at every altar, year in and year out. Pausanias says:

> They sacrifice in an antique style; they burn frankincense with honey-kneaded wheaten cakes on their altars and lay branches of olive on them and pour wine. It is only to the Nymphs and the Mistresses and on the common altar of all the gods that the practice is to pour no wine. The performance of the sacrifices is under a priest who holds that honor for a month, also prophets and wine-carriers, a sacred guide and a flute-player, and the woodman.[12]

The Temple of Hera is particularly associated with the women's or Hera's games, also held every four years, which consisted of a running match in the stadium between virgin girls: "They give the winners crowns made of olive branches and a share of the ox they slaughter to Hera."[13]

Many minor sacrifices were made by the athletes and their supporters during the festival, as the athletes prayed, made vows, and offered thanks.

Sometimes the entrails of sacrificed animals would be examined to see if they foretold victory;[14] this took place mainly during the morning of the first day of the festival.

Feasts and Celebrations

There were two forms of feast associated with the Olympic Games. The largest was the public banquet held in the Prytaneion on the evening of the middle day of the Games. At it were consumed the remains of the hundred head of oxen sacrificed to Zeus earlier in the day (Zeus being offered only the thighs). Pindar in the fifth century B.C. caught the atmosphere of the occasion: "and the whole company raised a great cheer, while the lovely light of the fair-faced moon lit up the evening. Then in joyful celebration the whole Altis rang with the banquet song."[15]

Apart from this main banquet, there were a large number of private celebrations in the evenings. The victors and their friends decked themselves in garlands and processed round the Altis singing victory hymns. The wealthier the victor, or his sponsor, the more luxurious the celebration. Alcibiades of Athens, the chariot-racer, clearly understood the impact on his own prestige and that of his home city, Athens, not only of being seen to be victorious—his chariots came in first, second, and third in 416 B.C.—but also of making lavish display. Isocrates describes it thus in a speech written for Alcibiades' son:

> My father, seeing that the festival assembly at Olympia was beloved and admired by the whole world, and that in it the Greeks made display of their wealth, strength of body, and training, and that not only the athletes were the objects of envy but that also the cities of the victors became renowned . . . [and] that expenditures in the Olympian Festival . . . enhance the city's reputation throughout all Greece, . . . [he] turned to the breeding of race horses . . . and he entered a larger number of teams in competition than even the mightiest cities had done . . . and they were of such excellence that he came out first, second, and third. Besides this his generosity in the sacrifices and in the other expenses connected with the festival was so lavish and magnificent that the public funds of all the others were clearly less than the private means of Alcibiades alone.[16]

Alcibiades, however, upset his fellow citizens by parading round the sacred enclosure with the ceremonial gold and silver vessels belonging to Athens, which he used for his own private victory celebrations.[17]

Empedocles of Agrigentum, a disciple of Pythagoras and a vegetarian, made an ox out of dough mixed with incense and garnished with expensive herbs and spices and distributed it among the spectators.[18] Often the victory celebrations lasted all night, and the following morning the victors made solemn vows and sacrifices to the appropriate gods.

Some idea of the rewards for the victors can be gleaned from two inscriptions found in Athens dating to 380 B.C. They concern the prizes given for athletic events in the Panathenaic festival in Athens. We learn that as many as 1,300 amphorae of olive oil were awarded to victors in prizes of from sixty to six jars, and if he chose to, the victor could have sold his prize at a price of twelve drachmas an amphora. One would expect that the magnificent Panathenaic vases hand-painted with pictures of Athena and an athletic scene became family heirlooms.[19]

The Spectators

Arrangements for competitors and spectators were left to private enter-prise. There was no shortage of local people anxious to earn a few drachmas by hiring out tents, mules, and donkeys, selling food and drink, and providing entertainment for the crowds when the Games were not in progress. Spectators were not exacting about accommodation at the Games. Aelian says that Plato shared a tent with strangers there.

This atmosphere of disorganized festivity is also reflected in Dio Chrysostom's account of the Isthmian Games:

> Round the temple of Poseidon you could see and hear the accursed sophists shouting and abusing one another, and their so-called pupils fighting each other, many authors giving readings of their works which no-one listens to, many poets reciting their poems and others expressing approval of them, many conjurers performing their tricks and many fortunetellers interpreting omens, thousands of lawyers arguing cases and a host of cheap jacks selling everything under the sun.[20]

When one remembers that at some Games there were about 40,000 spec-tators at Olympia, the problem of providing food and drink was clearly a massive one. At least the Games were held after the harvest, when the maximum amount of fresh fruit was available. There can be little doubt that the lot of the spectator was not always a comfortable one, as Epictetus wrote in his *Discourses:*

> Some unpleasant and hard things happen in life and do they not happen at Olympia? Do you not swelter? Are you not cramped and crowded? Do you not bathe badly? Are you not drenched whenever

it rains? Do you not have your fill of tumult and shouting and other annoyances? But I fancy you bear and endure it all by balancing it off against the memorable character of the spectacle.[21]

Nor were the proceedings free from massive infestations of flies. Pausanias reports that when Herakles was sacrificing at Olympia he was badly pestered by flies, and so he made a sacrifice to Zeus Averter of Flies (Apomyios) and the flies were turned away across the Alpheios.[22] The Eleans are said to have sacrificed in the same way to drive away flies from Olympia—but not even Zeus could do much against the lack of sanitation in such a large gathering.

One must imagine that the spectators fed rather like the people at Xenophon's Temple of Artemis at Skillos, not far from Olympia. Here all those taking part in the annual festival were given barley meal and loaves of bread, wine and sweetmeats, and a portion of the sacrificial victims as well as of game taken in hunting. There was a hunt during the festival on Mount Phloe, and boars, stags, and gazelles were caught. Fruit trees grew close to the temple precinct, providing fruit in season, and there was ample meadowland in the vicinity to feed cattle and especially horses and the draught animals which brought the spectators to the festival.[23]

Thus, although there is no direct treatise on or evidence for food at the ancient Olympic Games, it is possible to obtain an insight into various aspects of the victualing of the Games. There can be no doubt that the festival put a severe pressure on the local resources, and it was perhaps just as well that it only lasted for five days and that it only occurred once every four years.

Notes

1. Translated by R. S. Robinson, *Sources for the History of Greek Athletics in English Translation* (Cincinnati, Ohio, 1956), 224.

2. Philostratus *Gymn.* 34.

3. H. A. Harris, *Greek Athletes and Athletics* (London, 1964) 111.

4. Athenaeus *Deip.* 10.412.

5. Harris (supra n. 2) 172.

6. Pausanias 6.7.10.

7. Euripides *Autol.* fr. 282.

8. Harris (supra n. 3) 172.

9. Xenophon *Mem.* 3.14.3.

10. M. I. Finley and H. W. Pleket, *The Olympic Games* (London, 1976) 94.

11. Pausanias 5.13.1–7.

12. Pausanias 5.15.10. Translated by Peter Levi in *Pausanias, Guide to Greece* (Penguin 1971; rpt 1984).

13. Pausanias 5.16.3. Translated by Peter Levi (supra n. 12).

14. J. Swaddling, *The Ancient Olympic Games* (London, 1980) 39.

15. Pindar *Ol.* 10.73–78.

16. Isocrates *Syn.* 32–34. Translated by R. S. Robinson (supra n. 1) 120.

17. Swaddling (supra n. 14) 39.

18. Ibid. 76.

19. R. S. Robinson (supra n. 1) 119.

20. Dio Chrysostom *Or.* 8.9. Translated by H. A. Harris, *Greek Athletes and Athletics* (London, 1964) 159.

21. Epictetus *Disc.* 1.6.26–27. Translated by M. I. Finley and H. W. Pleket, *the Olympic Games: The First Thousand Years* (New York, 1976) 54.

22. Pausanias 5.14.1.

23. Xenophon *An.* 5.3.6–10.

Part Six

Beyond Olympia (2)

Local Rites and Festivals

Thomas F. Scanlon

Virgineum Gymnasium
Spartan Females and Early Greek Athletics

12

With typically erotic overtones Propertius sang the praise of Spartan maidens: "I marvel at the many rules of your palaestra, O Sparta, but even more at the blessings of your gymnasium for girls *(virgineum gymnasium)*, since a naked girl may take part in the well-known games amidst men as they wrestle" (3.14.1–4).

The study of female athletics in Archaic and Classical Greece offers a unique perspective from which to observe young women engaged in the rites of passage from adolescence to adulthood. Yet since men's physical initiatory tests and sports contest in general in ancient Greece were either a preparation for warfare or a reflection of the martial spirit, women's athletics for most Greeks, with the exception of Spartans, would have been a contradiction in terms. The present definition of women's athletics therefore includes girls' ritual contests of physical strength within the context of religious festivals, three of which are known—namely, those at Olympia, Brauron, and Sparta—and girls' physical education, which is found only at Sparta during the period under study. What all these instances of early female athletics have in common is that participation is limited to virgins, and they arguably serve as ritual, or, in the case of Sparta, actual tests of strength prior to marriage.[1]

Source material for this study poses two problems. First, it is scanty, since we have only a few clear examples of women's participation. And, secondly, it has relied upon men for transmission, which probably explains the paucity of evidence, since women's sports were both uninteresting and unimportant to men. We may infer from the few extant examples that women's athletic contests, particularly foot races in cult contexts, were probably more widespread than our sources indicate.[2]

I will merely mention here the ritual contests for women at Olympia and Brauron, before passing on to Sparta, where female participation was the earliest, most extensive, and possibly most influential as a model for the other rituals. My original contributions to this subject, which others have treated *pari passu,* are to put forth evidence for Spartan female athletics as part of a prenuptial initiation, to examine archaeological evidence for Spartan girls' physical education, and to suggest that Sparta may have influenced practice at Olympia.

In the context of his description of the sanctuary at Olympia in the mid-second century A.D., Pausanias gives the only extant account of a foot race for girls held at the quadrennial festival for Hera, the Heraia (5.16.2–3). Pausanias gives two accounts of the foundation of the festival, one attributing it to Hippodameia's thanksgiving for her marriage to Pelops, the other citing an Elean treaty of about 580 B.C. which occasioned the practice (5.16.4–6). I have argued elsewhere that the 580 date may allude to a reorganization of the Heraia under the influence of Spartan female athletics.[3] The festival structure is remarkably similar to that of the men's Olympics in its earliest period, consisting of a simple foot race followed by the awarding of an olive crown and the apportionment of the sacrificial cow at a final festival. The race was restricted to girls who ran in three (unspecified) age groups and wore special Amazon-style short chitons with one breast exposed, such as may be represented in a sixth-century Laconian bronze.[4] Age-grouping, restriction to maidens, and association with Hippodameia's marriage all suggest that the festival originated as a prenuptial initiation rite.[5] It is further appropriate that the so-called Sixteen Women who organized the Heraia constituted a college of married priestesses who also organized an Elean festival for Dionysus, the god of adult women. The Sixteen also organized a chorus to the local heroine Physkoa, who, together with the son Narkaios whom she bore to Dionysus, introduced the worship of Dionysus to the region.

The excavations of the sanctuary of Artemis at Brauron on the east coast of Attica have unearthed a series of locally produced ritual vessels evidently depicting scenes from the Brauronian Arkteia or "Bear Festival."[6] We know little about this festival except that Attic girls aged ten to fourteen called *arktoi* or "bears" were required to undergo certain rites before marriage. The vases, dated mostly between 490–420 B.C., show what are apparently races staged for the maidens, some dressed in short chitons, as in a lekythos of 490–470, some completely naked, as in a fragmentary krater of 430–420.[7] It is difficult to interpret the races further in the absence of literary testimony.

The case of Spartan women's athletics is strikingly anomalous among Greek *poleis,* since there the girls apparently took part in the famous education system, the *agoge,* an institution allegedly founded by the shadowy figure of Spartan reform, Lycurgus.[8] The dates and the existence of this lawgiver are justly doubted, and there are futher difficulties in our literary evidence for early Spartan society—namely, that the authors are all late, from the fourth century B.C. to the third century A.D., and that they each write with a particular *ira et studio* which strongly defends or condemns that communal *polis*.[9] Despite varying opinions on its origins and its success, the majority of authors agree on the form and purpose of Spartan education. Modern scholars maintain that the unique structure of the *agoge,* incorporating initiatory institutions found in other primitive cultures, suggests that its roots predate the Archaic period. Male messes, age classes, separation from society, and trials of strength are well documented for males and have analogues with initiation elsewhere. The system thus may have undergone an intensification in the mid-seventh century, a period identified with other Lycurgan measures.[10]

That Spartan girls were organized in age groups like the boys is indicated by references in Alcman *(Parth.* 52; second half of the seventh century B.C.), who calls a chorus of girls "cousins" *(anepsiai),* a term also used of boy colleagues, and Pindar (fr. 112; first half of the fifth century B.C.), who calls a Spartan girl chorus an *agela,* "horse-herd," the very term used for the boys' regiments in the *agoge.*[11] Other terms, namely *kasioi* or *kasen,* meaning "brothers," "sisters," or "cousins," appear in numerous inscriptions, mostly from the Roman period, and these suggest educational reform whose inception is possibly even datable to c. 184 B.C., when Spartans revived the archaic system after a crushing defeat.[12] Callimachus (ca. 305–240 B.C.) also refers to a group of Spartan maidens as an *ila* "company" *(Hymn* 5.33–34; cf. scholiast to *Hymn* 5, 33–34: ἴλα : ἡ τῶν νυμφῶν φρατρία καὶ ἄθροισις, *"ila:* the clan-division and collection of maidens"). One of the latest indications of the girls' *agoge* is a second-century A.D. inscription *(IG* 5.1.170) mentioning a board of six *guanikonomoi,* "regulators of women," corresponding to the young men's *paidonomoi.*[13] That Spartan girls are on occasion metaphorically compared to "fillies"—for example, in Alcman *(Parth.* 59) and Aristophanes *(Lys.* 1308–1313)—is further evidence that they belonged to "horse-herds" in Archaic and Classical times.[14]

Before looking at the widely attested physical education of Spartan girls, we should note that their education probably included "arts and letters" as well, since Plato mentions that they are all well schooled in philosophy and speaking, and there are other indications of their literacy. Their glibness in fact gave rise to a series of apothegms illustrating the free speech of Spartan women, many in the brassy spirit of the exhortation to warriors to come back "with your shield or on it."[15]

Theocritus (c. 300–260? B.C.)in his "Epithalamy of Helen" *(Hymn* 18) gives the best idealized portrait of the legendary Spartan beauty who doubtless served as a role model for younger girls. In the poem, twelve Spartan girls, former companions of the queen-to-be, praise her beauty, her skill at weaving, and her musical talent (26–37).[16] They recall their former activities: "We all as age-mates *(sunomalikes)* who practiced the

same running course and oiled ourselves down like men alongside the
bathing pools of the Eurotas, we are the four times sixty maidens, the
female corps of youth *(neolaia)"* (22–25).

The irony with regard to Spartan girls' physical education is that
however much it resembled that of the men in form, it was essentially
different in its goal of producing beautiful and fit young women, who
could endure childbirth and nourish their offspring until they, in turn,
could enter the *agoge.* Boys underwent the stages of initiation to become
strong and virtuous warriors; girls, to become wives. "Marriage is for the
girl what war is for the boy"—namely the fulfillment of their natures in
the service of the state.[17] The analogy of the types of education has led
authors, especially at Rome, to attribute to the female *agoge* the goal of
preparing female soldiers.[18] Plutarch (fl. 100–120 A.D.), for instance, in
the context of explaining that Spartan girls exercised to produce strong
offspring and contend with birth pains, adds "and moreover, if the need
arise, they might be able to fight for themselves, their children, and their
country" (*Mor.* 227 D.12). The corrective for this view is found in Plato
(*Leg.* 7.805E–806A; written c. 355–347 B.C.), who, in the words of the
Athenian interlocutor, complains that the Laconian system of female education is a "half-way measure" *(to . . . dia mesou)* in which girls share in
gymnastics and music, but women abstain from military service. Aristotle (384–322 B.C.), in a typical anti-Spartan tirade, gives a historical
exemplum: "Even in regard to courage, which is of no use in daily life, and
is needed only in war, the influence of the Lacedaimonian women has
been most mischievous. The evil showed itself in the Theban invasion
[370 B.C.], when, unlike most women in other cities, they were utterly
useless and caused more confusion than the enemy" (*Pol.* 2.6.7, 1269B).

Our earliest explicit source on the eugenic aim of Spartan female
education is Critias (*Const. Lac. DK,* II, 88, fr. 32, written c. 425–403
B.C.), followed by Xenophon (*Const. Lac.* 1.3–4, written c. 396–383 B.C.),
naming specifically "contests of running and strength" and first giving
Lycurgus credit for instituting the system. Plutarch (*Lyc.* 14.1–15.1) much
later (c. 100–120 B.C.) lists the fullest program of female sports:
"[Lycurgus] made the maidens exercise their bodies in running, wrestling, and the throwing of discus and javelin, so that the root of these born
might better mature by taking a strong beginning in strong bodies" (14.2).
By way of arguing against Aristotle's criticisms, Plutarch claims that the
girls were, no less than boys, "freed from all delicacy and effeminacy" by
requiring them without clothes to process, dance at certain festivals, and
sing in public. The nudity in fact inspired lofty sentiment "since they
partook no less than the men in bravery *(arete)* and ambition *(philotimia).*
Wherefore they were led to speak and think like Gorgo, the wife of
Leonides, is said to have done; when someone, apparently a foreigner,
said to her, 'You Spartan women alone rule over your men,' she answered,

'That's because only we give birth to men' "(14.4). Philostratus (*Gymn*. 27, written c. A.D. 230) echoes Plutarch's report by explaining that Lycurgus instituted female exercise to produce more and better "warrior-athletes" (*polemikous athletas*).[19]

The introduction of nudity to women's public events, as noted by Plutarch, may be an important clue to the ritual character and eugenic aim of their athleticism. Plutarch quotes Plato when he addresses the incentives to marriage in public nudity: "I refer to the processions of maidens, their undressing (*apoduseis*), and their games in the sight of young men drawn on by erotic, not geometrical, necessity!" (*Lyc*. 15.1; cf. Plat. *Rep*. 458D). It has been argued that nudity in these contexts can also mean "scantily clad"—that is, clad in the short Doric chiton, also called *chitoniskos*, the *monochiton*, or *chiton exomis*, which was worn without undergarment, pinned at the shoulder, open on one side exposing the thigh, and hemmed above the knees.[20] It is this scandalous garment which won them the epithet *phaineromerides*, or "thigh flashers," from Ibycus (sixth century B.C.)[21] and gave rise to the censorious words of Peleus in Euripides' *Andromache* (595–602), written ca. 430–424 B.C.:

> No Spartan girl could ever be restrained (*sophron*) even if she wanted to be; they desert their homes to go out with young men with their thighs bared and robes ungirt and they hold races and wrestling contests with them—I would not stand for it! Is it any wonder that you do not raise chaste women?

He goes on to compare the girls with their archetype Helen, who was also known as a home-deserter, a licentious and immodest woman, as Spartan females must have appeared to most Athenians.[22] How much more scandalous to imagine those girls entirely naked in public, as they probably were, in light of Plutarch's reference (*Lyc*. 15.1) to their "undressing" (*apoduseis*) before youths—namely, their removal of their *chitoniskos*. Similarly, Theocritus referred to girls "oiled down" for the foot race like men (18.23).

Athletic nudity in the Olympics allegedly began with Orsippus of Megara in 720 B.C. or possibly Acanthus of Sparta in the same year.[23] Plutarch (*Lyc*. 14.1–4) claims that Lycurgus introduced it at Sparta. But Plato suggests that it came to Sparta from Crete: "When first the Cretans, then the Lacedaimonians, began the practice of naked exercise, the wits of the time could have ridiculed this whole custom" (*Rep*. 5.425C). Whatever role the Spartans played in the institution of athletic nudity, the more important innovation was using the practice to further Spartan marriage. More than a simple athletic convenience, nudity is the primitive state of man in his natural innocence and passion—one is reminded of the sublime eroticism of Odysseus, brine-covered and washed up on the shores of Phaiakia, standing naked before the maiden Nausicaa.

Nudity is known to have served several religious and magic functions in ancient society, but cultic nudity among Greek girls and boys seems to have had the special significance of designating youths involved in special rituals at a stage prior to adulthood.[24] Spartan boys, for example, competed in age groups in the Gymnopaidia, or "Festival of Naked Youths," in honor of Apollo as a test of strength in preparation for real warfare.[25] Whether the boys were entirely naked or simply unarmed, their relative "undress" points to the special role of cultic nudity in the males' festival. Similarly, at Phaestus on Crete young boys practiced transvestitism at the Ekdysia, or "Festival of Undressing," in honor of Lato Phytia; new brides at the same festival slept next to the statue of Leucippus, patron hero of the festival.[26] The name of the Cretan festival and other references to "the undressed youths" (*ekdyomenoi*, vel sim.) suggest that cultic nudity played a role in this festival, which has the character of a prenuptial initiation for boys and girls, The recent finds of vases from Brauron in Attica showing girls, both naked and clothed in short chitons, running races for Artemis at the Arkteia Festival also suggest that cultic nudity played a role in this prenuptial ritual.[27] By analogy with customs elsewhere, we may assume that the athletic nudity of Spartan youths also served a religious and socializing function of preparing adolescents for marriage and adult life.

So when Plato recommended that youths associate in gymnastic exercise to be drawn by an erotic necessity, he may have been following the "Lycurgan" custom reported later by Plutarch. Euripides suggests that exercise in common may have been the rule, and he is followed by the less reliable, but perhaps here accurate, restatements of the principle by Propertius (3.14) and Ovid (*Her.* 16.149–52), the latter of whom addresses Helen: "And so Theseus rightly felt love's flame, for he was acquaint with all your charms, and you seemed fit spoil for the great hero to steal away, when, after the manner of your race, you engaged in sports of the shining palaestra, a nude maid mingled with nude men." Only Stobaeus writing in the fifth century A.D. explicitly denies this and states that the sexes exercised separately. And his claim is further weakened by the fact that only one exercise area, named the *Dromos* or "Track," is mentioned in Classical and Hellenistic times, and both boys and girls are said to frequent it.[28]

If the athletic nudity of Spartan females had deliberate erotic ends, they were certainly fostered by the legendary Spartan female beauty, perhaps comparable in our day to that of "California girls." "Sparta of the beautiful women" is first mentioned in the *Odyssey* (13.412; a *hapax* there), but the sensuous beauty of the chorus girls in Alcman's *Parthenion* of c. 600 B.C. carries on the legend. Similarly, Aristophanes' *Lysistrata* praises the beautiful skin and firm breasts as well as the virile muscularity of the

Spartan woman Lampito (*Lys.* 79–83); compare the similar remarks of
Athenaeus (12.566A) and Strabo (10.13). Beauty symbolizes the possession of virtue in the girl ready to marry. Physical exercise has bestowed on
her a quality which will find its culmination through the initiation process, in marriage perhaps at age eighteen to twenty, and then in the pro-
creation of beautiful infants. The whole educative process proceeds to the
acquisition of beauty for real, practical aims in the service of the state.
Whereas boys become good soldiers, girls become mothers who produce
good warriors.[29]

If beauty and the revealing Spartan costume, or lack of one, are
important or, indeed, essential elements of the Spartan female *agoge,* then
recognition of the Spartan ideal of female beauty by Homer and Alcman
suggests that Spartan society was at least predisposed to that ideal in the
seventh or even late eighth century. Ibycus' complaint about Spartan
"thigh-flashers," on the other hand, gives a *terminus post quem* of the 560s to
530s B.C. for the athletic costume, and hence for the social system of
female initiation.

This date in the sixth century is nicely supported by the archaeological evidence of a series of sixth- and early fifth-century bronzes, mirror handles and votive statues, apparently from Laconia or Laconian
workshops. They have been variously interpreted as dancers and acrobats—that is, secular entertainers—but in view of the literary evidence it
seems probable that they depict Spartan girls engaged in the dances, processions, and contests mentioned by Plutarch and others. Their existence
is all the more remarkable in view of the general absence of naked females
from sixth-century sculpture. I am not the first to suggest that the bronzes
represent Spartan female athletes, but I am the first, as far as I know, to
investigate the possibility fully and in some detail.[30]

Our discussion includes twenty-six bronzes of naked girls in the form
of both mirror handles and votive statuettes, whose provenances include
sites in Laconia (eight), elsewhere in the Peloponnese (two), Greece above
the Peloponnese (three), Ionia (two), and Italy (two). Nine are of
unknown provenance.[31] The fact that the majority of the bronzes with
known provenances come from the Peloponnese, and indeed from Laconia, suggests a Laconian origin for the style. It has been argued that
many of those from outside Laconia show Laconian influence. If, indeed,
the naked girls are not entertainers or *hetairai* of some sort, as will be
argued below, it would be difficult to explain their presence in the sixth
century as anything but a reflection of the cultic and athletic nudity best
known from Sparta.

Praschniker discusses thirteen mirror handles or statuettes representing naked females (Appendix I infra, nos. 1, 3, 4, 10, 12, 13, 14, 15, 19,
20, 22, 25, 26) which he considers to have been manufactured by Spartans or by others working under Laconian influence. Langlotz discusses

five mirror handles of naked females as Laconian bronzes, although he does not identify them as representations of athletes or of entertainers (Appendix I, nos. 3, 15, 20, 25, 26).[32] Richter discusses two of the naked figures (Appendix I, nos. 17 and 18) and argues against Praschniker and Langlotz that this type of mirror handle need not be Spartan in style, since individual features can be found elsewhere in Greek sculpture and painting of the period.[33] Yet the Peloponnesian provenance of the majority of the statuettes, along with other factors, indicates Spartan influence if not Spartan workmanship. Richter observes that the girls do not answer to the description of Aristophanes' firm-breasted Lampito, but we should remember that Lampito was married and older and so more full-breasted than the Spartan maidens possibly represented by the mirror handles: "They are not muscular athletes, but dainty dancing girls, as shown by the fact that three of them hold castanets. Probably they are *hetairai.*"[34] Häfner notes that the cymbals held by the girls in fact contradict the notion that they are *hetairai,* since *hetairai* first appear with cymbals in Roman times.[35] The natural wiriness of contemporary young female athletes, like the Rumanian gymnast Nadia Comaneci or the American track star Mary Decker, corresponds closely to the images of the Greek bronzes. Jantzen suggests that naked male figures on Locrian mirror handles were devised in imitation of naked girl figures, of which eleven are mentioned.[36] Of the eleven, Jantzen classifies five as Spartan work, one other as being from Hermione in the southeastern Peloponnese (Appendix I, no. 14), one possibly a Cheronese product (no. 8), and three of unknown provenance. He mentions one other freestanding votive statuette from Sparta (p. 67, sec. D.5 = Appendix I, no. 6). No dates are given for any of the above. The five which Jantzen identifies as Spartan are listed in Appendix I (nos. 3, 9, 10, 15, and 25).

Häfner identifies only three mirror handles as certainly Spartan (Appendix I, nos. 3, 14, 21).[37] She is reluctant to ascribe all thirteen under discussion to Sparta: "To consider the mirror handles as Laconian creations, since dances for naked girls are attested only for Laconia, is a hasty conclusion. Similar dances may have been practiced in other places, only the traditions of them have perished. Also it is questionable whether one should ascribe the creation of such costly objects to Sparta, a state little inclined to luxury." Rather, Häfner would relate the mirror handles "to the realm of Aphrodite." Yet Spartan preoccupation with physical beauty as manifest in the mirrors is a sign not of societal luxury, but of concern with health, childbirth, and the eugenic aims of female education. Similarly, the absence of testimonia concerning female public nudity elsewhere in Greece does not argue strongly *ex silentio* against identification of the naked-girl handles with Spartan girls, since the multitude of testimonia recording Spartan female nudity in public is a much stronger argument in favor of this identification. Häfner notes that, on stylistic grounds, the handles are too varied to be assigned to one common Laconian workshop, and that certain features are not otherwise common in Laconian art (pp. 13 and 36). She presumes an austerity in Laconian art and postulates that certain Ionian features in the treatment of hair, eyes, dress, or body on Spartan figures are a result of Ionian influence and perhaps of the Ionian origin of the mirror-handle style. Yet we may ask why Sparta, if it was so disinclined to refinements and luxury, ever bothered to produce even a few bronze female figurines. How could a sixth-century Spartan *not* identify the naked figures with the practice of female nudity in contemporary Sparta? It is easier to postulate Spartan influence on Ionian-style handles, since the actual models for such figurines were evident in Spartan daily life. Or there may have been Ionian stylistic influence on an originally Laconian subject. Herodotus (1.70; 3.39, 44ff., 55, 148) mentions Spartan relations with Samian and Ionian oligarchs in the late sixth century and the bronze mixing bowl once sent to King Croesus of Lydia. Laconian pottery and bronzes have been found on Samos.[38] The reason why Spartan nude female mirror handles were exported and perhaps even copied by non-Spartan artists abroad cannot be known for certain, but their popularity can plausibly be ascribed to their attraction as novelty items. It may be more than coincidence that the only other widespread representation of a female nude in the sixth century is the popular portrayal of Atalanta wrestling with or standing in the palaestra beside Peleus.[39] Most of the Atalanta wrestling vases date from 550 to 500 B.C.— that is, exactly the same period within which most of the naked female bronzes were produced. The novelty value and perhaps subtly erotic appeal of the Atalanta illustrations contributed to their popularity independent of numerous other depictions of heroic athletic contests in funeral games. So too the nude female bronzes, which may have originated as representations of actual or ideal Spartan athletes, were copied by non-Spartans when the subject gained trendy popularity. Therefore, despite Häfner's objections, it seems probable that the bronze representations of naked females on mirror handles and statuettes from the mid-sixth to the early fifth centuries B.C. originated as portraits of contemporary Spartan girls performing athletics or cult dances. The fact that the majority of those whose provenance is known came from Laconia and the unique and widespread renown of Spartan girls' nudity from literary sources of the sixth century and later argue in favor of identifying the bronzes as portraits of Spartan girls.[40] Regarding the bronzes Cartledge conjectures: "They were almost certainly made by men, some of whom could have been Spartan citizens. But the mirrors at least could have been commissioned and/or dedicated by women."[41]

A few of the figures have musical accoutrements, which were probably used in the public dances mentioned by Plutarch.[42] There is a badly preserved girl flautist from Sparta, and a mirror handle from Amyklaion shows a girl holding cymbals and wearing a mysterious baldric or shoulder strap seen on five other statuettes.[43] The long hair which was a mark of Spartan maidens was shorn at marriage, and wives wore only short hair.[44] Incidentally, the reverse is true for Spartan boys who had to wear their hair short until manhood, when, as warriors, they were to keep it long. Hair length is in fact an important indicator of the status of initiates in many societies.[45] The cymbals are also in evidence in a figure from Curium (Cyprus) (fig. 12.1). Her hair has been bound up in a net or cap of the type also worn by male athletes.[46] Among these bronzes I have counted nine female figures with hair similarly bound up by a headband, net, or cap in athletic style.[47] The cymbals, besides being instruments used to accompany the cult dance, were common as the toys of maidens dedicated to Artemis Limnates at Sparta.[48] They might thus be called symbols of the transition to adulthood. This statuette is also of interest because on the baldric can be seen a lunate crescent object which has gone unidentified but could be a strigil, used by athletes for cleaning themselves after exercise, or, more likely, a sickle of the sort found on late Spartan stelai.[49] The sickles were dedicated to Artemis Orthia by boy victors in athletic contests, so that their presence on the naked girl may be an identification of that girl as a victor in a certain competition. The girls thus wear their prizes around their chests, an unusual custom to my knowledge, otherwise found only much later among those practicing Greek athletics in Rome.[50] We do know, however, that children sometimes wore their favorite amulets on a shoulder strap.[51]

Another mirror handle of unknown provenance now in New York also shows the shoulder strap with the curious crescent (fig. 12.2). Note again the athletic hair net. Also of interest is the spherical object in the girl's left hand, which has been identified as some piece of fruit, but is more likely an oil flask, again a common implement for athletes and found on at least three of the girl statuettes.[52] A mirror handle from Cerveteri also holds the oil flask in her left hand, but here with a blossum in her right. The blossom, commonly identified as a lotus, is found on six mirror handles and is seen on numerous other clothed figures, male and female, from bronze sculpture and vases.[53] It may be a victory prize similar to the more usually awarded palm branch, or it may be a symbol of the maidens' fertility, vitality, and virginal purity. Compare our expression "to deflower" and the Greek expression "to lose one's bloom" (*apanthein*), applied to athletes debilitated as a result of sex. Further examples of girls holding the blossom are a votive statuette from Sparta wearing the athletic cap and a mirror handle from Hermione. One example of a peplos-clad Spartan maiden with flower is a statuette of unknown provenance but showing Ionic influence.[54]

Most of the bronze maidens—seventeen altogether—are without any clothing, but six do wear the *diazoma*, or trunks, which are otherwise

Fig. 12.1.
Nude female bronze mirror handle from Curium, Cyprus, c. 530 B.C. The Metropolitan Museum of Art, The Cesnola Collection; purchased by subscription, 1874–1876. (74.51.5680) (formerly no. 447); (photo courtesy of the museum) all rights reserved, The Metropolitan Museum of Art. Note "hair net" of type also seen on male athletes, and sickle (?) on shoulder strap, a possible prize for victory in a contest.

Fig. 12.2.
Nude female bronze mirror
handle (unknown prove-
nance) possibly from a
Spartan workshop, c. 550
B.C. The Metropolitan
Museum of Art, Fletcher
Fund, 1938. (38.11.3);
(photo courtesy of the
museum) all rights
reserved, The Metropolitan
Museum of Art. Note ath-
letic "hair net," sickle
"prize" on shoulder strap,
and oil flask (?) in left hand.

shown on sixth- and fifth-century vase paintings of the legendary
Atalanta as she wrestles Peleus.[55] This is a clear indication of athletic
garb, seen in the mirror handle now in New York (fig. 12.3) and also in the
mirror handle now in the Trent Museum (fig. 12.4) as well as the figure in
the Hamburg Museum (fig. 12.5).[56] The Hamburg girl is unique and
noteworthy in that she is holding up a strigil in a victorious attitude also
seen in a mid-fifth-century statuette group from Delphi.[57] That the
Delphic victor has won in the pentathlon is evident from the jumping
weight he carries. The implication is that the Hamburg girl is perhaps the
only certain female victor statuette.

The nudity or near nudity of these girls recalls the nudity of girls in
the Brauronian rites, where girls "play the bear." Separation from society

Fig. 12.3.
Nude female bronze mirror handle (unknown provenance), c. 540 B.C. The Metropolitan Museum of Art, Rogers Fund, 1946. (41.11.5a); (photo courtesy of the museum) all rights reserved, The Metropolitan Museum of Art. The *diazoma* or trunks are of a type worn by Atalanta depicted in wrestling scenes on Greek vases of this period.

and existence "in the wilds," literally or symbolically, is typical of initiatory rites for youths.[58] The "wild" element is represented on many of the mirror handles by lion or griffin supporting struts, but also by animals under their feet, like turtles, or the frog under a Laconian figure from Cyprus.[59] The marsh animals may be an allusion to the fact that the girls danced and ran near the bathing pools of the Eurotas River, as mentioned by Theocritus (18.22–25) and Aristophanes (*Lys.* 1308–1313).

Among the contests for girls, the foot race, like those held at Olympia and Brauron, had a special, sacred prestige. The *Dromos* or "Track" at Sparta also served as the gymnasium in the probable absence of any proper building before Roman Imperial times.[60] We may locate the *Dromos* on the banks of the Eurotas in the vicinity of the sanctuary of Artemis Orthia. The Eurotas is mentioned as the place of girls' exercise

Fig. 12.4.
(a, front; b, back) Nude
female bronze mirror han-
dle (unknown provenance),
sixth century B.C. Trent,
Italy, Museo Provinciale
d'Arte—Castello del Buon-
consiglio inv. no. 3061
(photo courtesy of the
museum). Figure wears
athletic *diazoma;* cp. figure
12.3.

a

not only by Aristophanes and Theocritus, but also by Cicero and
Pausanias.[61]

In addition to the naked female bronzes studied above, there are five
bronzes of girl runners apparently in Laconian style.[62] Besides an Amazon-style girl wearing the dress of the Olympian Heraia, now in London,
there is the female runner from Dodona in a similar pose in a short chiton,
one from Palermo, and two others in the Delphi and Sparta museums.

Pausanias relates the only detail we have for the actual ritual of a race
for girls at Sparta (3.13.7).[63]

b

At Sparta next to the Temple of Dionysus Colonatas there is a precinct of the Hero, who, they say, guided Dionysus on his journey to Sparta. The Dionysiades and Leucippides sacrifice to this Hero before they do to the god. As for the second group of eleven women called "Dionysiades," for them they hold a foot race. The custom for them to run a race came from Delphi.

Whether the Delphic origin indicates imitation of an actual race at Delphi or merely the institution of the custom at the behest of the Pythian

Fig. 12.5.
Nude female bronze figu-
rine. Hamburg, Museum
für Kunst und Gewerbe inv.
no. 1917.362 (photo cour-
tesy of the museum). The
figure wears an athletic
diazoma and victoriously
holds up a strigil.

oracle is unclear. More informative are the two colleges of priestesses who
organize the race. The Leucippides are maidens, namesakes of the mythical brides of the Tyndaridai, Castor and Pollux, who are local Spartan
heroes.[64] The duties of the two priestesses are to attend the shrine of the
mythical sisters and to weave a tunic for Apollo Amyclae each year. The
Palermo runner, it has been said, was modeled on a metope of the Silaris
Treasury near Paestum, which may well represent the mythical Leucippides in flight from their husbands-to-be, the Tyndaridai.[65] Castor and
Pollux are said to have caught the maidens and carried them away as
brides. Thus, the priestesses of the Leucippides are natural overseers of
the race of the maiden Dionysiades, a race with probable prenuptial
significance.[66]

The identity of the Dionysiades is less clear, since they are otherwise unknown and the worship of Dionysus at Sparta outside of this temple is restricted to mountainside *orgiai*. Nilsson has suggested that their number, eleven, may indicate one leader who is chased by ten runners in a rite for the salvation of the state, as in the foot race of the Spartan *Staphylodromoi*, or "Grape-runners," which is held during the Carneia.[67] Calame has proposed that the presence of Dionysus, as the divinity of the adult female, indicates that the foot race of the Dionysiades is an initiatory race for maidens moving from adolescence to adulthood.[68]

We find in the Dionysiades race striking formal and structural parallels with the Heraia at Olympia which characterize both as prenuptial rites.[69] Cult affiliations of the colleges organizing both races include a hero or heroes who introduce Dionysus to the region and a young bride or brides devoted to a maternal goddess, thus tracing the progress of girls to the married state. The mythical affiliations of the Leucippides at Sparta and Hippodameia at Olympia include the winning or carrying off of a young bride. Participation in both foot races is limited to maidens. And the organizers in both cases hold special rites for Dionysus as well as for the hero or heroes who introduced him.[70] Finally, the name "Leucippides," or "daughters of Leucippus," literally means the "white mares," whereas their spouses, the Tyndaridae, are known by the epithet *Leukopoloi*, or "white colts."[71] The association with horses recalls the organizational term *agelai*, or "horse-herds," used to designate companies of girls and boys in the Spartan *agoge* and is further supported by metaphors in Alcman (*Parth.* I.59) and Aristophanes (*Lys.* 1308–1313) which compare the troops of dancing or racing girls to fillies. There may be a similar metaphorical association of maidens with horses in the name of Hippodameia, literally "tamer of horses," a possible allusion to her direction of young maidens with their original institution of her foot race to Hera.[72] The equine image in the realms of matrimony is not new to us who compare the equine image in English "bridegroom," derived by folk etymology from Middle English *bridegome*, meaning simply "bride man."

The Sparta-Olympia parallels in the cult race suggest at least a similar cult environment which fostered prenuptial trials for girls devoted to heroines, to Dionysus, and to a maternal goddess. I have suggested elsewhere that the Heraia may have been reorganized c. 580 B.C. under contemporary Spartan political influence in Elis.[73] If that is so, the parallels between the Olympian Heraia and the Spartan foot race evidence the influence of Spartan female athletics over cult practices for girls elsewhere. Sparta was a natural model in the area of progressive social reform for women, as Plato amply illustrates.

So the foot race stands out in the Spartan athletic program for girls as one way to foster progress toward womanhood in a religious and athletic context. The other contests listed in Appendix II (infra), including wrestling and discus- and javelin-throwing as well as the exercises of *bibasis* (jumping in place) and dance, are to be distinguished as religiously less significant, but important in eugenic terms for the service and preservation of the state.[74] Sources indicate that Spartan girls' and boys' physical education waned between the fourth and second centuries B.C., when there was a renewal of the vigor of the Lycurgan system, and the legend of the muscular vigor of Spartan women lived on until Philostratus in the third century A.D.[75] Despite the *de facto* and *de iure* suppression of Spartan women's rights in our own terms, the fact that we still marvel at the Spartan female in an age of progressive liberation is a testimony to their unique social achievement in Western history. To which Gorgo might have added, "Because only we give birth to men."

Naked Female Bronzes

The following is a catalogue of bronze figurines representing young girls, naked or wearing only the *diazoma,* and used mostly as mirror handles or mirror supports. Those few which are statuettes not attached to mirrors are so designated. Museum, inventory number, and provenance are followed by approximate date and suggested origin according to Charbonneaux (= Ch; see n. 53 infra); Häfner (= H; see n. 4 infra); Jantzen (= J; see n. 36 infra); Langlotz (= L; see n. 4 infra); Praschniker (= P; see n. 30 infra); Richter (= R; see nn. 20, 30, and 33 infra); Schröder (= S; see n. 1 infra). Numbers indicate pages of the works cited.

1. Athens, National Museum (no number or provenance given) (with *diazoma*). Sixth-century, Spartan: P. 226–27.
2. Athens, NM 6631 from the Acropolis. c. 525–500, uncertain origin: H. 12, 90–91.
3. Athens, NM 7548 from Amyklaion. c. 530–320, Spartan: H. 117–18, J. 9–10, L. 87, P. 229.
4. Athens, NM 7703 from Aegina (with *diazoma*). Sixth-century, Aeginetan: L. 99, P. 239–40.
5. Athens, NM 13975 from Argos. c. 525–500, Magna Graecia (?): H. 90–91.
6. Athens, NM 15897 from Sparta (statuette). Late sixth-century, Spartan: H. 34–35, 123.
7. Athens, NM 15900 from Sparta. c. 520, Spartan: H 123–24.
8. Berlin, Charlottenberg 10820 from Anaktorion, Akarnania. Sixth-century, Spartan: L. 86; N.W. Greece (?): H. 132–33, J. 66.
9. Berlin, Charlottenberg 31084 (unknown provenance). Sixth-century, Northeast Peloponnese: H. 133, J. 116–17.
10. Dresden, Skulpturensammlung H⁴ 44/16 from Cerveteri. c. 500, East Ionic: H. 137–38, J. 9–10, P. 227.
11. Hamburg, Museum für Kunst und Gewerbe 1917.362 (with *diazoma*), from Egypt (?): Roman, of Spartan type, uncertain origin. S. 196, pl. 110b.
12. Leningrad, Hermitage (no number) from Odessa. Aeginetan: L. 99, P. 240–42; c. 500–475 Ionian (?): H. 144.
13. Collection Löser (unknown provenance) (statuette). c. 490–480, Spartan (?): H. 158–59, P. 236.
14. Munich, Museum der antike Kleinkunst 3482 from Hermione (Southeast Peloponnese). c. 510, Spartan: H. 147–48, J. 9–10 and 66, P. 236.
15. New York, Metropolitan Museum C.B. 447 from Curium, Cyprus. c. 530, Spartan: J. 9–10, L. 87, P. 222; Ionian (?): H. 148.
16. New York, Met. Mus. 06.11.04 (unknown provenance). Sixth-century, Spartan: L. 87, R(1915) 11–2; South Italian/Etruscan (?): H. 149.
17. New York, Met. Mus. 38.11.3 (unknown provenance). c. 550, Corinthian: R(1938) 344; South Italian/Etruscan: H. 149.
18. New York, Met. Mus. 41.11.5 (unknown provenance) (with *diazoma*). c. 540: R(1942) 324.
19. Paris, Louvre (no number) (unknown provenance ex Coll. Gréau). Early sixth-century, Spartan: Ch. 69, H. 157, P. 240 no. 40.

20. Paris, Louvre 138 from Amyklai. Mid sixth-century, Spartan: Ch. 69 and 141, H. 157, L. 87 and 94, P. 251.
21. Sparta Museum 27 from Sparta. Early fifth-century, Spartan: H. 173.
22. Sparta Mus. 28 from Sparta. Fifth-century, Spartan: H. 173, P. 238.
23. Trent, Museo Provinciale d'Arte inv. no. 3061 (Magna Graecia) (with *diazoma*). Sixth-century: J. 9 no. 1, P. 240 no. 41, S. 196 and pl. 110a.
24. Versailles, Coll. Morgenroth (unknown provenance) (with *diazoma*). c. 525–500: H. 12, 90–91, J. 66.
25. Vienna, Kunsthistorisches Museum VI 2925 from Nemea (?). c. 500, North Peloponnese: H. 176–7, J. 9–10, P. 219; Spartan: L. 86.
26. Vienna, Kunsthist. Mus. VI 4979 from Sparta (?) (statuette). c. 500, Spartan: H. 177, L. 86, P. 235.

Appendix Two

Spartan Female Physical Activities According to Sources Chronologically Arranged

Source	Date	Activities R	E	W	Di	J	Da	O
Euripides *Andr.* 595–602	430–424 B.C.	X	X					
Critias DK2.88 fr. 32	425–403 B.C.	X	X					
Aristophanes *Lys.* 78–84, 1308–1313	413 B.C.						X	X (bibasis)
Xenophon *Const. Lac.*	393–383 B.C.	X	X					X (strength)
Plato *Rep.* 458D	c. 375 B.C.		X					
Plato *Leg.* 7.805E–806A	c. 355–347 B.C.		X					X (music)
Theocritus *Id.* 18	300–260 B.C.	X						X (music, weaving)
Cicero *Tusc.* 2.15.36	45 B.C.		X					
Propertius 3.14	c. 23 B.C.				X	X		X (ball, hoop, pankration, boxing, hunting, equitation, military drills)
Ovid *Her.* 16.149–52	A.D. 2–18	X						
Schol. to Juvenal 4.53	A.D. 54–68			X				
Martial 4.55.6–7	A.D. 88	X						
Plutarch *Lyc.* 14.1–15.1	A.D. 100–120	X		X	X	X	X	
Pollux *Onom.* 4.102, I, 231(13)	3rd quarter of 2nd c. A.D.							X (bibasis)
Philostratus *Gymn.* 27	A.D. 230	X	X					

Activities key: *R* = running; *E* = exercise (unspecified); *W* = wrestling; *Di* = discus-throwing; *J* = javelin-throwing; *Da* = dance; *O* = other (specified).

Notes

1. The following give general surveys of women's role in Greek athletics: J. Krause, *Die Gymnastik und Agonistik der Hellenen* (Leipzig, 1841; repr. Wiesbaden, 1971) vol. 1, 31–33; L. Grasberger, *Erziehung und Uterricht im klassischen Altertum,* III (Würzburg, 1881) 498–508; L. Meyer, *De virginum exercitationibus gymnicis apud veteres* (Klausthal, 1872); B. Schröder, *Der Sport im Altertum* (Leipzig, 1927) 162–66; O. von Vacano, *Das Problem des alten Zeustempels in Olympia* (Cologne, 1937), Suppl.: "Über Mädchensport in Griechenland," 51–58; J. Juethner, *Die athletischen Leibesübungen der Griechen,* ed. F. Brein, *SB Wien* 249, 1 (Vienna, 1965) 100–102; H. A. Harris, *Greek Athletes and Athletics* (London, 1964) 179–86. For interpretations of women's sport as part of initiatory ritual, see H. Jeanmaire, *Couroi et couretes* (Lille, 1939) 413–18; A. Brelich, *Le iniziazione,* pt. 2 (Rome, 1962) 72–74, 83–105, and 127–46; idem, *Paides e parthenoi* (Rome, 1969) 449–56; W. Burkert, *Griechische Religion der archaischen und klassischen Epoche* (Stuttgart, Berlin, Cologne, Mainz, 1977) 390–95; C. Calame, *Les choeurs de jeunes filles en grèce archaïque,* I and II (Rome, 1977) esp. vol. 1 350–57, re Spartan girls; L. Kahil, "L'Artémis de Brauron: rites et Mystère," *AntK* 20 (1977) 86–98; P. Perlman, "Plato *Laws* 833C–834D and the Bears of Brauron," *GRBS* 24 (1983) 115–30. I wish to thank John Mansfield for sharing with me the text of a lecture he delivered at the University of California, Berkeley, in February 1981, "Women in Greek Athletics: A Man's View," and the very useful collection of sources appended to it, "Women in Greek Athletics: Sources and Materials" (unpublished). Also of interest is the consideration of boys' and girls' complementary roles in rites of passage to adulthood as discussed by P. Vidal-Naquet, "Le cru, l'enfant grec et le cuit," in *Faire de l'histoire: Nouveaux objets,* ed. J. le Goff and P. Nora (Paris, 1974) 137–68, esp. 156–62.

2. Mansfield (supra n. 1)

3. T. F. Scanlon, "The Footrace of the Heraia at Olympia," *Ancient World* 8 (1984) 77–90. Spartan affinities with the Olympian Heraia include: resemblances in the roles of priestess-organizers, associations with Dionysus in both cult complexes, age classes among maiden-participants, similarity in girls' dresses, and contemporary Spartan influences in art and politics at Olympia.

4. London, British Museum 208 from Albania (?). See U. Häfner, *Das Kunstschaffen Lakoniens in archaischer Zeit,* Diss. Munich, 1965, 144–45; E. Langlotz, *Frühgriechischen Bildhauerschulen,* I and II (1927; repr. Rome, 1976) vol. 1, 86ff., and vol. 2, no. 41, pl. 48a. Dated by Langlotz to c. 560 B.C. and by Häfner to the second half of the sixth century B.C.

5. Jeanmaire (supra n. 1), 413–18; Brelich, *Le iniziazione* (supra n. 1) 270; Calame (supra n. 1) vol. 1, 210–14.

6. Perlman (supra n. 1); Kahil (supra n. 1); idem, "Quelques vases du sanctuaire d'Artémis à Brauron," *AntK* Beih. 1 (1963) 13–14, pl. 6.1–2; idem, *Greece and Italy in the Classical World,* Acta XI International Congress of Classical Archaeology (London, 1979) 73–87; idem, "Le 'craterisque' d'Artémis et le Brauronion de l'Acropole," *Hesperia* 50 (1981) 253–63.

7. Kahil, "Autour de l'Artémis attique," *AntK* 8 (1965) pl. 10, 6–7, and idem, "Le Artémis" (supra n. 1) fig. B, pl. 19. Perlman (supra n. 1) 123 n. 42, suggests that the distinction between clothed and unclothed girls on the vases is one of respectively older and younger girls, specifically above and below thirteen years of age, corresponding to Plato *Leg.* 833C–834D, where it is recommended that older girls compete "properly dressed" in short chitons. This is, however, untenable, since the nude girls in the above vase include those visibly younger and older together, both with and without well-developed breasts and figures. This does not exclude, but rather supports, initiatory motives for the nudity, which is dictated by reasons other than the "propriety" with which Plato is concerned.

8. H. Jeanmaire, *REG* 26 (1913) 134–35; M. P. Nilsson, "Die Grundlagen des spartanischen Lebens," *Klio* 12 (1912) 308–40, reprinted in *Opuscula Selecta,* 3 vols. (Lund, 1951–60) vol. 2, 826–69 at p. 848; P. Vidal-Naquet (supra n. 1) 160; P. Cartledge, "Spartan Wives: Liberation or Licence?" *CQ* 31 (1981) 84–105, esp. 91–93.

9. See generally F. Ollier, *Le mirage spartiate* (Paris, 1933; repr. New York, 1973); A. Andrewes, *The Greek Tyrants* (New York and Evanston, 1956) 66–77; E. N. Tigerstedt, *The Legend of Sparta in Classical Antiquity* (Stockholm, 1965) vol. 1, 70–78; W. G. Forrest, *A History of Sparta: 950–192 B.C.* (London, 1968; repr. 1980) 35–60; Panel Oliva, *Sparta and Her Social Problems* (Amsterdam and Prague, 1971) 63–70. See also A. Szegedy-Maszak, "Legends of the Greek Lawgivers, *GRBS* 19 (1978) 199–209.

10. Tigerstedt (supra n. 9) 38, 68–69, places the intensification of the *agoge* in the mid-seventh century, since it would have been called for after the serious Spartan defeat at Hysiae (699/698? B.C.) and after the Second Messenian War. Brelich, *Le iniziazione* (supra n. 1) esp. 48–74, discusses initiatory characteristics and function of Sparta (and Cretan) *agoge* and festivals. Regarding the *agoge* he concludes (57–58): "The summary illustration of the Spartan *agoge* given above seems to answer most perfectly to the social institution of the primitive type hinged on initiation at most stages: after the first years of infancy, the individual is separated from the family and entrusted to the community; he lives with his *coetanei* ("age equals") under the control of male adults; he is subject to deprivations, vigorous discipline, and to an especially harsh test, while at the same time he is placed outside the normal laws which are enforced in society; he passes from year to year . . . into a new category of age where he can strengthen himself by means of agonistic combats with his peers. Only at a relatively late age (corresponding to Spartan gerontocratic ideals) does he acquire the normal status of an adult."

11. D. Page, *Alcman: The Parthenion* (Oxford, 1951) 67–68; C. Calame (supra n. 1) vol. 2, 84–85 re *anepsiai* in Alcman, and vol. 1, 372–85 on "L'*agélé* spartiate" and "Les choeurs de jeunes filles lacédémoniennes." On other terms associated with Spartan education and on the *agoge* in general, see Grasberger (supra n. 1) 57–60; C. Forbes, *Greek Physical Education* (New York and London, 1929) 12–43; H. Michell, *Sparta* (Cambridge, 1952) 165–204; K. M. T. Chrimes (Atkinson), *Ancient Sparta: A Re-examination of the Evidence* (Manchester, 1952) 84–136; H. I. Marrou, *A History of Education in Antiquity,* trans. G. Lamb (London and New York, 1956) 14–25; J. T. Hooker, *The Ancient Spartans* (London, Toronto, Melbourne, 1980) 132–44.

12. Plutarch *Phil.* 16. Chrimes (supra n. 11) 97ff., 221ff., and 442ff.; Forbes (supra n. 11) 38.

13. C. Wehrli, "Les gynéconomes," *MusHelv* 19 (1962) 33–38.

14. On equestrian metaphors for girls' organizations, see Calame (supra n. 1) vol. 2, 67–72, and Page (supra n. 11) 89–90. Neither of these notices the metaphor in Aristophanes *Lys.* 1308–1313.

15. On Spartan women's education in philosophy and speaking, see Cartledge (supra n. 8) 92 and idem, "Literacy in the Spartan Oligarchy" *JHS* 98 (1978) 25–37 (re apothegms). On apothegms illustrating the free speech of Spartan women, see Tigerstedt (supra n. 9) vol. 2, 16–30. Contrast male Athenian attitudes to women's free speech in public: Sophocles *Aj.* 293; Euripides *Heracl.* 476–77 and fr. 61; Thucydides 2.45.2–46.1.

16. On Spartan women's music and gymnastics, see Plato *Leg.* 806A, where, however, it is suggested that slave girls did the weaving. But their weaving skills are alluded to by Pausanias 3.16.2, where Spartan women are said to weave a *chiton* for Apollo of Amyclae each year. Re their freedom from other sedentary domestic tasks, see Cartledge (supra n. 8) 91 and n. 40, citing Heraclides Lembus 373.13 (baking), and the discussion in P. Herfst, *Le travail de la femme dans la Grèce ancienne* (Paris, 1922) 18–24 (weaving), 24–32 (cooking), and 112–13 (Spartan women's exemption).

17. J.-P. Vernant, *Problèmes de la guerre en Grèce ancienne* (Paris, 1968) 15, cited by P. Vidal-Naquet (supra n. 1) 149: "le mariage est á la fille ce que la guerre est au garçon: pour tous deux, ils marquent l'accomplissement de leur nature respective, au sortir d'un état où chacun participe encore de l'autre." See Vidal-Naquet's further comments on pages 156–61, where he concludes his discussion of the similarity between boys' and girls' education by stating: "En tout cas, l'impression qu'on peut retirer des rares données de la tradition antique est moins celle d'un "parallelism" entre éducation des jeunes filles et éducation des jeunes gens, que celui d'un décalque. . . . La jeune fille spartiate était, au sens plein du terme, un 'garçon manqué.'" See Cartledge (supra n. 8) 94.

18. Cicero *Tusc.* 2.15.36; Propertius 3.14.1ff. Cartledge (supra n. 8) 87–88.

19. J. Juethner, *Philostratus über Gymnastik* (Leipzig and Berlin, 1909; repr. Stuttgart, 1969) 242 ad. loc.

20. J. H. Krause (supra n. 1) vol. 2, 682–86, argues for total nudity, but allows that they may have later worn the short chiton for certain exercises. W. A. Becker, *Charicles,*[3] trans. F. Metcalfe (New York and Bombay, 1906) 297–300, also maintains that Spartan girls exercised in total nudity, but G. M. A. Richter, "An Archaic Greek Mirror," *AJA* 42 (1938) 337–44, esp. 342, no. 4, wants *gymnos* to mean "lightly clad" with reference to Spartan girls. The archaeological evidence from the sixth century, examined below, shows girls totally naked, wearing trunks only, and wearing the Doric *chiton*. For discussion of the latter form of dress, see M. Johnson, *Ancient Greek Dress* (Chicago, 1964) 52–53.

21. Ibycus fr. 58 Page; cf. Euripides *Hec.* 933f.; Pollux *Onom.* 2.187, 7.54f.; Clement *Paed* 2.10.114.1. Cartledge (supra n. 8) 92, no. 46, cites Athenaeus 13.602E for thighs as an erotogenic feature and proposes that "thighs" may have also been a conventional euphemism for female pudenda. This would leave unresolved the ambiguity between being literally naked and scantily

clad, and would, in any case, not contradict the evidence of bronze statuettes to be examined below.

22. Cf. Plutarch *Comp. Lyc. et Num.* 3.3.4, citing Sophocles fr. 788 Nauck.

23. Dionysius of Halicarnassus 7.72.3–4.

24. F. Pfister, s.v. Nacktheit, *RE* 16.2 (1935) 1541–49; Brelich, *Paides e parthenoi* (supra n. 1) 157–58, 171–73, 200–201.

25. Xenophon *Hell.* 6.4–16; Plutarch *Ages.* 29; Plato *Leg.* 633 B–C; Athenaeus 678C. Bölte, "Zu Lakonischen Festen," *RhM* 78 (1929) 124–43; H. T. Wade-Gery, "A Note on the Origin of the Spartan Gymnopaidiai," *CQ* 43 (1949) 79–81; M. P. Nilsson, *Griechische Feste von religiöser Bedeutung* (Darmstadt, 1957) 140–42.

26. Antoninus Liberalis 17. Nilsson (supra n. 25) 370–71; R. F. Willetts, *Cretan Cults and Festivals* (London, 1962) 173–79; Burkert (supra n. 1) 392.

27. Kahil (supra n. 1); Perlman (supra n. 1) esp. 125–27.

28. Aristophanes *Lys.* 1308–1313; Theocritus *Id.* 18.39; Cic. *Tusc.* 2.15–16; Pausanias 3.14–6. The Ovid *Heroides* translation is by G. Showerman in the Loeb Library edition (1968).

29. See Cartledge (supra n. 8) 93–96, who discusses beauty as an important, and possibly an essential, ingredient in Spartan matrimony, as suggested by Alcman's poems and by an anecdote in Plutarch (*Mor.* 1D). The anecdote relates the story of King Archidamos II (reigned c. 469–427 B.C.), who was fined for marrying an ugly (or small—cf. Plutarch *Ages.* 2.6) woman. Cartledge (94–95) estimates the marriage age of girls as between eighteen and twenty.

30. C. Praschniker, "Bronzene Spiegelstuetze im Wiener Hofmuseum," *Österreichisches Archaeologisches Institut, Wien. Jahreshefte* 15 (1912) 219–52, presents the first extensive treatment of the bronzes and, largely on the basis of their youthful physique, identifies them with the Spartan girls of Plutarch *Lyc.* 14 (esp. pp. 250–51). Cf. W. A. Müller, *Nacktheit und Entblössung in der altorientalischen und älteren griechischen Kunst* (Leipzig, 1906) 142; S. Heckenbach, *De nuditate sacra: Religionsgeshichtliche Untersuchungen und Vorarbeiten*, vol. 9, pt. 3, 15f., cited by Praschniker, 250 nn. 72–73. Lists of bronze girl handles are also given in U. Jantzen, *Griechischen Griff-Phialen*, Winckelmannsprogramm 114 (Berlin, 1958) 7, and P. Oberländer, *Griechische Handspiegel* (Ph.D. Dissertation, Hamburg, 1967) 211, 275–76 n. 147. K. Schefold, "Griechische Spiegel," *Die Antike* 16 (1940) 24ff., and idem, *Orient, Hellas und Rom* (Bern, 1949), sees the bronze mirror handles as representations of handmaidens or attendants of Artemis. L. O. K. Congdon in a thorough and important study, *Caryatid Mirrors of Ancient Greece: Technical, Stylistic and Historical Considerations of an Archaic and Early Classical Bronze Series* (Mainz, 1981) 13ff., sees the girls as maidens related to cult practices, but not as goddesses themselves. Congdon, who studies the naked-maiden-with-trunks type on pp. 136–37, no. 14, pl. 10 and pp. 211–12, no. 16, pl. 95, identifies products of the Laconian workshops as the earliest and most enduring type of female handle forms. H. Jucker, "Der archaische griechische Standspiegel in Cincinnati," in L. Bonfante, H. von Heintze, and C. Lord, eds., *In Memoriam O. J. Brendel: Essays in Archaeology and the Humanities* (Mainz, 1976) 25–35 (seen too late to be incorporated into my text), discusses a naked female bronze handle in Cincinnati which may

be added to the items discussed in this study; most important, the Cincinnati piece is, according to Jucker, the earliest Greek mirror handle and from a Laconian workshop.

31. Those from Laconia: Appendix I, nos. 3, 6, 7, 14, 20, 21, 22, 26. From the Peloponnese outside Laconia: nos. 5, 25. From Greece above the Peloponnese: nos. 2, 4, 8. From Ionia: 12, 15. From Italy: 10, 13. Of unknown provenance: 1, 9, 11, 16, 17, 18, 19, 23, 24. See G. M. A. Richter, *Greek, Etruscan, and Roman Bronzes* (New York, 1915) 11–12 for a discussion of Appendix I, no. 16.

32. Langlotz (supra n. 4) vol. 1, 86–98 and vol. 2, pl. 44b and c, 45b, 46, 48a and b.

33. Richter (supra n. 20) and idem, "Another Archaic Greek Mirror," *AJA* 46 (1942) 319–24.

34. Richter (supra n. 20) 343.

35. Häfner (supra n. 4) 88–89, no. 20.

36. U. Jantzen, *Bronzewerkstätten in Grossgriechenland und Sizilien* (Berlin, 1937), *JDAI Erganzungsheft* 13, 9–10 and 66, app. I: Standspiegel A and C. The eleven female mirror handles mentioned by Jantzen include Appendix I (infra) nos. 3, 9, 10, 15, 25 (all Spartan) and 8, 12, 14. The votive statuette is no. 13.

37. Häfner (supra n. 4) 12–38.

38. Cf. L. Jeffery, *Archaic Greece: The City States c. 700–500 B.C.* (London and Tonbridge, 1976) 213, 217; U. Jantzen, *Aegyptische und orientalische Bronzen aus dem Heraion von Samos, Samos* 8 (1972) on bronzes.

39. L. E. Roller, "Funeral Games in Greek Art," *AJA* 85 (1981) 107–119, pls. 19–20, esp. 111–12. Vases from the second half of the sixth century show scenes of Peleus and Atalanta wrestling in similar poses. Fifth- to fourth-century vases show the pair in a more relaxed palaestra setting.

40. Most recently Cartledge (supra n. 8) 92 no. 47 has cited eleven bronzes as confirmation of Spartan girls' public nudity; the bronzes he mentions are those in Appendix I, nos. 6, 7, 8, 9, 16, 17, 19, 25, and 26. He also cites Sparta 594 and 3302, and publication of the latter by Th. Karageorgha, *Deltion* 20.1 (1965) 96–109, which I have not seen.

　　It is beyond the scope of this study to trace the ultimate origins of nude female figurines and mirror-handles from possible Near Eastern or Egyptian prototypes. J. Broadman, *The Greeks Overseas* (Baltimore, 1964) 81–82, pl. 1a and fig. 12d, discusses five nude female figures in ivory found in a grave in Athens dated to the third quarter of the eighth century, but these "clearly imitate the eastern 'Astarte' type of the nude fertility goddess" known from Nimrud, Assyria, and do not otherwise resemble the later bronzes in question. Boardman, pp. 163–64 and figs. 44a and b, in reference to the Greek girl bronzes and certain Egyptian counterparts, concludes that the motif is ultimately Egyptian, possibly transmitted in part via the Near East. But "the number of Egyptian traits in sixth-century Spartan art," Boardman notes, "may be due to her close relations with Cyrene in North Africa" as well as other individual instances of Spartan trade with Egypt in this period. Even if Egypt initially inspired Sparta to produce the statuettes and mirrors, the public nudity of girls at Sparta seems to have further encouraged manufacture of images otherwise generally absent from Greek sculpture of this period.

41. Cartledge (supra n. 8) 92 n. 47; cf. 93 n. 54, where Cartledge notes that "from the late seventh century onwards we have *ex votos* from Sparta inscribed with the name of a dedicatrix. Since the recipient deities were also female and a fair proportion of the uninscribed offerings have feminine associations, many of the dedications were probably offered by women." Cf. idem (supra n. 15) 25–37.

42. Plutarch *Lyc.* 14.2 Cf. Theocritus *Id.* 18.26–37, alluding to Helen's musical talent, and Plato *Leg.* 771E–772A, where he proposes public dances for youths and maidens for the new city so that they could view one another, "each of them naked, within the limits of sober modesty." In general on the make-up and activity of Spartan girls' choruses see Calame (supra n. 1) vol. 1, esp. 381–385, and vol. 2 on the chorus in Alcman's *Parthenion.*

43. Girl flautist from Sparta: Athens, National Museum (NM) 15900, c. 520 B.C.; mirror handle from Amyklaion: Athens, NM 7548, c. 530–520 B.C. The shoulder strap is also seen on nos. 8, 15, 17, 21, 25 in Appendix I. To the strap are usually attached small objects (amulets?) and one larger crescent-shaped object (seen on nos. 15, 17, 25), to be discussed below. The "amulets" on a shoulder strap are identified by Häfner as the usual accoutrements of children: (supra n. 4) 88 n. 18, citing a terracotta statuette of a child from Paestum, *AA* 71 (1956) 446, pl. 156, and a bronze statuette of a boy in Kassel, M. Bieber, *Die antiken Skulpturen und Bronzen in Cassel* (Marburg, 1915) no. 214, pl. 44. The strap thus argues against identifying the bronze girls as *hetairai* and in favor of seeing in them representations of young Spartan maidens at some stage before marriage.

44. Plutarch *Lyc.* 15.3 relates the cutting of a Spartan girl's hair on her wedding night. Cartledge (supra no. 8), 101, cites the following additional literary evidence for the fact that Spartan females wore their hair long only while *parthenai* or *korai,* but had it shorn at marriage and kept it short thereafter: [Aristotle] *Lac. Pol.* ap. Heracleides Lembos 373.13 (Dilts); Lucian *Fugitivi* 27; Xenophon of Ephesus 5.1.7. For short hair on Spartan boys and long hair on their men, see Cartledge, "Hoplites and Heroes," *JHS* 97 (1977) 11–27, esp. 15 n. 39, quoting Plutarch *Lyc.* 16.6: "As they grew in age, their bodily exercise was increased and their heads were close-clipped," and Plutarch *Lyc.* 22.1: "They [the boys] wore their hair long as soon as they ceased to be youths."

45. Brelich *Paides e parthenoi* (supra n. 1) 71–72 n. 59, 80–81 n. 88, re other cultures; 115, 129, 358, 447, 464 re Greek custom of tonsure in ritual contexts. In Athens young boys about to become members of the Phratria during the Apaturia dedicated their hair to the god: H. W. Parke, *Festivals of the Athenians* (London, 1977) 89 and n. 101; Burkert (supra n. 1) 384 n. 18; J. Labarbe, "L'age correspondant au sacrifice du κούρειον et les données historique du sixième discours d'Isée," *Bulletin de l'Académie Royal de Belgique* 39 (1953) 358–94. In general on the significance of hair in ritual: L. Sommer, *Das Haar in Aberglauben und Religion der Griechen,* Diss. Münster, 1912; P. Schredelseker, *De superstitionibus Graecorum ad crines pertinent,* Diss. Heidelberg, 1913; Burkert (supra n. 1) 120–21 and n. 29. G. Thomson, *Aeschylus and Athens* (New York, 1940; repr. 1967) 108 (cf.

438 n. 19) remarks that in Greece and elsewhere "hair was cut on two distinct occasions—the attainment of puberty by a boy or the marriage of a girl and the death of a relative." These crises, or cruces, of life require some outward manifestation of commemoration of loss, but also a sense of renewed identity by those cutting their hair.

46. Figure from Curium: New York, Metropolitan Museum 447, c. 530 B.C. (= n. 15 in Appendix I) The best-attested type of cap was known as the *amphotides* or *apotides* (ear-guards), which J. H. Krause (supra n. 1) vol. 2, 517–18, discusses as a late innovation for the palaestra, but E. N. Gardiner, *Greek Athletic Sports and Festivals* (London, 1910) 433, n. 2, adds: "The evidence for these lappets is all late, but the caps belong to the fifth century B.C." See Gardiner figs. 17, 149, and 150, but note that only in fig. 149, a Roman imperial sculpture, are the ears covered by the device. In the other illustrations, sixth- and fifth-century vases (London, British Museum 326 and Munich 795), as well as in numerous sculptures, notably the famous stone base from Athens with pentathletes (late sixth-century B.C.), the athletes wear caps or hair nets which do not cover the ears but do keep the hair in place. On the stone relief base with athletes, see S. Casson, "The New Athenian Statue Bases," *JHS* 45 (1925) 164–79, and L. Gründel in *AA* (1925) col. 87. The cap or net worn on the heads of male athletes from the sixth to fifth centuries is probably reflected also in the bronzes of girls from the same period.

47. Appendix I, nos. 6, 7, 11, 13, 15, 17, 22, 25, 26.

48. *Anth. Pal.* 6.280; *IG* V.1, 225–26. Perlman (supra n. 1) 125 n. 52 and 126 n. 57, notes other prenuptial dedications in Archil. fr. 18 Bergk (veil to Hera), *Anth. Pal.* 6.276 (snood to Artemis), Pausanias 2.33.1 (girdles of Troizenian maidens to Athena Apatouria *pro gamou*), and *IG* II², 1514, lines 60–62, and 1516, lines 35–38 (saffron-colored robe to Artemis Brauronia in fourth century).

49. For sickles as prizes in the *paidikos agon,* see Chrimes (supra n. 11) 1 and 87–88, 94, 98–99. See also N. D. Papachatze, *Pausaniou Ellados Periegesis Biblio 2. kai 3.: Korinthiaka kai Lakonia* (Athens, 1976) vol. 2, 372, pls. 386 and 387.

50. Juvenal 3.67–68: rusticus ille tuus sumit trechedipna, Quirine, / et ceromatico fert niceteria collo. ("O Romulus, that country bumpkin now wears the parasite's dinner outfit, and carries his athletic prizes around his neck annointed for wrestling.")

51. See n. 43 supra.

52. Mirror handle with crescent on shoulder strap: New York, Metropolitan Museum 38.11.3, c. 550 B.C. Statuettes with an oil flask (lekythos or aryballos): Sparta Museum 27; New York, Metropolitan Museum 38.11.3; Dresden, Skulpturensammlung H⁴ 44/16. Cf. Jantzen (supra n. 36) pl. 4, nos. 18–19, showing a male athlete holding an oil flask. On the use of oil by athletes, see Harris (supra n. 1) 158–59; Gardiner (supra n. 46) 476–78 and figs. 175, 176, and 177; idem, *Athletics of the Ancient World* (Oxford, 1930; repr. Chicago, 1980); and C. Ulf, "Die Einreibung der griechischen Athleten mit Öl: Zweck und Ursprung," *Stadion* 5 (1979) 220–38. A naked woman is shown anointing herself with the aryballos amidst other women swimming (*hetairai?*) on Paris, Louvre F203, a red-figure amphora of c. 530–515; cf. N.

Yalouris, ed., *The Eternal Olympics* (New York, 1979) 261, pl. 151. for depictions of male athletes using the aryballos fastened to the wrist with a looped strap, see Yalouris 119, pl. 48; R. Patrucco, *Lo sport nella Grecia antica* (Florence, 1972) figs. 161, 162, and 163a (= Berlin, terracotta figure, winter *Typenkatalog* II 383.2; Leiden XVe 28 [PC 63] black-figure hydria; Berlin 2180, red-figure krater); and Schröder (supra n. 1) pl. 104 (alabastron and aryballoi) and 106a (Berlin 2180).

53. Mirror handle from Cerveteri: Dresden, Skulpturensammlung H⁴ 44/16, c. 500 B.C. The flower is in the hand of nude female bronze figures Vienna VI 4979; Sparta Museum 27; Paris, Louvre (no number; see J. Charbonneaux, *Les bronzes grecs* [Paris, 1958] pl. 7.1); Munich Museum der antike Kunst, 3482; New York, Metropolitan Museum, 38.11.3; New York, Metropolitan Museum 06.11.04; and Dresden, Skulpturensammlung H⁴ 44/16. We may note that the lotus is also seen in the lotus palmette frieze from Amyklaion, Sparta Museum, Wace and Tod, *Cat*. 206, no. 731a and b, 732. If the flower in the girls' hands is a lotus, the blossom may have had a special (sacred?) local significance in Sparta.

54. Athletes "losing their bloom": Philostratus *Gymn*. 48. Votive statuette from Sparta: Vienna, KM VI 4979, c. 500; mirror handle from Hermione: Munich, Mus. Ant. Kleinkunst 3482, c. 510; peplos-clad Spartan maiden: Berlin, Staat. Mus. 7933, c. 500.

55. Munich amphora c. 550–520: Munich, Antikensammlungen 584J. See supra n. 39, esp. Roller, 111, n. 31, whence E. Gerhard, *Auserlesene Vasen* (Berlin, 1847) pl. 177, and Yalouris (supra n. 52) fig. 13. For three of the bronzes under consideration (Appendix I, nos. 2, 5, and 8), I could not determine whether there is a *diazoma* or not because of the absence of photographs or mention of the fact in the publications I surveyed.

56. Mirror handle in New York, Metropolitan Museum 41.11.5, c. 540 B.C.; in Trent, Museo Provinciale d'Arte 3061, sixth century, B.C.; in Hamburg, Museum für Kunst und Gewerbe 1917.362, nude female bronze figurine, Roman, of Spartan type. Cf. Schröder (supra n. 1) pls. 110a and b and p. 196. Schröder cites the parallel to the Hamburg statuette of a Lucanian calyx krater (c. 380–360? B.C.) from Epizephrian Locri, Reggio Calabria 5014; cf. P. Orsi, "Locri Epizephri," *NSc* (1917) 110, fig. 12; Trendall, *The Red-figured Vases of Lucania, Campania and Sicily* (Oxford, 1967) 76 and 386, Locri Group, showing a girl wearing trunks and holding a strigil in a palaestra setting with a naked young man. Cf. the similar statuette of a nude girl with a strigil in Coussin, "Deux statuettes antiques du musée de Rennes," *RA* 5th ser. 19 (1924) 215–22. Although the Hamburg figure has been identified as a Roman statuette, it bears comparison with the Spartan girl mirror handles from which it may have been directly or indirectly derived. A. Kossatz-Diessmann, "Zur Herkunft der Perizoma im Satyrspiel," *JdI* 97 (1982) 79 and n. 50, and pl. 17 on p. 80, discusses the Hamburg girl in this connection and generally sees the *perizoma* (= *diazoma* of my discussion) as "anfangs eine weibliche Sportracht" (90) which was later adapted for female dancers and acrobats in secular contexts and then for male actors, including satyrs. For earlier publications of the Hamburg girl, see E. von Mercklin, "Antiken im Hamburgischen Museum für Kunst und Gewerbe," *AA* (1928) 434–35 and fig. 147, and H. Hoffmann, *Kunst des Altertums im Hamburg* (Mainz, 1961) fig. 49. For

recent publications of the Trent girl, see E. Walde Psenner, *I bronzetti
figurati antichi del Trentino* (Trent, 1983) 122, 123 n. 103; and G. Cuirletti, ed.,
Divinità e uomini dell'antico Trentino, Quaderni della Sezione Archeologica,
Museo Provinciale d'Arte 3 (Trent, 1986) 61. I wish to express my appreciation to Dr. Hornbostel of the Museum für Kunst und Gewerbe, Hamburg,
and to Sr. Ciurletti of the Museo Provinciale d'Arte of Trent for their gener-
ous assistance and helpful references.

57. Charbonneaux (supra n. 53) pl. 22, no. 2, and p. 144.

58. Burkert (supra n. 1) 391 with further references; Brelich, *Paidec e parthenoi*
(supra n. 1) 29–30 and passim: see index under *segregazione.*

59. Laconian figure from Cyprus: New York, Metropolitan Museum C.B. 447, c.
530 B.C. (= Appendix I, no. 15).

60. Pausanias 3.14.6; J. Delorme, *Gymnasion* (Paris, 1969) 72–74; W.
Zschietzschmann, *Wettkampf- und Übungsstätten in Griechenland,* II: *Pal-
aestra—Gymnasion* (Stuttgart, 1961) 37–39. Xenophon, Euripides,
Aristophanes, and Theocritus omit any mention of palaestrae or gymnasia
in their discussion of Spartan exercise. Delorme discounts Plutarch's report
(*Cim.* 16.5) of a gymnasium building in 464 B.C. The two buildings seen by
Pausanias (3.14.6) are dated by Delorme to the first centuries B.C. and A.D.,
while the *dromos* is considered to be a simple *campus* in its earlier form.

61. Aristophanes *Lys.* 1308–1313; Theocritus *Id.* 18.39; Cicero *Tusc.* 2.15.16;
Pausanias 3.14.6.

62. The five bronze statuettes of female runners are as follows. (1) Athens,
National Museum Carapanos 24, female runner from Dodona, c. 600 B.C.:
see Langlotz (supra n. 4) 88 and 93; Häfner (supra n. 4) 127–28; Jantzen
(supra n. 36) 39, 70, and 71. (2) Delphi Inv. no. 3072. (3) London, British
Museum 208, female runner from Albania (?). The short chiton with one
breast exposed is reminiscent of the girl runners in the Olympian Heraia
mentioned in Pausanias 5.16.3. See Häfner (supra n. 4) 144–45, who
believes that the piece is not Laconian, since the modeling is too lively;
Langlotz (supra n. 4) 94, dates the piece to c. 560 B.C. (4) Palermo, Museo
Nazionale, "maenad" from Collection Salnitrano. See Jantzen (supra n. 36)
27, 39, and 70–71, who sees the piece as a decorative figure on a vessel
and judges it to be from a South Italian workshop (Tarentum?) but with
Peloponnesian influences. (5) Sparta, Museum 3305, female runner from
Sparta.
    The figures of running girls have been called "maenads" by Jantzen
(supra n. 36) 70–71. Cf. four known figures of running Amazons clearly
distinguished by their dress and headdress: Athens, National Museum
6589, 6622, 6624 (all from the Acropolis) and 13230 (from Thessaly); D. von
Bothmer, *Amazons in Greek Art* (Oxford, 1957) 122–23, nos. 8 and 9; A. de
Ridder, *Catalogue des bronzes trouvés sur l'acropole d'Athènes* (Paris,
1896) 327–29, nos. 815–17, fig. 321; H. A. Shapiro, "Amazons, Thracians,
and Scythians," *GRBS* 24 (1983) 105–115, pls. 3 and 4.

63. Cf. Hesychius, s.v. *Dionysiades,* and Calame (supra n. 1) 323–33; Nilsson
(supra n. 25) 298; S. Wide, *Lakonische Kulte* (Leipzig, 1893) 160–161.
Hesychius, s.v. *en Drionas* (E 2823 Latte), merely mentions "a race of girls
in Sparta," apparently in honor of the Driodones, divinities worshipped in
Sparta; idem, s.v. *triolax* (IV, p. 197 Schmidt): "a running contest for maid-

ens" seems to have been a race of three stades' length (cf. the *diaulos* of two stades), but its location is uncertain.

64. Pausanias 3.16.1–2.

65. P. Zancani Montuoro and U. Zanotti-Bianco, *Heraion alla Foce del Sele,* II: *Il Primo Thesauros* (Rome, 1964), ch. 31. "Leucippidi," 339–349 and pls. 49.2 and 97–100.

66. Calame (supra n. 1) vol. 1, 323–33; see also E. Kuhnert in Roscher, s.v. Leukippiden, col. 1992.

67. Nilsson (supra n. 25) 298.

68. Calame (supra n. 1) vol. 1, 333.

69. Pausanias 5.16.2–3. On the Heraia, see Nilsson (supra n. 25) 62; and Calame (supra n. 1) vol. 1, 67 and 211–14.

70. The Sixteen women of Elis who organized the Heraia and the chorus for Physcoa (Paus. 5.16.6) also held a special Thyia or rite for Dionysus in which they invoked him as a bull (Plutarch *Quaest Graec.* 299 and *De Is. et Os.* 364F). Compare the sacrifice and foot race staged by the Dionysiades and Leucippides at Sparta (Pausanias 3.13.7).

71. Calame (supra n. 1) vol. 1, 332, no. 315, cites references to the Dioskouroi as *leukippoi* or *leukopoloi*: Pindar *Pyth.* 1.66; Euripides *Hel.* 638; Euripides *Ant.* fr. 223 (Suppl. C55 Nauck); Hesychius s.v. *Dioskouroi* (D1929 Latte).

72. Pausanias 5.16.4. L. Drees, *Der Ursprung der olympischen Spiele (Stuttgart, 1962) 28 n. 62.*

73. Scanlon (supra n. 3) 77–90.

74. Besides wrestling by Spartan women, there is evidence that it was practiced by Etruscan women in the fourth century B.C. (Theopompus *ap.* Athenaeus 13.517D), by Roman women at the Floralia festival (Juvenal 6.246–52), and by women in Antioch at the Olympic festival held there (Malalas *Chronographia* 12, p. 288; 10–13 Dindorf). Wrestling between girls and boys seems to have been practiced occasionally, but was regarded as a curiosity: schol. to Juvenal 4.53 mentions that "Palfurius Sura, the son of a man of consular rank, during the reign of Nero once wrestled with a Lacedaemonian maiden in an athletic contest"; Athenaeus *Deip.* 12.566E (200 A.D.) reports with lascivious interest the fact that boys and girls wrestle together in the gymnasium on Chios. L. B. Warren, "The Women of Etruria," *Arethusa* 6 (1973) 91–101, on 92–93, attributes, without good reason, the report on Etruscan women's wrestling to Theopompus' imagination. There is, for instance, a fourth-century B.C. Etruscan strigil with a handle in the shape of a naked girl holding a strigil and crowning herself: London, British Museum; cf. H. A. Harris, *Sport in Greece and Rome* (Ithaca, 1972) fig. 43; H. Walters, *Catalogue of the Bronzes, Greek, Roman, Etruscan,* Department of Greek and Roman Antiquities, British Museum (London, 1899) 110, no. 665; cf. 104–105, no. 640, showing a female wrestler on the handle of an Etruscan cista.

On *bibasis,* see Pollux *Onom.* 4.102, I, p. 231 (Bethe) (third quarter of second century A.D.): "The *bibasis* was a kind of Laconian dance. Contests were held in it not only for boys, but also for young women. You had to jump up and touch your buttocks with your feet and they counted the number of leaps, which is the explanation for the epigram of one girl, who '. . . once did the *bibasis* a thousand times, the most of anyone ever.'" For Spartan female dances, see H. Michell (supra n. 11), 188, who mentions five cult dances for girls.

75. See Appendix II, where sources and events are listed chronologically. It is beyond the purview of this paper to discuss the two Spartan female chariot victors who are known to have won Olympic crowns in the fourth century, since the women only sponsored the chariots, which were driven by men: Kyniska won in 396 and 392 B.C. and Euryleonis in 368 (?). See L. Moretti, *Olympionikai: I vincitori negli antichi agoni* MemLinc ser. 8, vol. 8.2 (Rome, 1957) 114–15, 121.

Kostas J. Gallis

The Games in Ancient Larisa
An Example of Provincial Olympic Games

13

Surely the Greeks in Classical antiquity, when the Olympic Games were taking place in Olympia, could not have foreseen that there would come a time, two and a half millennia later, that this kind of contest would be held in places far away from Olympia of which they could not have had the foggiest idea. Nor could they have imagined that they would be repeated every four years in the same spirit of peaceful and honorable competition, solely to win the glory of victory.

The Olympic Games were the best-known games in Classical antiquity. But games took place in other parts of Greece as well. Apart from the almost equally celebrated Pythia, Nemea, and Isthmia, there were local games in many cities. Every city in ancient Greece had its theater and its stadium. The Olympic Games were, we can say, the culmination of this kind of contest of a Panhellenic character.

It is not accidental that the spirit of such contests reached a high level in ancient Greece. It has to do with the character of the Greeks themselves, who have been described as the least gregarious nation in the world. This, in turn, is probably due—among other factors—to the geographic formation of Greece itself. This country has a diverse landscape, divided by mountain ranges and a very irregular coastline into many small geographic units; it has also many islands. All these areas have been inhabited since prehistoric times. This geographic arrangement caused the development of the independent and autonomous ancient Greek state and a national character expressed by a tendency to compete. This spirit of competition was a decisive factor in Greek history.

In the Olympic Games competitors came from all over the Greek world, not only from the mainland but also from the Greek colonies. Although a good deal of evidence exists for the program of the Olympic Games, the ways and conditions of participation, the awarding of prizes, and the honors reserved for the victors in their own cities,[1] we lack adequate evidence about the stages prior to participation in the Games: how the athletes were selected to represent the various cities and the circumstances of their going to Olympia to compete. We do not know if there existed a system for the selection of the athletes who would represent a city or economic support for their travel to Olympia. So it is supposed that they went to Olympia at their own expense and that anyone could participate, if he was capable of doing so.

Surely many of these athletes would have already tested their abilities by participating in local games. We do not have a great deal of information about these local games. Thus, I shall here focus on the events taking place in Larisa—one of the major cities of Thessaly—during the Classical, Hellenistic, and Roman periods. Our evidence about the games in ancient Larisa derives from certain passages of ancient writers and also from archaeological finds: that is, inscriptions (such as lists of victorious athletes or grave stelae of athletes) and local coins, which bear relevant representations. Through this evidence I shall try to reconstruct a picture of the games in that part of Thessaly.[2]

In Classical times Larisa was the seat of the Thessalian League. In this city two major sets of games took place. One was local—only Larisaeans participated—and was probably conducted every year; we do not know its name. In the inscriptions these games are simply referred to as the *agon*—"the games."[3] The other games had a Panthessalic character and were conducted every four years in honor of Zeus Eleutherios (Zeus the Liberator). They were called *Eleutheria*.

Eleutheria

The Eleutheria, or "Liberation Festival," was initiated in 196 B.C., a year after the Macedonian king Philip V, under whose influence Thessaly was at that time, was defeated by the Romans in the battle of Kynoskephalai, an event considered to be the start of the liberation of Thessaly from Macedonian rule.[4] Most of the Thessalian cities had at that time gone over to the side of the Romans against Philip, not suspecting that by doing so they were preparing their own subjection, and consequently that of all Greece, to the Romans half a century later. Hence this major festival to commemorate their liberation from Macedonian suzerainty. There was even a great temple in Larisa devoted to Zeus Eleutherios.[5]

That this festival took place every four years, like the Olympic Games, can be concluded from a Thessalian insciption dating to the beginning of the first century B.C.[6] These games were an important event in Thessaly, as can be deduced from the fact that the *agonothetes*—the person responsible for organizing the games, was the *strategos* of the Thessalians, the highest political and military authority in Thessaly at the time of the Thessalian League.

Many inscriptions preserve the names of the victors in the various competitions. These inscriptions always start by giving the names of the *strategos* and of the priest of Zeus the Liberator as well as identifying the particular game in a succession of games to which reference is made.[7]

Gymnastic Competitions

According to the evidence of the inscriptions, the various kinds of gymnastic competitions were as follows:[8]

Several types of foot races—the *stadion* (a distance of about 200 meters) and the *dolichos* (a distance of about 2 kilometers), in both of which young boys, "beardless" young men (adolescents), and men competed separately; and the *hoplites dromos* (race in armor), in which armed men competed.

The pentathlon, which consisted of running, jumping, discus-throwing, javelin-throwing, and wrestling. There were separate events for boys, adolescents, and men.

The famous *pankration,* a combination of wrestling and boxing, again divided into three categories according to the age of the participants. This was the most dangerous and toughest of all events, since the competitors sought to win by any means necessary, regardless of the danger to the bodies and even the lives of their opponents.

Equestrian Events

Even more important were the various equestrian events, which gave the particularly Thessalian color to these festivals and formed the most spectacular and interesting part of the games.[9] As Thessaly, the largest plain in Greece, was famous for its horses and its cavalry, these games gave the Thessalians an opportunity to display their riding abilities and foreigners an opportunity to admire the famous Thessalian horsemen and chariot-drivers.

The events connected with chariot races perhaps have their origins in the warlike life of the Mycenaean period. In historical times they offered an opportunity to demonstrate one's wealth and even political power. The chariot races held in Larisa, according to the evidence of the inscriptions, were of the following kinds:

Synoris polike: a chariot pulled by two foals

Synoris teleia: a chariot pulled by two horses

Harma polikon: a chariot pulled by four foals

Harma teleion: a chariot pulled by four horses

There were also two kinds of horse races: for foals and for horses separately. There were also two other kinds of horse racing, spectacular and very characteristic of Thessaly: the *aphippolampas* (a torch race on horseback) and the *aphippodroma* (mounting competitions). In these games the Thessalians were adept, particularly those coming from the areas of Larisa and Pherae.

The *aphippolampas* had its origins in Thrace, whence it was introduced into Athens, or more accurately Piraeus, in the fifth century B.C. The idea was a novel one, and the nocturnal horse race with lighted torches held a special fascination.[10] This sport spread to other parts of Greece, and it was very popular in the Hellenistic and Roman periods. Thus, it was also held in Larisa during the Eleutheria as well as in the annual local games.

More original and particularly popular in horse-breeding places such as Thessaly, Cyrene, Sicily, and southern Italy was the *aphippodroma.* In this complex and dangerous race the rider had to dismount at several points in the course, run alongside the horse without letting go of the reins or losing speed, and mount again.[11] This event was also part of the local games, at least since the fourth century B.C.

Its importance as a Thessalian tradition and also as an event with great appeal to the public can be seen in the fact that it was represented on Larisaean coins of the fourth century B.C. On the obverse of a silver drachma of Larisa from the first half of the fourth century B.C. (figure 13.1),[12] we see a representation of the head of the nymph Larisa, the per-

Fig. 13.1.
Silver drachma of Larisa, of the fourth century B.C., with representation on the reverse of an equestrian event

sonification of the city, wearing a band on her hair; on the reverse is a youth wearing a petasos and a chlamys and holding a whip and the reins of a horse. The depiction of the horse as galloping fast suggests that the scene is a representation of the horse-mounting competitions. The most critical and dangerous point of the event was, of course, the moment at which the competitor jumped to the ground. The rider turned, swung one leg over the horse's neck, and sat facing the side. Then he allowed himself to slide down, either with both legs together or with one bent (the one toward the horse's head) and the other stretched out, ready to hit the ground. He held the reins with one hand and steadied himself on the animal's back with the other, to make it easier to throw himself foward and upward when he jumped. There were no stirrups, and the riders practiced mounting and dismounting from either side.

Bull-Wrestling

Both the Eleutheria and the annual local games included the *taurotheria,* "bull-wrestling." This was similar to the *taurokathapsia* of Minoan Crete, but in Larisa the bull was pursued by a horseman who at the critical moment would jump off the horse and grasp the bull by the horns.

In this event the horseman closely pursued the bull, and provoked him to make him tired. In a silver drachma of the fourth century B.C. (figure 13.2),[13] we see on one side the horseman galloping in full charge, chasing the bull, which is depicted on the other side running at full speed. Gradually the horseman came closer to the bull, running beside him. A very vivid account of this phase is given to us by Heliodoros in his *Aithiopika,* written in the third century A.D.: "and now Theagenes was riding on the galloping horse, just beside the bull, keeping exactly the

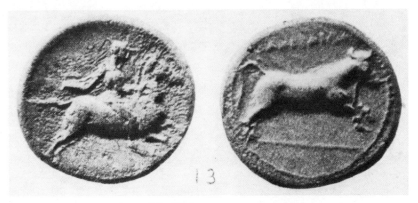

Fig. 13.2.
Silver drachma of Larisa with representations of bull wrestling

same speed with him, so that the distant spectators thought that the backs of the two animals were united and they applauded Theagenes as if he had yoked a strange *'synoris'* driven by a horse and a bull."[14] Finally there followed the *salto mortale*. In a climax of agony and fear, the spectators would see the rider jump from horse's back onto the bull, while the riderless horse turned aside.[15] On another Larisaean drachma, of the second half of the fifth century B.C. (figure 13.3),[16] we see on the obverse the youth who has grasped the running bull by the horns; he wears the chlamys, and his petasos is flying backward. On the reverse the horse is depicted running away with reins flying loose. The inscription reads: ΛΑΡΙΣΑΙΑ.

In the final, very dangerous phase of the game, the youth wrestled with the bull, holding him always by the horns, till the bull was exhausted. Then he would twist the bull's head and thus force the animal down, thrusting its horns into the ground.[17] A very rare representation on a Larisaean coin shows this moment, when the youth is bending the bull's head down.[18] The scene is also vividly described by Heliodoros: "And the bull, prevented from going forward and restricted by the tight clasping and the weight of the youth's body, bends forward and falls over, head first, onto the ground and lay there. As he fell with all his weight, his horns stuck in the earth and his head remained motionless, while he moved his legs in the air helplessly."[19]

Very instructive about the various phases of the game is a relief from Smyrna, now in Oxford (figure 13.4).[20] It bears the inscription: Ταυροκαθαψίων ἡμέρα B (the second day of the *taurokathapsia*). It represents five horsemen engaged in bull-wrestling. They are dressed in short chitons. The first horseman, riding at full gallop and extending his right hand forward, gives the impression that he is in full pursuit of the bull,

Fig. 13.3.
Silver drachma of Larisa with representations of bull wrestling

Fig. 13.4.
Relief from Smyrna, now in Oxford, with a sequence of
scenes of bull wrestling

which is supposed to be in front. The second horseman turns toward the
left (toward the spectator) and with his hand seizes the bull by the horns.
The third competitor is galloping. In the fourth group the horse is standing without its rider. To the right the competitor is sitting on the bull,
whom he has turned over on the ground, with its back legs in the air. It is
the scene described by Heliodoros, the most dramatic moment of the
game.[21] In the last group the competitor is ready to abandon the horse,
passing over its neck and jumping onto the bull, whom he has seized by the
horns. Finally, according to the account in Heliodoros, servants would
run toward the defeated bull, tie his neck with loops, and drag him to the
altar to be sacrificed.

The Thessalian bull-wrestlers are praised by Philip Thessaloniceus
as subduing the bulls without use of weapons:

> Thessalians with good horses, pursuing the bulls, these men strug-
> gling against the animals with only their bare hands, they
> synchronized their horses with the movement of the bulls, hurrying
> to clasp the bull's front by a tight hold; having bent to the earth the
> bull's head by the pressure of this tight hold, they neutralized the
> great strength of the animal.[22]

It seems that in Thessaly there was a strong tradition of this kind of bull-
wrestling, created by the hard pastoral life in the vast Thessalian plain.
Perhaps it is not accidental that the background of the myths concerning
the Centaurs is staged there, showing the close relationship of its old
inhabitants with horses in their everyday life.[23]

The accuracy with which the die-engravers represented these scenes
of bull-wrestling is impressive. The muscles of the competitor's body as

well as the characteristic folds in the neck of the bull are depicted clearly (cf. fig. 13.3). Such scenes were depicted even on smaller coins, such as triobols (half-drachmas), where, because of the narrow space, only the front half of the bull and of the horse is depicted.[24] On the even-smaller surfaces of the triemiobols (one quarter of a drachma), only the head of the bull is depicted, in front view, with the upper part of the youth hanging from his horns; on the reverse is depicted the head of the horse (fig. 13.5).[25]

It has been suggested that the *taurokathapsia* had a religious significance. According to Cook, it was a ritual having to do with fertility.[26] But adequate evidence to prove this view does not exist. It seems more probable that the religious festivals and particularly the worship of Zeus the Liberator in Larisa, the capital of the Thessalian League, only afforded the background within which the various national and social events of Thessalian life took place in the form of games and cultural competitions.[27]

It has also been suggested that the bull-wrestling in Thessaly derives from the Minoan *taurokathapsia,* but there are some basic differences. First, in the Minoan *taurokathapsia* there is no horse, and it seems that these contests had mainly an acrobatic character, whereas in Thessaly competitors chased the bull on horseback and finally subdued him for sacrifice. Moreover, we have no evidence for chronological continuity between the height of Minoan civilization c. 2,000 to 1,400 B.C., and the bull games of the Classical period in Thessaly, leaving a gap of several centuries in addition to the geographic distance. It seems more probable that these bull games, in the form in which they were practiced in Thessaly— that is, with the use of horses—originated in Thessaly itself because of the region's social conditions and natural environment: specifically, the big landowners, the riding skill of the Thessalians, and need in everyday life for herdsmen to catch their bulls on the vast Thessalian plain. Later on

Fig. 13.5.
Thessalian triemiobol (one quarter of a drachma) with representations of bull wrestling

these games spread to the east coast of the Aegean, with which Thessaly was in close contact in Hellenistic and Roman times.[28]

In the Roman period, this sport spread west to Rome. Pliny says that this spectacle was introduced to Rome by Caesar, who apparently witnessed it during his campaign in Thessaly against Pompey. Suetonius attests that Claudius gave this spectacle in his turn.[29] It seems that in Roman times bull-fighting became popular throughout the Empire and spread as far as France and Iberia. In Spain it remains popular.[30] It has been argued that the sport was transmitted by the Spanish to America, where it is still practiced in some western states in the form of steer-wrestling.[31] So perhaps something of the Olympic spirit crossed the ocean long before the Olympic Games were revived in Athens in 1896 on the initiative of Baron Pierre de Coubertin.

Cultural Competitions

Apart from various kinds of athletic events, the program of the Eleutheria included contests for trumpeters and heralds. If these contests were similar to those held at Olympia, the trumpeters and heralds competed to see whose trumpet or voice carried the farthest.[32] The winners would have the honor of calling out the names of the athletes and blowing the trumpet throughout the games. In Larisa there were also musical contests—specifically flute and kithara playing and singing—as is attested by various inscriptions referring by name to the victors.[33]

Participation in the games at Larisa was not limited to athletes and artists from Thessaly, but included those from other areas of the Greek world, even from the most remote colonies. The various lists mention victors from Boeotia; from cities of Asia Minor, such as Ephesus, Magnesia-on-Meander, Miletus, Cyzicus, and others; from Cyme, Syracuse, Patras, and Corfu; from Epirus; and from the islands of the Aegean, such as Thasos and Cos.[34]

Many victors came from Thessalian cities other than Larisa: from Metropolis in Western Thessaly, Kierion, Atrax, Pherae, and Gyrtoni; but the greatest number of victors mentioned came from Larisa. Among them the majority distinguished themselves in equestrian games, like the *synoris, aphippodroma,* horse racing, and chariot racing.[35] In the last category are mentioned two women, both Larisaeans: Aristokleia, daughter of Megakles, who won in the *polike synoris* (i.e., a chariot drawn by two foals), and Hepione, daughter of Polyxenos, who won in the *harma teleion* (i.e., a chariot drawn by four horses).[36]

Among the victors in the Eleutheria were athletes who had won distinction in famous games in other parts of Greece. An epigram on the base of a statue of an athlete in Larisa, of the first century B.C., informs us that he was crowned victor five times in his life, twice as a youth and three times as an adult: in Nemea, in Delos, in Alea, in the Eleutheria in Larisa, and in Levadia in Boeotia.[37]

An honorary decree of Larisa of the first century A.D. provides evidence for the existence in Larisa of two other games or festivals: the Thessalon Poseidonia in honor of the god Poseidon and the Caesareia in honor of the Roman emperors.[38] It seems probable that these games were also organized by the Thessalian League, but we know nothing about their program or how often they took place.[39]

Local Games

As we have noted, some games other than the Eleutheria occurred in Larisa, perhaps annually. These games were local.[40] The general responsibility for these games was held by the presiding five *tagoi*, who were the city authorities in Classical and Hellenistic times. We do not know the name of these games; as mentioned earlier, in the inscriptions they are referred to simply as the *agon*. Nor do we know the deity in whose honor they were held. It is possible that they were in honor of either Athena Polias or Apollo Kerdoos, who were the two major deities worshipped in the city.

The temple of Athena Polias in Larisa (as in Athens) was on the acropolis.[41] The worship of this deity was connected with the mythological traditions about Akrisios, the mythical founder of the city.[42] According to the myth, Akrisios had come from Argos to Larisa because the Delphic Oracle had predicted that he would be killed by the son of his daughter Danaë. Later Perseus, the son of Danaë and Zeus, went to Larisa and there met his grandfather, and they were about to return together to Argos. The Larisaean youth organized games to honor them before their departure; during these games Perseus, throwing the discus, accidentally hit his grandfather in the foot, and from this wound he died. Akrisios was buried in Larisa, and later he was honored by Larisaeans as their hero.[43] This myth later formed the plot of Sophocles' tragedy *The Larisaeans,* of which only a few fragments have survived.[44]

On the other hand, the local games could also very well have been associated with the worship of the god Apollo, whose important temple was in the agora of Larisa.[45] The worship of Apollo in Larisa was connected with the Delphic celebration called Septeteria; during this festival the sacred laurel of Apollo was transferred from the Valley of Tempe to Delphi by a holy procession, at the head of which was a youth of aristocratic birth, symbolizing the reincarnation of Apollo.[46] This procession went from Tempe through Larisa, Mount Oeta, and the district of Doris to reach Delphi, following the same route that Apollo was supposed to have followed after he killed Python, the mythical dragon of Delphi, and purified himself in the waters of Tempe. At a short distance from Larisa there was a small village called Deipnias, where the youth representing Apollo would have dinner and rest during this procession to Delphi.[47]

Athletic Events

Whatever deity these local games honored, their program seems to have been rich and to have included various races, musical competitions, and equestrian games, some of which seem not to have been included in the Panthessalic games of the Eleutheria. In the inscriptions listing the names of the victors in these local games are mentioned the following events:[48]

Two foot races—the *stadion* and *diaulos;*

The torch race for youths;

The *hoplites dromos* (race in armor);

The *prosdrome:* an imitation of a military assault involving three successive waves of horsemen, infantry, and chariots drawn by two horses,[49] perhaps representing the three main forms of warfare;[50]

Boxing and the *pankration,* with separate competitions for youths and men;

Archery competitions, with separate events for men on foot and on horseback;[51]

Bull-wrestling, which always appeared first in the various lists;[52]

The *aphippolampas* and the *aphippodroma.*[53]

Another complex game—mentioned in inscriptions only in relation to the local games, but probably included also in the Panthessalic games of the Eleutheria—was a variation of the mounting competition involving the use of chariots. The game was called *apobatikos agon* (dismounting competition). There were two people in the chariot: the man who had to jump down from the chariot, run, and then get back into it again before the race was over, and the man who held the reins and had to drive the chariot in such a way as to assist the movements of the other.[54] In Larisa it seems that victory in this kind of competition might be claimed separately by the man who jumped from the chariot, called the *apobates,* and the chariot-driver, the *eniochos,* since an inscription has been found of a victor list which makes a clear distinction between these victors; the *apobates,* named Dionysios, son of Zenon, was victor in the main dismounting competition, while the chariot-driver, named Timasitheos, son of Gorgopas, was victor in the *synoris tou apobantos:* that is, in the two-horse chariot from which the *apobates* had jumped.[55]

Cultural Competitions

As in the Panthessalic games of the Eleutheria, some cultural competitions were included in the local games. From the inscriptions we know that they included *logika enkomia* (i.e., narrations in prose), *epika enkomia* (i.e., epic narrations), and various epigrams.[56]

There were also competitions in poetic composition, divided into two categories: *palaia kataloge* and *nea kataloge* (the old and the new languages).[57] (It seems that the Greeks had the problem of two languages—ancient and modern Greek—even in antiquity.) The inscriptions referred to date to the Roman period. At that time the Greek spoken everywhere was the so-called *koine.* Thus, it seems that the competitors in Larisa could present poetry according to the rules of the old metrical system as well as poetry adjusted to the pronunciation of the language spoken in Roman times.[58]

From our knowledge of both the Panthessalic Eleutheria and the local games, its seems that Larisa played an important role in athletic activities in Thessaly, mainly because of its central position in the region. Athletes from all over the Greek world participated in the Panthessalic games. The Eleutheria was the most glorious festival of Thessaly, something like the Panathenaea for Attica. The cultural events associated with the games—for example, the competitions in various forms of literature—show that the region also had a developed cultural life.[59]

Roman Times

The period following the subjection of Greece by the Romans in 146 B.C. was crucial for sport and the sporting ideal. During this period there was a general economic, moral, and social collapse; most of the local games ceased to be held, and the Panhellenic games fell into decay.

Moreover, the character of the games gradually changed. Whereas the ancient games were closely connected with religion and the heroic past, in Late Roman times they became simply imposing spectacles which the subjects of the vast Roman Empire came from east and west to see. The taste of this public was affected, as time went on, by the preferences of the Romans, who delighted not only in the heavy events (wrestling, boxing, and the *pankration*), to which the professionals had already largely turned in the Hellenistic period, but also in the more bloody contests between gladiators, or between men and wild beasts. Thus, in some places armed combat came to be included in the program of the games.[60] Larisa was no exception to this: it became famous for its gladiatorial combats. According to Apuleius, famous gladiators were recruited from Thessaly in general.[61]

A recent find that is very illuminating for this aspect of the games in Roman times is the grave stele of the gladiator Phoibos, which was found in Larisa in 1978.[62] It was a chance find from the acropolis of Larisa, not far from the Peneios River. The stele, dated to the second half of the second century A.D., bears the representation of a heavily armed gladiator, with helmet, shield, and sword. The three laurel wreaths, to the left, and the three palm branches framing the gladiator symbolize his victories (fig. 13.6). The inscription is instructive. Written in the first person, it says:

I lie here, Phoibos the gladiator, proved strong in various stadiums ar:d loved by all. My previous name was Lagenis; I was from Cyzicus and, having wrestled in Asia, Thrace, and Macedonia, competing in Larisa I met my fate. Having lived well, having lived together with other friends, I lie here, having drawn my opponent down with me.

A complementary inscription on the left side of the stone, in verse, written in the third person, gives some more information: "Phoibos had many spectators in stadiums, as he was a friend to everybody. And now, by the banks of the river Peneios, he lies not alone but together with the man who killed him."

From the inscription we realize that the gladiator's nickname was Phoibos—the name attributed to Apollo—whereas his real name was Lagenis. Victorious in many contests in Asia, Thrace, and Macedonia, he fought his fatal match in Larisa. Both opponents were killed and buried in the same place.

Apuleius, the Roman writer of the second century A.D., mentions one Socrates, who, returning from Macedonia, where he had gone for business, planned to stop in Larisa to watch its famous gladiatorial combats. It is possible that one was the combat in which Phoibos lost his life.[63]

Topographical Evidence

We do not know exactly where in Larisa these events took place. The stadium is supposed to have been near the Peneios to the west side of the city. In this area there recently came to light a structure related to spectacles, with two rows of seats (fig. 13.7). A part of it was destroyed during excavations for the foundations of a modern block of flats to be erected

Fig. 13.6.
Grave stele from Larisa of the gladiator Phoibos, second
half of the second century A.D.

Fig. 13.7.
Two rows of seats of an open air structure in Larisa, of the
Late Hellenistic period (second century B.C.)

there, but all the stones of the seats have been recovered and will be used
for its restoration. It is near the eastern bank of the Peneios, just southwest
of the citadel. At first it was thought to be the *sphendone* of the stadium of
Larisa. But in the course of the excavations this structure proved to have a
horseshoe-shaped arrangement of seats. From its dimensions it seems that
it was an open-air structure, definitely used for certain kinds of spectacles, but its exact purpose remains unclear.

However, another relevant structure of ancient Larisa is certainly
known, and this is its theater. It lies on the southern slope of the acropolis
of ancient Larisa, now under buildings of the modern city. Parts of it have
already been revealed by excavations—namely, the western part of its
skene and part of its *koilon* (fig. 13.8).[64] The whole theater was constructed
of white marble and is estimated to have provided seating for about 6,000
spectators. The Archaeological Service of Greece plans the gradual
expropriation of all private property coinciding with the extent of the theater, so that it will be explored in the future and, after its restoration, will
be used again for festivals, like other ancient theaters in Greece.

The theater as it is preserved now dates to Hellenistic times (third
century B.C.), and it was in use till Late Roman times, as can be seen from
various inscriptions from that time on the upper surface of the seats. It is
fairly certain that some of the cultural competitions associated with vari-

Fig. 13.8.
Part of the ancient theater of Larisa, in the course of the
excavations

ous games in Larisa took place in this spot. Moreover, plays with Thessalian themes, such as *The Larisaeans* of Sophocles or the *Alkestis* of
Euripides, were very likely staged in this theater.

Concluding Remarks

Games were in many cases combined with cultural competitions and cultural events in general. Such are attested even from Early Classical
times—for example, Isocrates wrote his *Panegyrikos* to be delivered at a
Panhellenic gathering at Olympia, just as his teacher Gorgias had done in
408 B.C., and just as Lysias did when he delivered his Olympic speech
before the Panhellenes assembled at Olympia in 388 B.C. At these Panhellenic gatherings, athletics and music delighted the hearts of the Greeks
and reminded them of their ancient roots. Their wise men came to win
glory and praise and to speak to them of their past. Here the Greeks forgot
their own particular city and all that divided them; full of elation, they
lived a common life, albeit ephemerally, and began to speak of a moth-
erland bounded only by the hearts of men.[65]

I find it suitable to finish this chapter by quoting some of the intro-
ductory words from a recent publication on the Olympic Games: "It was

this spirit, born in Greece and perfectly expressed in the Olympic Games, which Baron de Coubertin wanted to revive in the modern Olympic Games—a belief in man, in his physical strength and moral worth, in human brotherhood, peace, and love throughout the world."[66]

Notes

1. A good summary of the existing evidence has been published by N. Yalouris et al., *The Olympic Games in Ancient Greece,* Ekdotiki Athenon (Athens, 1982).

2. T. D. Axenidis' publication on the ancient Thessalian games is still the only substantial work about the games in ancient Larisa; see T. D. Axenidis, *Oi archaeoi Thessalikoi agones kai i politistiki ton simasia. Istoriki kai Laographiki Etaireia ton Thessalon* (Athens, 1947).

3. E.g., *IG* IX.2, 531, lines 5ff.; 536, lines 6ff.

4. Axenidis (supra n. 2) 9.

5. See T. D. Axenidis, *I Pelasgis Larisa Kai i Archaea Thessalia, II* (Athens, 1949) 170–71.

6. *IG* IX.2, 528; Axenidis (supra n. 2) 10.

7. *IG* IX.2, 525 and 528; Axenidis (supra n. 2) 10–11.

8. Axenidis (supra n. 2) 11–12.

9. Ibid. 12–15.

10. Cf. Yalouris et al. (supra n. 1) 251.

11. Ibid. 246.

12. P. Gardner, *A Catalogue of the Greek Coins in the British Museum: Thessaly to Aetolia* (London, 1883) pl. V, 11.

13. Ibid. pl. V, 13.

14. Heliodorus *Aithiopika* 10.28ff.

15. Axenidis (supra n. 2) 16.

16. C. M. Kraay and M. Hirmer, *Greek Coins* (New York, 1966) pls. 148, 466.

17. Axenidis (supra n. 2) 16; L. Robert, "Deux épigrammes de Philippe de Thessalonique," *JSav* (April–June 1982) 139–162, esp. 148ff.

18. *Sylloge Nummorum Graecorum,* Danish National Museum, Thessaly-Ill-yricum (Copenhagen 1943) pl. 3, 113.

19. Heliodorus *Aithiopika* 10.30.

20. Robert (supra n. 17) 152 ff.

21. Heliodorus *Aithiopika* 10.30; Robert (supra n. 17) 152–54.

22. *Anth. Pal.* 9. 543.

23. Axenidis (supra n. 2) 19 and 23.

24. Gardner (supra n. 12) pl. IV, 9; *Sylloge Nummorum Graecorum* (supra n. 18) pl. 3, 102–4.

25. Coin in Volos Museum, inv. no. 406. I thank the director of Volos Museum, Mrs. Roula Doulgeri-Intzesiloglou, for the photograph of fig. 13.5.

26. A. B. Cook, *Zeus: A Study in Ancient Religion,* I (Cambridge, 1914) 499ff.

27. Axenidis (supra n. 2) 22.

28. Ibid. 22–23.

29. Robert (supra n. 17) 151.

30. Cook (supra n. 26) 498.

31. C. Seltman, *Greek Coins* (London, 1965) 160.

32. Yalouris et al. (supra n. 1) 128–29.

33. *IG* IX.2, 525, lines 4–12; 528, lines 6–15; 534, lines 1–8.

34. Axenidis (supra n. 2) 26–28.

35. Ibid. 28–32.

36. Aristokleia: *IG* IX.2, 526, lines 18–19; Hepione: Axenidis (supra n. 2) 28–29.

37. *IG* IX.2, 614, lines 4ff.; Axenidis (supra n. 2) 31.

38. *IG* IX.2, 614b.

39. Axenidis (supra n. 2) 36–37.

40. Ibid. 37–44.

41. *IG* IX.2, 517, lines 22 and 45; Axenidis (supra n. 5) 162–65.

42. Hellanikos from Lesbos in schol. to Apollonius Rhodius 1.40 (*FGrHist* I.4.91); Stephanus Byzantios s.v. Larisa.

43. Clemens Alexandrinus, *FGrHist* I.184; ibid. I.29.2; Pherekydis of Athens in schol. to Apollonius Rhodius 4.1091 (*FGrHist* I.3.10, 12); Apollodorus 2.4.4; Pausanias 2.16.2; J. Toepffer, s.v. Akrisios, *RE* 1.1 (1958) 1196–97.

44. Aug. Nauck, ed., *Tragicorum Graecorum Fragmenta*[2] (Leipzig, 1889) 213ff., frags. 347–52.

45. *IG* IX.2, 512, lines 18–21 and 31–32; 517, lines 22 and 44; 521, lines 4–5; Axenidis (supra n. 5) 166–70.

46. Plutarch, *Quaest. Graec.* 12.202 c (p. 293 c); *De mus.* 1136A; Aelian *VH* 3.1.

47. Kallimachos in Stephanus Byzantios s.v. Deipnias.

48. *IG* IX.2, 527, 531, and 532.

49. *IG* IX.2, 531, lines 13–17; 532, lines 13–16.

50. Axenidis (supra n. 2) 41.

51. *IG* IX.2, 527, lines 14–19; 531, lines 40–43.

52. *IG* IX.2, 531, line 11; 532, lines 9–10.

53. *IG* IX.2, 531, lines 18 and 37–38; 532, lines 17–18.

54. Yalouris et al. (supra n. 1) 246–47.

55. *IG* IX.2, 527, lines 8–11.

56. *IG* IX.2, 531, lines 43–46 and 48–49.

57. Ibid. lines 12 and 46–47; 532, lines 11–12.

58. Axenidis (supra n. 2) 42.

59. Ibid. 44–45.

60. Yalouris et al. (supra n. 1) 282–84.

61. Apuleius *Met.* 10–18.

62. A. A. Kontoyannis, "Epitimbio yia ena monomacho," *ArchEph* (1981) 37–52.

63. Ibid. 52.

64. A. Arvanitopoulos, *Praktika* (1910) 174ff.; Chourmouziadis, *AAA* 2 (1969) 167–69; K. Gallis, *Politeia* 6 (Dec. 1982) 52–53; K. Gallis, *ArchDelt* 35 (1980), Chronika (in press).

65. Yalouris et al. (supra n. 1) 73.

66. Ibid. 9.

Daniel P. Harmon

The Religious Significance of Games in the Roman Age

14

In a sense my subject, the religious significance of games in the Roman age, represents the decline and fall of athletic festivals in the Greek and Roman world. There is some irony in this development because it was the official policy of several Roman emperors to promote Greek athletics. Perhaps the keenest Roman patron of Greek sports was the emperor Nero, who added the magnificent gymnasium to the complex of baths on the Campus Martius in Rome, where he even erected a great bronze statue of himself to commemorate his patronage of athletics.[1] After the battle of Actium, the emperor Augustus initiated Greek games, the Actia, to celebrate and immortalize his military victory. Nero followed this precedent and started his own festival, the Neronia, which fell into obscurity after his death.[2] But Nero really did fancy himself an athlete and participated not only in the chariot races of the Circus Maximus, but even in the Olympics, where he won victories in the chariot races, in the contest for heralds—during which he proclaimed his own victories—and also in the special dramatic and musical events which were added for the first—and only—time to the Olympic Games on his insistence.[3]

Juvenal's famous phrase *mens sana in corpore sano* has been quoted through the ages in the support of programs in athletics and physical exercise for the young. But as scholars have frequently noted, those who quote Juvenal in defense of such programs are usually unaware that Juvenal had little, if anything, favorable to say about Greek athletics and athletes.[4] Horace and Vergil seem on the whole to take a positive view of athletics; and certainly the imagery of athletic games is used with a favorable meaning in the scriptural writings of St. Paul.[5] But many upper-class Romans must have shared with Cicero and Juvenal an ambivalence toward the Greek athletic festivals. On the other hand, if the games had not appealed to the masses, the Roman emperors would hardly have sponsored them.

There had, of course, been a change since the time of the old celebrations of the Olympic festivals in Classical Greece. By the late Republic and early Empire, guilds (along with the stables that provided horses and riders for the circus) traded and sold their athletes in a manner that must not have been very different from what happens in professional athletics today.[6]

In many respects the old athletic festivals had become a form of public entertainment. The eternal symbol of Rome is its Colosseum (the Flavian Amphitheater); and it is again a phrase of Juvenal's, "bread and circuses," which more than any other sums up Roman life in the early Empire. If St. Paul in many respects exhibits a favorable attitude toward the classic form of Greek athletics, the Latin Christian writer Tertullian (of the second century) found the Roman games an abomination, symptomatic of all that was wrong in the secular life of his times.[7]

But there is a sense in which the public games, even when they took a turn for the worse in Rome, continued to have some religious significance. Tertullian himself saw a religious meaning in these games. This realization in part explains his aversion to the "spectacles"—the *spectacula,* as he and his contemporaries named them. The old-style Olympic program could not compete (as many scholars have concluded) with the growing appeal of the *spectaculum*—the fantastic, eye-dazzling spectacle—which drew the masses together in common experience. But the people were not watchers in a wholly passive sense. The horse races of the circus had the greatest appeal, from the early Empire to the Byzantine Age. The people identified with and became adherents of one circus faction or another, known from the color of the cloaks which its jockeys wore.[8] This loyalty to the Reds or Whites, the Blues or Greens, or (for a short time) the Purples or Golds was of enormous social importance.[9] The great victors of these races, such as the famous Porphyrius, were idolized as immortal heroes.[10] They took the place of the demigods and old heroic warriors of the Classical Age; and the games which formed a common experience of society were under the patronage of the emperor. In a famous relief from Byzantium, we see him in his imperial box, holding out the wreath of victory, which he is about to confer. There is a nearly liturgical air about the scene, which shows musicians, dancers, and apparently a choir along with the spectators. The emperor, who bestows the symbol of victory, takes on a godlike role, analogous at least in some degree to the function which the great Zeus of Olympia or Athena of the Acropolis fulfilled in acknowledging human victory. It is impossible to imagine the races and the spectacles of Rome or Byzantium without the patronage and frequent presence of the emperor. Tiberius avoided the circus, though he had himself participated as a contestant in the races when he was young. But Augustus, Claudius, Nero, and most of the others were often to be seen in the imperial box.[11]

Many scholars, as I have noted, remark that the Olympic program could not compete with the appeal of the racetrack, the circus, and the spectacles of the Colosseum; and it is often supposed that the reason for this difference in taste is to be found in the Roman temperament, which had (it is usually implied) a penchant for the sadistic, and which lacked (as some have stated) that admiration or yearning for the ideal which lies at the basis of Greek athletics in the Classical Age. This hypothesis is an oversimplification. Much of the population of Rome at this time came from the Greek world and from other parts of the Mediterranean. The fundamental cause of the shift of interest away from individual accomplishment, which was rewarded in the old Olympic program, to the more spectacular—and at times grotesquely spectacular—events of the circus or amphitheater must have been the change in the social structure and in the human condition which had taken place in the Hellenistic and Roman ages. In the Classical Age the accomplishments of the individual were prized and celebrated. The athlete won glory for himself, for his family, and for his city state. In the Imperial Age, the excitement of the spectacular, the exhilaration and even the shock that one experienced at the games, the vicarious sense of victory shared with one's faction at the races, were all thrills that became a way of life—even if they were pathetic substitutes for the adulation which the glorious achievements of athletes inspired in the Classical ages of both Greece and Rome. Still, there remained a substratum of religious meaning in the imperial sports. It is this religious meaning—the pagan element in the Roman games—which so profoundly disturbed Tertullian. And this core of religious meaning was inherited from the athletic festivals of the Archaic and Classical ages.

There are three religious motifs or themes from the Greek games which are continued in the Roman athletic festivals; and the Greek influence, as is so often the case at Rome, comes in large part through the Etruscans. The first of these themes which the Romans share with the Greeks is that the celebration of games initiates a new era, a new period of time. Most of the Greek athletic festivals were recurring, tied in some way or another to the agricultural cycle, even to the cycle of life and death. The four-year interval between the games at Olympia came to be recognized, at least from the fourth century, as the Olympiad, the most common mode of dating important events throughout the Greek and Roman world.[12]

The second of these themes is reflected in monuments, on coins, and in the odes of Pindar: victory brings man close to the gods. The very foundation myth—the story of the abduction of Hippodameia by Pelops—exhibits the same theme, but carries it a step further: victory in a race brought Pelops not only recognition by the gods, but a form of immortality.[13] The story of Pelops' abduction of Hippodameia from her father, Oinomaos, in the chariot race—a feat which resulted in the death of the father—was represented on the east pediment of the Temple of Zeus at Olympia.[14] There is a famous representation of the story in a red-figure vase from the late fifth century, now in the Museo Archeologico of Arezzo.[15] The story is certainly an old one and already occurs in the pseudo-Hesiodic *Great Ehoiai*.[16] We know that it also appeared on the Kypselos chest from about 570 B.C.[17] The myth emerges in the Archaic period and comes to be of fundamental significance for the cult in Olympia. Yet it also seems clear that the story was a later addition to the mythic lore of the games. It is, of course, the foot races which are the more ancient in the Olympic competitions: it was not until 680 B.C. (in the twenty-fifth Olympiad) that chariot racing was introduced.[18] A study by Devereux suggests that the myth of Pelops and Hippodameia reflects the strange taboos of Elean animal husbandry rights.[19] What is important for our consideration is the fact that in the Olympic sanctuary a hero shrine of Pelops lies in close proximity to the altar of Zeus, which is itself the ritual center of the sacred precinct, the Altis.

If the Pelops myth came to be localized in Olympia, it seems likely from his importance in Argos and elsewhere that his mythic association with Olympia is a later development.[20] How and when the Pelops story came to be attached to the games is less important than the fact that games and hero cults go hand in hand. And hero cults are localized in a particular place. The name Pelops (as linguists have concluded) must have arisen as an eponym of a people: analogy supplied by other forms (like Dolopes and Druopes) suggests that at one time there must have existed a word **Pelopes;* and there is general agreement that this word would have been related to *pelios* and *pelitnos,* meaning "dark."[21] The **Pelopes* should have been dark-featured, and perhaps dark-haired.

Thus, Burkert has advanced a theory that in the name of Pelops we see the reflection of a polar tension which lies at the very basis of the Olympic cult.[22] Whereas the sacrifice of Zeus was accomplished by the blazing light of torches at the height of his sacrificial altar, the offerings to Pelops were made in a sacrificial pit, downward. The name Pelops (Burkert concludes) can be understood to mean "dark face" and thus expresses the antithesis of the god of daylight.[23] Certainly the tale of Pelops belongs to the deepest and darkest levels of myth. It deals in some way with the beginnings of the sacrificial ritual and its paraphernalia (hence the importance of the sacrificial cauldron in the story of Pelops).[24] The myth has to do with a form of "original sin," which results in the ancestral curse upon a royal house and its people. The details of the story are well known, but I call attention to the fact that, as Burkert explains the origin of sacrifice, the ritual is concerned not only with the destruction of life, but with its restoration and with the continuation of the cycle which is so important in the life of the hunter, where Burkert sees the beginnings of all ritual sacrifice.[25] Tantalus destroyed Pelops. By a special act of grace he was restored to life by Zeus. And since ivory was a precious material used in creating images of the gods, it seems clear that the ivory shoulder of the restored Pelops (which replaced the shoulder eaten by Demeter) makes Pelops an immortal figure. It is of importance that Demeter, the sorrowful mother who mourns for her missing daughter, plays a role in this myth: Demeter is concerned with human longings for immortality.

There is surely (as Burkert emphasizes) a polar tension between the Olympic cult of Zeus—carried out by torchlight on an altar that looks to the skies—and the chthonic or hero cult of Pelops. It is Zeus who grants victory to humankind, as the gold and ivory statue in his temple at Olympia emphasized. Pelops, who becomes a prototype of the Olympic victor, is an immortal figure, through the special grace and favor of Zeus. The figure of Pelops, however, ties the theme of immortality to victory in a horse race. Horse racing, in turn, was at first the special preserve of the nobility: horse racing and victory, nobility and immortality thus go hand in hand. This striving for immortality is the last of the three important themes which Roman agonistic festivals shared with the Greek.

The popularity of Olympic-type events in the Hellenistic and Roman ages is evident from the number and exquisite quality of representations of such contests from those periods.[26] There is ample evidence that the enthusiasm for Olympic-style games goes back to very early stages in the development of Italic and Roman culture. Etruscan tomb painting reflects most of the events of the Olympic program. There are, for example, the wrestlers in the Tomb of the Augurs, an event which is featured again at Chiusi in the Tomba della Scimmia (the Tomb of the Monkey).[27] From the beginning of the fifth century we have scenes with horse races, wrestlers, boxers, javelin-throwers, and aquatic sports.[28] There are a number of indications that the Etruscans erected temporary grandstands for both judges and spectators.[29] It has usually been supposed that the Etruscans took over this feature of Greek life, as they did so many others, from their contact with Greeks, especially in southern Italy. It is probable, of course, that some of the interest in the athletic contests was of native origin; nonetheless, that Greek influence was of great importance seems obvious. But even if nearly the whole Olympic program is represented in Etruscan monuments, the equestrian events are especially prominent. There is a splendid representation of a youth with his race horse in the Tomb of the Funeral Couch at Tarquinia, and an even more beautiful representation on a sarcophagus of Amazons driving the four-hourse chariot.[30]

But the most striking memorial to the Etruscans' love for the games is the Tomba delle Olimpiadi discovered in Tarquinia on March 26, 1958. It is named not only from the events depicted but from the fact that the preparation for the 1960 Olympics in Rome was underway when it was discovered.[31] The tomb dates to the second half of the sixth century B.C. and lies not far from the well-known Tomb of the Augurs. Practically nothing was left of its contents. It had already been sacked by tomb robbers in antiquity. But as Bartoccini, Lerici, and Moretti, the scholars who published the tomb, have remarked, it is distinguished from all the other tombs in the cemetery—and indeed from any Etruscan tomb so far discovered—by the remarkable artistic personality of the painter, which reveals a sense of style and a feeling for color which are altogether out of the ordinary.[32]

On the right-hand wall we see a discus-thrower, with the left arm extended in front of him and the right drawn backward, about to balance himself before hurling the discus. In this figure (as in nearly all), the artist has taken special care to portray muscular structure. The first figures that we see upon entering the chamber are two runners, the position of their arms and legs indicating that they are in movement. The expression on the face of the older man, who is bearded, would seem to indicate that he is already the winner. The panel shows various types of athletes. A man behind the discus-thrower is apparently a jumper.

But it is the left-hand wall, with its magnificent chariot races, that is the most striking. Four chariots coming from the right are racing to a goal post. The first charioteer is a young man without a beard. He turns his head to look behind him, afraid that his rival will pass him just before he comes to the finish line. The second charioteer is leaning forward over the pole to speed his team on during the crucial finish. The third charioteer is beginning to pass the second, and he will apparently be the winner. The chariot wreck of the fourth shows that there is a tragic side to the games, which reminds us that victory in the games is ultimately to be seen as a victory over death. That theme is underscored by another scene in the murals of this tomb, to which I shall return.[33]

The French scholar Piganiol has called attention to an element in two representations of festive games among the wall paintings in Etruscan tombs.[34] One tomb in Tarquinia has paintings of various types of athletes, but once again racing is so prominent that the tomb is named *La Tomba delle Bighe*. The frescoes of this "Tomb of the Two-Horse Chariot" show riders, a runner, and a javelin-thrower. But at the center of attention in the small frieze of this tomb are a pyrrhic dancer and an athlete, who are at the head of a procession which has arrived at what must be not a raised altar or a table, but a low retaining wall of some kind. Piganiol has seen evidence of a similar structure in the Tomb of the Monkey in Chiusi.[35] The flute-player stands on the other side of another low wall, and a woman standing on a platform before the structure wears her hair in a *tutulus*. There are athletes on the other side of the low wall, and a curious figure—who has been interpreted in various ways—is obviously seated and wearing a hooded cloak. She rests under an umbrella. A woman on the left seems to await the arrival of others at this central point of interest in the series of friezes, which show athletes involved in various games.

The scene is outdoors, and the woman protects herself from the sun. She must be of some importance. Is she a priestess? Are these perhaps funeral games, and is she the widow or the mother of the deceased? Or is she to be interpreted as the deceased person herself, attending her own funeral games? These details perhaps lie beyond recall, but it seems likely (as Piganiol has suggested) that both this scene and that from the Tomba delle Bighe represent a chthonic ritual.[36] The low wall, then, surrounds some form of pit. It would seem to be a *bothros* or eschara, a communication with the Lower World.

Etruscan art shows a growing preoccupation with death and themes of the Underworld. In the Tomba dei Caronti (from the end of the third century B.C.), figures of the Underworld flank the doorway, which represents either the entrance to the tomb or perhaps the gateway to Orcus, the Underworld itself. On the right, we see the figure of Charun, who wields the hammer; and on the left, a winged figure like Vanth.[37] The François tomb at Vulci, dating from the end of the second to the beginning of the first century B.C., has a famous depiction of the demon Charun, a blue-faced creature with hooked nose who (unlike the Greek Charon) carries a mallet and is a *psychopompos*—one who conducts the souls of the dead to the next world.[38] The evidence points in the direction of Capua and Paestum as the source of the gladiatorial games which became increasingly popular at Rome from the second century B.C. onward.[39] Tertullian derides the games of the amphitheater by saying, "We have seen Jove's brother, too, hauling out the corpses of gladiators, hammer in hand."[40] The reference is apparently to a circus figure whose task it was to carry off the corpses of gladiators. He must have worn the costume and carried the mallet of the Etruscan Charun, whom Tertullian confuses with Dis (the Roman translation of Greek Plouton).

The paintings of the François tomb depict the sacrifice of a Trojan prisoner, a theme which recurs frequently in Etruscan art. Charun the *psychopompos* there anticipates the role of the clown of the amphitheater to which Tertullian refers: his presence suggests that he will soon lead the Trojan prisoner to the Underworld. Though many scholars have supposed that these morbid preoccupations of Etruscan art prefigure the Roman gladiatorial games, there is curiously little evidence of such games in Etruria itself. But as Bloch has noted, we do seem to have distant prototypes of the Roman gladiatorial games in the curious figures which appear on frescoes at Tarquinia dating from the sixth century.[41] In the Tomb of the Augurs, we see one of these masked figures, who is called Phersu. There is another such figure in the Tomb of the Pulcinella.[42] In the Tomb of the Augurs, Phersu—the masked figure—executes the punishment of a man, whose head is covered with a sack.[43] Unable to see, he tries to defend himself with a club against the attack of a savage dog. When we return to the Tomba delle Olimpiadi, once again we see Phersu and a victim, again with his head in a sack, playing the cruel game of Phersu.[44] Phersu is the masked character, and the Latin word *persona* is certainly derived from the Tuscan term. The *-na* suggests an Etruscan name, a personification of the mask—that is, of the death mask. In the Tomba delle Olimpiadi, this gruesome figure occurs in the midst of the lively gymnastic and equestrian games. Even in this sixth-century tomb there is a preoccupation with death: victory in the games is contrasted with the helpless struggle of the victim of Phersu and with the tragic accident of the loser in the chariot race. The *agon* of the games represents a struggle between the forces of life and death. The brightness, the color, the sense of exuberance in the liveliness of the athletes and the race horses is counterbalanced by a grim fascination with the Underworld and its tortures. There are, it is true, savage elements in the myth of Pelops, which lies at the foundation of the athletic festivals of Olympia. But these details were kept on the whole in the background. Pindar denies the relevance of the more gruesome stories about Pelops to the Olympic Games.[45] The preoccupation with the Underworld becomes more and more pronounced in the Etruscan tomb paintings, and the games themselves are often depicted as a matter of life and death.

It is significant, then, that Roman tradition looks to the Tarquins, the Etruscan kings of Rome, and thus to Tarquinia as the originators of the great games of Rome. The Ludi Magni were celebrated to commemorate the dedication of the great Capitoline temple.[46] They were indeed the forerunners of the Capitoline games; and there is a story, preserved by Plutarch, that when Tarquin was still king, he had nearly completed the Temple of Jupiter Capitolinus when he commissioned an Etruscan craftsman from Veii to make a chariot of terra cotta for its roof.[47] It was not long after this that he was expelled from the throne. But when the Etruscans had modeled the chariot and put it in the furnace to fire it, the clay expanded and swelled to such an extent that the furnace had to be torn down to remove it. This, of course, was interpreted as a sign by the divine seers—a promise of Rome's majesty and future power. The city of Veii decided, for understandable reasons, to keep the chariot. Plutarch goes on to say:

A few days later, there were chariot races at Veii. Here the usual exciting spectacles were witnessed, but when the charioteer with his garland on his head was quietly driving his victorious chariot from the Hippodrome, his horses were suddenly frightened for no obvious reason, but either by some divine order—or else by chance—and they dashed off at top speed to Rome, charioteer and all. It was useless for him to try to rein them in or to calm them with his voice. He was whirled helplessly along until they reached the capitol and threw him out there at the gate now called Ratumena.

The people of Veii were perplexed and terrified at this occurrence, and they allowed the workmen to deliver the chariot of terra cotta.[48]

In this legend which recounts the crowning of the great Roman temple with its chariot—the symbol of victory—Jupiter Optimus Maximus is himself the victor. Jupiter, like Zeus, confers victory upon men. It was at his Capitoline temple that the triumphal procession found it culmination. There has been some disagreement as to whether the triumphal general—whose face was reddened with a dye called *minium*, like the faces of images of the gods—was supposed to enjoy godlike status during the ritual. The triumph certainly did bring him divine recognition: when he had ascended the capitol, he laid his laurel branch in the lap of the statue of Jupiter. The triumph, which brings recognition from Jupiter himself, creates a bond between the human and the divine; and in works of art the triumphal chariot becomes a symbol of apotheosis.[49] The association of the victorious charioteer with immortality, whether he rides his chariot in the horse races or in the military triumph, is expressed by the elegist Propertius of the Augustan Age: "It is by my verse that fame lifts me aloft from the earth and my daughter the Muse triumphs with garlanded horses. Tiny *Amores* ride with me in my chariot. And a mob of authors follow behind my wheels like captives. Why do you loosen the reins and try to beat me in the race?" The poet goes on to describe his ascent of the Mount of the Muses, where he receives the crown of immortality as a victor in the race. The triumphal chariot, then, becomes a familiar symbol of victory and immortality.[50]

Although the Capitoline temple with its ornamental chariot was meant to be the crowning accomplishment of the Tarquin dynasty, it was by tradition initiated in the first year of the Republic and became the symbol of the new era of freedom. The inauguration of the temple on the Ides of September was renewed at an annual rite in which a large nail was driven and fixed into the wall of one of its chambers, symbolizing the fixed and inescapable nature of destiny. The rite was apparently borrowed from the Etruscan goddess Nortia.[51] This ritual (which may have been abandoned in the third century) and the annual "great games" (the Ludi Magni) were meant to ensure that the new epoch, for which the temple of Jupiter Optimus Maximus came to stand, would endure. The temple, the ritual, and the annual games guaranteed that the Republican era was always new and forever young. Jupiter's cult partners in the Capitoline triad were Minerva (in her capacity as goddess of craftsmen) and Juno, whose very name is related to *junior* and *juvenis,* "youth."[52] The statues of Minerva and Juno occupied cells on either side of that of the great Jupiter. But the Capitoline temple also housed the cult of the goddess Juventas, the personification of youthful beauty itself. It was to her that the Roman youths made a special offering when they came of age and assumed the *toga virilis,* "the gown of manhood."[53] In the cult of the Temple of Jupiter on the Capitoline there is, then, a mystic blending of youth, victory, and the promise of immortality: the great god and his Capitoline temple were the guarantee that Rome would endure forever.

The Capitoline temple and its cult became symbolic of Rome's destiny to be the master, first of Latium, then of Italy, then of the Empire. The hill upon which the temple stood was orginally called the Mons Tarpeius. The change of the name to Capitoline was explained as the result of a prodigy: when excavating to lay the foundations of the temple, the workmen found a head *(caput)* which was interpreted as a sign that Rome would become head or governor of an empire.[54] The name Tarpeius is usually now explained as a dialectical form related to Tarquinius: the Capitoline originally, then, belonged to the Etruscan kings.[55] And so, too, did the great stretch of fertile land along the banks of the Tiber belong to the Etruscan royal house, according to a Roman tradition. In this plain, which was under the protection of Mars, the Tarquins had their fields of grain. When the Etruscan kings were expelled, the Campus Martius became the common property of the Roman people.[56] But an old ritual which was continued into the Republican era and beyond recalled that the Campus Martius had special meaning to the king. From Plutarch and others we learn that after a chariot race on the Campus Martius during the Ides of October, the right-hand horse of the winning team was sacrificed to Mars.[57] A runner carried its tail to the altar of the Regia (a royal building, perhaps at one time a kingly residence), while men who lived on the Via Sacra (i.e., close to the king and therefore representatives of the city) fought for possession of the horse's head with men from the area called Subura. This team must represent the outsiders. If they won, they fixed the horse's head to the Turris Mamilia, a building within their territory. When the team of the Sacra Via was victorious, they nailed the trophy to the wall of the Regia. Festus notes that the sacrifice was made *ob frugum eventum,* "for the success of the crop."[58] The very sustenance of life and the success of the crops seem to have depended upon the king's victory. The annals make it clear that early Roman history was one of constant raids and annual conflicts between neighboring peoples. The sacrifice of the winning race horse and the capturing of its head as a trophy in the ritualized battle were apparently meant to ensure victory and thus the protection of the crops for the king and his people. The October Horse, an offering to Mars, was decked with garlands and loaves of bread as a sign that the god would protect the crops and ensure a good harvest. Scholars have usually assumed that the race from which the October Horse was taken preceded the sacrifice.

We also know that horse races called the Equirria took place on February 27, just before the Kalends of March (the first day of the month of Mars), and again on March 14, the day before the Ides or full moon, which was, in the fullest sense, the religious New Year.[59] In the Republican Age there was a racecourse on the Campus Martius, the plain of Mars, somewhere between the Tiber and the present Piazza Navona (which itself lies upon the remains of the racetrack built by Domitian).[60] It was in this old racecourse that the Equirria of February 27 and that of March 14 were held. The second Equirria coincided with the Mamuralia, when a curious New Year's ritual was enacted: a man clothed in skins was led out, whipped, and driven away with long wands; the people shouted his name "Mamurius!" as they chased him—the incarnation of the Old Year— from the city.[61] During almost the whole of the month, the Salii, the leaping priests of Mars, enacted their pyrrhic dance to awaken the spirit of the new Mars.[62]

Several Etruscan artifacts represent what appears to be the birth of Mars, the warrior god. A cista from Praeneste of the fourth century pictures the goddess Minerva holding the boy Mars over a vessel. She has laid her helmet and shield down behind her on the rocks. This Minerva appears in the guise of Athene Polias, with the *aegis* and the figure of winged Victory hovering over her.[63] But the pithos must be symbolic in some manner of death and burial. The representation of the three-headed dog Cerberus clearly gives the scene a relation to the Underworld; the boiling water (or fire?) which is indicated at the opening of the pithos apparently represents the waters of the River Styx: Minerva, it would seem, is about to dip the child Mars in the Styx to endow him with immortality, as Thetis had done to Achilles. Her hand puts a stylus to his lips. Does she also anoint his lips with ambrosia? Or is she the craftsman who shapes his lips? Two Etruscan mirrors of the third century, one from Chiusi and the other from Bolsena, show what must be related scenes, although in one Mars (Maris) is doubled. There is much about these later representations of Etruscan Maris that remains unclear: his various epithets, which may express different functions or relationships which he fulfilled, have yet to be explained. All three monuments, however, show the birth or rejuvenation or rebirth of Mars. The spirit of the Roman Mars, we know, was periodically stirred up by the ritual cry *"Mars, vigila!"* ("wake up, Mars!").[64] His rebirth, at the beginning of the archaic New Year (in the month of March), was celebrated on the Campus Martius with horse races, which opened the season of military campaigns and the agricultural year. It was a time of rebirth in the world of nature itself. The rebirth of the god Mars reassured the continuation of the Roman people.

There has been much discussion about whether Mars was, in origin, a warrior or an agricultural god.[65] The former, in my view, remains the most likely. For the Romans, he was above all the ancestral god from whom the Roman people sprang. The story of the Vestal Virgin Rhea Silvia from Alba Longa, of her mating with the god Mars, of the birth of

Romulus and Remus, and of their exposure and miraculous salvation by the she-wolf, who suckled them, ties the Romans to the warrior god. The Romans were children of Romulus; and Romulus was the son of Mars. The wolf was their totem animal, and sacred to Mars himself. But the Romans were hardly alone among ancient Italic peoples in tracing their origin to this god, as is clear from the names of groups such as Marsi, Mamertini, Marrucini; or from the Picentes, named for the sacred wood-pecker of Mars.[66] The frequency of the names Marius, Marcus, Mamercus (all derived from Mars) reminds us that this god was of much broader importance in Italic life than was Ares (his counterpart) in Greek life.

A constant tradition emphasizes that his sacred plain, the Campus Martius, belonged to the people.[67] An important legend tells us that the courtesan Acca Larentia made a fortune in her profession and willed it, along with her land on the banks of the Tiber (i.e., the Campus Martius), to Rome.[68] A variant story tells us that a Vestal Virgin, one Gaia Tarracia, owned the fertile plain and that it was she who gave the land to Rome.[69] Acca, which means "mother," and Gaia, "earth," are names appropriate to goddesses.[70] Both the courtesan and the Vestal Virgin have associations with fertility. Larentia, as Radke has shown, means "causing to become green."[71] Her name, then, refers to the greening or ripening process. And Tarracia is clearly related to the placenames Taras and Tarentum, the name of the most fertile and well-watered stretch along the banks of the Tiber.[72]

Games, especially horse races, were celebrated on this ground: they were called the Ludi Tarentini, and according to tradition they go back to the regal period.[73] The Tarentum was so fertile that according to ancient lore the crop of wheat harvested after the expulsion of Tarquin the Proud was thrown into the Tiber, where it formed the Tiber Island.[74] The Tarentum, then, was the fertile plain of Mars on the banks of the Tiber. As far as we know, neither the name of the place nor the games called Tarentini come from Tarantum, the Spartan colony in southern Italy (Apulia), which is described in an ancient Delphic oracle as "the rich land of Taras."[75] Rather, the syllable *tar* in Tarentum of Rome and in Tarantum of Apulia, which is found in a host of Italic placenames, seems to mean "rich," "well-watered" earth.[76] The Ludi Tarentini, then, belong to a cult of the earth on the plain of Mars at Rome. Mars had his altar there; and the ancient sources relate that the first Roman consul, following the advice of a Sibylline oracle, consecrated an underground altar to Dis and Proserpina on the plain of Tarentum. *Dis* is a translation of the Greek *Plouton* (the wealth of the earth), and Persephone is the goddess of the Eleusinian mysteries.[77] The old Etrusco-Roman cult of Mother Earth was given a new, Greek interpretation.

We can conclude that the great Roman horse races which were celebrated in the worhip of Mars at the beginning of the agricultural season belonged to a fertility or "earth" cult. In both Greece and Rome the horse belongs to the chthonic realm; in myth, the horse was born from the earth: the horse seems to incorporate the very power and vitality of the earth itself, so that victory in the horse race somehow assures victory—or success and survival—for mankind in a bountiful harvest.[78] At the other end of the Roman agricultural cycle, horse races were celebrated again. In July, sacrifices were offered to Consus, the god of the stored harvest—once more on an underground altar, which was uncovered only for the offerings of sacrifice.[79] But the great altar of Consus was on the Circus Maximus, at the first turning point of the race track: on August 21, the soil was once again removed, sacrifices were offered to the god, and the Consualia—the majestic horse and chariot races—were celebrated.[80] The theme of victory, we have seen, is attached to the beginning and to the end of the agricultural cycle, upon which the very survival of the people depended.

These old Roman games, like their Olympic counterparts, recurred in a regular pattern. At their basis was a cult of the earth, attached in part to the god Mars, the divine ancestor of the Roman people—much as Pelops, the eponymous ancestor of the Peloponnesians, received his worship in the Olympics. The reinterpretation of the old cult on the Campus Martius along Greek lines, with the foundation of an underground altar to Dis and Proserpina, gave the Roman institution an Eleusinian dimension: it was the first stage of a transformation which made the games of the Campus Martius an expression of Rome's aspirations to immortality.

At the end of the third century B.C., in the course of the Punic wars, the Roman authorities took extraordinary measures because of the unusual nature and number of bizzare omens. Stones rained from the sky at Veii. Lightning struck temples and damaged city walls. At Frosinone, a child as large as a four-year-old was born, and it was unclear whether the child was male or female. In 200 B.C., flames were seen in the sky in Lucania. Another child of uncertain sex was born. A lamb with a pig's head and a pig with a man's head were born. All of these monstrous events were signs that nature was confusing species.[81] On both occasions, the officials in charge of the Sacred Books called for propitiatory rites. First Livius Andronicus and then the poet Licinius Tegula were called upon to compose hymns.[82] These songs were the forerunners of Horace's *Carmen Saeculare.* They were sung by choirs of twenty-seven youths and maidens as part of a purificatory ritual in a rite of renewal. From the Etruscans, the Roman had learned the concept of the *saeculum,* which was defined as a span of time equal to the longest human life in a particular generation of men. The *saeculum* came to be fixed first as 109, then as 100 years in the late Republic and early Empire.[83] But among the Etruscans and their earlier Roman students, it was considered impossible for ordinary mortals to know the beginning and end of these ages (when the old generation ended and the new one began), except by signs, prodigies, and omens in the realm of nature. The fires in the heavens and the contradictions of nature, which called for hymns and purificatory rituals in the late third century, were signs that the end-time was near. The singing of the hymns by choirs of innocent youths and virgins, the celebration of games and theatrical performances, were all offerings to the gods, meant to ensure the peaceful transition to a new era.[84] These celebrations came to be styled the Ludi Saeculares, the Secular Games; and the underground altar of the Tarentum on the Campus Martius was originally the focal point of their celebration.[85] The notion remained that new life springs from the old.

Augustus renewed and expanded these games, for which Horace's famous *Carmen Saeculare* was composed.[86] Claudius (on the pretext that Augustus had miscalculated the date of the new *saeculum*) celebrated them again.[87] In the Imperial Age, nearly every emperor wanted his subjects to imagine that his rise to power heralded the dawning of a new age. The emperor became a sign of the new epoch, a promise that life would go on. Salvation and survival came to be identified with the emperor, as the imperial titles such as "savior" and "father of the country" make clear.[88] Hope for the future depended upon the imperial house, and the emperor became a *divus*, a god himself. Hence, he was patron of the great games, which ritualized victory and survival.

This relationship between the great games and the imperial household is expressed in a most striking way in the Lusus Troiae, the so-called Game of Troy, an ancient equestrian custom which extends back at least to the sixth century B.C. Sulla revived the Troia, but it was Augustus who elaborated it.[89] Vergil describes the Lusus Troiae in the fifth book of the *Aeneid* as a part of the funeral games of Anchises, the father of Aeneas.[90] He describes the youths riding in double columns, then wheeling suddenly around—half to the left and half to the right—in the ritualized mock battle: "Just as the labyrinth held a path woven with blind walls . . . even in such a course do the Trojan children engage their steps, weaving in sport their flight and conflict." The poet could have had no knowledge of a late seventh-century Etruscan vase from Tragliatella (near Caere).

The vase shows a number of scenes, but the most important is that of youths emerging on horseback from a labyrinth, which contains the inscription *TRUIA,* "Troy." There was, we learn from ancient sources, a place named Troia on the Mediterranean shore near Lavinium, where the Trojan Aeneas was thought to have landed.[91] Did this pre-Indo-European placename Troia, which was found elsewhere in Italy as well, prompt the localization of the Aeneas legend in this area? Does the word *troia* mean "a passageway" of some kind? Archaic Latin preserves the related words *amptruare* and *redantruare,* used of the repeated back-and-forth motions of the Salii.[92] And Plutarch preserves the information that the youths of Delos even in his own day performed "a dance in imitation of the circling passages of the labyrinth, and consisting of various rhythmic involutions and evolutions." These were apparently done in connection with certain athletic contests at Delos.[93] The story of Theseus, who returned from the labyrinth after killing the Minotaur, is probably an aetiological myth for such a contest. The labyrinth dance and the Lusus Troiae must have celebrated a return from danger, a triumph of life over death. During the Imperial Age the youth of the imperial house led the performance of the equestrian display called the Lusus Troiae.[94] It was offered on the birthday of the emperor, as a part of the funeral games for deceased members of the imperial house, and during extraordinary *spectacula* of the circus and later of the amphitheater. It played a special role in the Secular Games, just as it once had in funeral games.[95] The victories of these ceremonial games, performed by young men (or even boys) of the imperial house, were a symbolic assurance of the continuity of the state, which depended for its welfare, or even "salvation," upon the emperor.

Some later writers described the circus as a microcosm: the chariots represented the sun and the celestial bodies, the colors worn by the factions represented the seasons of the year. Every feature of the circus was drawn into this symbolic interpretation. The provider of this microcosm, where the Romans passed the hours in a life of leisure, was their godlike emperor. It is probably no accident that the circus lies below his palace. Not only is the circus at Rome below the Domus Augustana, but the circus of Maxentius is adjacent to and below the emperor's palace on the Appian Way. The proximity of circus and imperial palace is best explained not by the emperor's need to make a quick exit when the crowd became unruly, but by the fact that he had so often to be in attendance at the games.[96] Each emperor in succession offered games and spectacles as a sign of his epoch or era, often surpassing those who had gone before him. At the basis of all these spectacles, which were often so grandiose and extravagant that they were witness to the godlike majesty of the emperor, lies the notion that victory—even if only a ritual victory experienced at second hand— holds out some share in immortality.

Notes

1. Suetonius *Ner.* 12. G. Piccaluga, *Elementi spettacolari nei rituali festivi romani,* Quaderni di Studi e Materiali di Storia delle Religioni (Rome, 1965), remains an excellent theoretical discussion on the significances of the word *ludus.*

2. Piccaluga (supra n. 1); Suetonius *Ner.* 12 and 21.

3. Suetonius *Ner.* 23–24.

4. H. A. Harris, *Sport in Greece and Rome* (Ithaca, N.Y., 1972) 64, makes this observation.

5. On the Roman authors' attitudes toward Greek athletics, see Harris (supra n. 4) 49–74.

6. Ibid. 184–211; R. Auguet, *Cruelty and Civilization: The Roman Games* (London, 1972) 120f.

7. Tertullian *De Spect.* 5; 7; and passim.

8. See A. Cameron, *Circus Factions: Blues and Greens at Rome and Byzantium* (Oxford, 1976); Harris (supra n. 4) 193–211; Auguet (supra n. 6) 135.

9. A. Cameron, *Porphyrius the Charioteer* (Oxford, 1973) 232f.

10. Cameron (supra n. 9).

11. Harris (supra n. 4) 59f.

12. A. E. Samuel, *Greek and Roman Chronology,* Handbuch der Altertumswissenschaft 1.7 (Munich, 1972) 189–94.

13. Sources for the myth of Pelops are collected by Bloch, s.v. Pelops, in W. H. Roscher, *Ausführliches Lexikon der griechischen und römischen Mythologie* 3.2 (Stuttgart, 1902–1909) 1866–75

14. M. L. Säflund, *The East Pediment of the Temple of Zeus at Olympia,* Studies in Mediterranean Archaeology 27 (Göteborg, 1970).

15. See, e.g., the illustration in G. A. Christopoulos and J. C. Bastias, *Athletic in Ancient Greece* (Athens, 1976) 83, pl. 32.

16. Hesiod, fr. 259; Pausanias 6.21.10f.; H. G. Evelyn-White, trans., *Hesiod: The Homeric Hymns and Homerica* (Cambridge, Mass., 1914) 261.

17. Pausanias 5.17.6–7.

18. Pausanias 5.8.7.

19. G. Devereux, "The Abduction of Hippodameia as 'Aition' of a Greek Animal Husbandry Rite," *Studi e Materiali di Storia delle Religioni* 36 (1965) 3–25; see also W. Burkert, *Homo Necans: The Anthropology of Ancient Greek Sacrificial Ritual and Myth,* trans. Peter Bing (Berkeley, 1983) 95–96.

20. A. Mallwitz, *Olympia und seine Bauten* (Munich, 1972) 79–84 and 133–37; H.-V. Herrmann, "Pelops in Olympia," in *Stele: Tomos eis mnemen tou Nikolaou Kontoleontos* (Athens, 1980) 59–74.

21. J. B. Hoffman, *Etymologisches Wörterbuch des Griechischen* (Munich, 1949) s.v. *pelitnos.*

22. Burkert (supra n. 19) 96–103.

23. Ibid. 97.

24. Pausanias 5.10.4; Burkert (supra n. 19) 100–101.

25. Burkert (supra n. 19) 1–82.

26. See, e.g., B. Kyrkos, "Sport in the Hellenistic and Roman Periods," in *Athletics in Ancient Greece,* ed. I. Douskov (Athens, 1977) 275–87.

27. See L. Banti, *Etruscan Cities and Their Culture,* trans. E. Bizzarri (Berkeley and Los Angeles, 1973) pls. 31 and 78; M. Pallottino, *Etruscan Painting,* the Great Centuries of Painting, directed by A. Skira (New York, 1952) 39 and 65.

28. For illustrations, see, e.g., M. Moretti, *Nuovi monumenti della pittura etrusca* (Milan, 1966) 104–116, 124–31.

29. J. Heurgon, *Daily Life of the Etruscans,* trans. James Kirkup (London, 1961) 207f.

30. Pallottino (supra n. 27) 83 and 94.

31. R. Bartoccini, C. M. Lerici, and M. Moretti, *Tarquinia: La Tomba delle Olimpiadi* (Milan, 1960) 5f.

32. Ibid. 67.

33. Ibid. 55–58.

34. A. Piganiol, *Recherches sur les jeux romains: Notes d'archéologie et d'histoire religieuse,* Publications de la Faculté des Lettres de l'Université de Strasbourg 13 (Strasbourg and Paris, 1923) 1–14. For illustrations of these tombs, see F. Poulsen, *Etruscan Tomb Paintings: Their Subjects and Significance,* trans. I. Andersen (Oxford, 1922) 24, fig. 20, and 27, fig. 22.

35. Piganiol (supra n. 34) 3–4.

36. Ibid. 4–14.

37. On Vanth and Charun, see M. Pallottino, *The Etruscans,* trans. J. Cremona (Bloomington, Ind., 1975) 149.

38. Pallottino (supra n. 27) 115–24.

39. See J. Heurgon, *Recherches sur l'histoire, la religion et la civilisation de Capoue Préromaine des origines à la deuxième guerre punique,* Bibliothèque des Écoles Françaises d'Athènes et de Rome 154 (Paris, 1942) 429f.; G. Ville, *La gladiature en occident des origines à la mort de Domitien,* Bibliothèque des Écoles Françaises d'Athènes et de Rome 245 (Paris, 1981) 1–56.

40. Tertullian *Apol.* 15.5, trans. T. R. Glover (Cambridge, Mass., 1931) 79.

41. R. Bloch, *The Etruscans,* trans. S. Hood (New York, 1958) 134–35.

42. See Poulsen (supra n. 34) figs. 4–6.

43. Ibid.

44. Bartoccini et al. (supra n. 31) 87.

45. Pindar *Ol.* 1.30–58.

46. On the relationship between the Ludi Magni or Romani, see G. Wissowa, *Religion und Kultus der Römer,* Handbuch der klassischen Altertumswissenschaft 5.4 (Munich, 1912) 126, 451–53. Habel, s.v. *ludi publici, RE* 5 Suppl. (1931) 617–20.

47. Plutarch *Publ.* 13.

48. Ibid. Cf. *Plutarch's Lives* I, trans. B. Perrin (Cambridge, Mass., 1914) 535–36.

49. G. M. A. Richter, *A Handbook of Greek Art* (London, 1959) 355; I. S. Ryberg, *Rites of the State Religion in Roman Art,* MAAR 22 (Rome, 1955) fig. 28A; P. Mingazzini, *Le rappresentazioni vascolari del mito dell' apoteosi di Herakles,* MemLinc, ser. 6, vol. 1 (Rome, 1925) 419–21, 449–50.

50. Propertius 3.1.9f. On this theme, see D. P. Harmon, "The Poet's Initiation and the Sacerdotal Imagery of Propertius 3, 1–5," in *Studies in Latin Literature and Roman History,* Collection Latomus 164 (Brussels, 1979) 321f.

51. Livy 7.3; A. J. Pfiffig, *Religio Etrusca* (Graz, 1975) 258–59; G. Radke, *Die Götter Altitaliens,* Fontes et Commentationes: Schriftenreihe des Instituts für Epigraphik an der Universität Münster 3 (Münster, 1965) 232.

52. G. Dury-Moyaers and Marcel Renard, "Aperçu critique de travaux relatifs au culte de Junon," in *Aufstieg und Niedergang der römischen Welt* II.17.1, ed. Wolfgang Haase (Berlin and New York, 1981) 143–46, with bibliography.

53. Dionysius Halicarnassus *Ant. Rom.* 3.69.5; Pliny *NH* 35.108; Livy 5.54; Augustine *De Civ. D.* 4.23; Lucius Piso *apud* Dionysius Halicarnassus 4.15.5–6.

54. Livy 1.55.6.

55. G. Radke, "Acca Larentia und die fratres Arvales: Ein Stück römisch-sabinischer Frühgeschichte," in *Aufstieg und Niedergang der römischen Welt* I.2, ed. H. Temporini (Berlin and New York, 1972) 429–30.

56. Livy 2.5.2–5; Dionysius Halicarnassus *Ant. Rom.* 5.13; Plutarch *Publ.* 8; Zosimus 2.3. See F. Castagnoli, *Il Campo Marzio nell' antichità,* MemLinc, ser. 8, vol. 1.4 (Rome, 1946) 93–193, especially 100f.; F. Coarelli, *Guida archeologica di Roma* (Verona, 1975) 239.

57. Plutarch *Quaest. Rom.* 97.287a; Timaeus *apud* Polybius 12.4b; Festus 190L = p. 295 L²; *CIL* 1², p. 274. On Equus October, see U. W. Scholz, *Studien zum altitalischen und altrömischen Marskult und Marsmythos* (Heidelberg, 1970) 9f., 81f.; and, above all, C. B. Pascal, "October Horse," *HSCP* 85 (1981) 261–91.

58. Festus 246 L = p. 326 L².

59. H. H. Scullard, *Festivals and Ceremonies of the Roman Republic* (Ithaca, N.Y., 1981) 82 and 89.

60. Castagnoli (supra n. 56) 136; S. B. Platner, *The Topography and Monuments of Ancient Rome*² (Boston, 1911) 341; Coarelli (supra n. 56) 239.

61. Scullard (supra n. 59) 89; H. Stern, "Note sur deux images du mois de Mars," *REL* 52 (1974) 70–74.

62. On the dance and hymns of the Salii: B. Maurenbrecher, *Carminum Saliarium Reliquiae,* Jahrbücher für klassische Philologie, Suppl. 21 (Leipzig, 1894) 315–18; Rappaport, s.v. Salii, *RE* 1A.2 (1920) 1874–99; W. W. Fowler, *Roman Festivals of the Period of the Republic* (London, 1899) 37–44.

63. These are discussed by H. Wagenvoort, "Origin of the Ludi Saeculares," in *Studies in Roman Literature, Culture and Religion* (Leiden, 1956) 213–32, figs. 1–3; Scholz (supra n. 57) 141f.

64. Servius *Aen.* 7.603, 8.3; Wissowa (supra n. 46) 144.

65. For a review of the discussion, see Scholz (supra n. 57) 34–45, and G. Dumézil, *Archaic Roman Religion,* trans. P. Krapp (Chicago, 1970) 205f.; J. H. Croon, "Die Ideologie des Marskultes unter dem Principat und ihre Vorgeschichte," in *Aufstieg und Niedergang des römischen Welt* (supra n. 52) 260–68.

66. E. T. Salmon, *The Making of Roman Italy* (Ithaca, N.Y., 1982) 7, 22–23; Giacomo Devoto, *Gli antichi italici*[2] (Florence, 1951) 124–127, 233–34. See also Radke (supra n. 51) 199–205. Whether the Marrucini belong to Mars is unclear.

67. See supra n. 56.

68. Aulus Gellius 7.7; Pliny *NH* 34.6.11; Macrobius *Sat.* 1.10.15–16; Plutarch *Rom.* 5; idem *Quaest. Rom.* 35; *CIL* 1[2], p. 238; Castagnoli (supra n. 56) 101f.

69. Aulus Gellius 7.7; Pliny *NH* 34.6.11.

70. Radke (supra n. 51) 55.

71. Radke (supra n. 55) 422 f.

72. Castagnoli (supra n. 56) 98f.

73. Wissowa (supra n. 46) 309, with ancient sources.

74. See n. 56 supra.

75. Strabo 6.279; H. Nissen, *Italische Landeskunde* 2.2 (Berlin, 1902) 865–76.

76. C. Battisti, *Sostrati e parastrati nell' Italia preistorica* (Florence, 1959) 132–35, gives a full etymological discussion of *Tarentum* and related words.

77. K. Latte, *Römische Religionsgeschichte,* Handbuch der Altertumswissenschaft 5.4 (Munich, 1960) 247.

78. The horse represents the elemental power or forces of the earth and sea; cf. W. Burkert, *Griechische Religion der archaischen und klassischen Epoche,* Religionen der Menschheit 15 (Stuttgart, 1977) 218–19.

79. Scullard (supra n. 59) 163.

80. Ibid. 177–78.

81. Livy 27.37, 31.12.

82. Ibid.

83. The standard work on the suject is J. B. Pighi, *De Ludis Saecularibus Populi Romani Quiritium Libri Sex*[2] (Amsterdam, 1965). See the more recent work, with full bibliography, of P. Brind' Amour, "L'Origine des Jeux Séculaires," in *Aufstieg und Niedergang der römischen Welt* 2.16.2, ed. W. Haase (Berlin and New York, 1978) 1334–417.

84. For a review of the relationship between the Secular Games and the Ludi Tarentini, see P. Weiss, "Die 'Säkularspiele' der Republik—eine annalistische Fiktion," *RömMitt* 80 (1973) 205–17.

85. Ibid. 207f.

86. For bibliography, see Brind' Amour (supra n. 83) 1354f.

87. Suetonius, *Claud.* 21.2.

88. L. R. Taylor, *The Divinity of the Roman Emperor* (Middletown, Conn., 1931) 35f., 47, 69f., 200, 218, 241f.

89. See H. v. Petrikovits, "Troiae Lusus," *Klio* n.s. 14 (1939) 209–20; J.-P. Neraudau, *La jeunesse dans la littérature et les institutions de la Rome républicaine* (Paris, 1979) 227–34; J. Toutain, s.v. Troja, Trojae lusus, *Dar-Sag* 5.493–96.

90. Vergil *Aen.* 5.545–603.

91. The vase is published and fully discussed by G. Q. Giglioli, "L'Oinochoe di Tragliatella," *Studi Etruschi* 3 (1929) 111–59, esp. table 24. Cf. also L. R. Taylor, *"Seviri Equitum Romanorum* and Municipal *Seviri,"* *JRS* 14 (1924) 158–71.

92. *Antroare,* Paulus-Festus 9 L; *redantruare,* Festus 334 L; Pacuvius trag. fr. 106. On the Italic place and placename *Troia,* see G. Dury-Moyaers, *Enée et Lavinium,* Collection Latomus 174 (Brussels, 1981) 146–55; and Battisti (supra n. 76) 27.

93. Plutarch *Thes.* 21.

94. Toutain (supra n. 89) 494–95.

95. Ibid.

96. Cameron (supra n. 8) 182.

Wendy J. Raschke

Epilogue

The archæological investigation of the ancient Olympic Games and of ancient sport in general involves a fragile tension between the "expectations engendered by modern experiences," as Glass observes, and the puzzling material remains multilated by ancient alterations and "friendly" modern archaeologists. Hard material evidence, however fragmentary, and literary sources, however ambiguous or late, must be reconciled in our search for the truth. Since classical archaeologists are at a greater disadvantage than many in having largely incomplete physical remains and written records at their disposal, any conclusion regarding ancient culture must be taken as a more or less provisional understanding based on the best current evidence. Miller aptly suggests that "archaeology is the laboratory of history," and so it happens that ancient historians and archaeologists are forced not only to creatively reconstruct the monuments, but also to hypothesize what typically and specifically took place within the walls of a gymnasium or the borders of a stadium. Conclusions, such as they are, often amount to an admission of negative results or a disavowal of other implausible theories. It is difficult, then, to put forth definitive, general statements about the nature of the ancient Olympics based on the studies in this collection. It will be appropriate, however, to distinguish the major contributions of each study to the scholarship on Olympic questions; thereafter elucidation will be attempted of some general truths which appear to emerge.

Despite the proliferation of scholarly theories on the origins of the Olympics and Greek athletics during the past century,[1] C. Renfrew and Puhvel demonstrate that some headway can be made by the application of new methods and new cross-cultural evidence to the questions of aetiology. After a survey of the primary sources of evidence for athletics in Minoan-Mycenaean times, Renfrew reminds us of the necessarily dim state of our knowledge concerning traditional Greek athletics prior to the eighth century B.C. But by his rejection of later legends and his emphasis on religious and, to some extent, athletic continuity from late Mycenaean times to the late Dark Ages, he places in proper perspective the remarkable synthesis of traditional religion, sports, and cooperation between the *poleis* which was achieved by the institution of the Panhellenic Olympics in the eighth century B.C. Renfrew's skepticism and his isolation of Minoan-Mycenaean elements which have survived are properly cautious correctives to the far-reaching hypotheses which characterize previous scholarship.

Renfrew's conclusions are indeed complemented by Puhvel's most enlightening exposition of parallel Hellado-Anatolian practices combining athletics in festival contexts. Puhvel's original juxtaposition of Hittite and Homeric descriptions of games shows that "many of the organized events which gradually were incorporated into the Olympic Games were neither new nor specifically Greek." The very presence of Hittite games in cult contexts points to an ultimate Indo-European heritage for the Mediterranean athletic tradition, but it still leaves open the question of when and where this tradition was adopted by the Greek peoples. Although Puhvel's findings make it more tempting to retroject the origin of festival games such as the Olympics to the second millennium B.C., the total lack of reliable evidence for such phenomena, as Renfrew has argued, makes it more likely that the Greeks were late in adopting athletic festivals, at least at a national level. It may have been the cultural blight of the Dark Ages which in fact inhibited the flowering of this aspect of Hellenic culture.

Whatever the origins of the Olympic Games, their wide-reaching cultural and political significance is clear in historical times. Renfrew characterizes Panhellenism as an original contribution of the Games; Raubitschek discusses the importance of the Panhellenic ideal in the aetiological legends of the Olympics and in their later history. Ironically, the idea of peace and Hellenic unity is almost completely overlooked in the Classical period, but gains new life after the trauma of the Peloponnesian War. Raubitschek's archaeological and literary evidence for political trends gives a novel insight into one of the core concepts of the ancient Games admired by the moderns—namely, peaceful competition among states which are otherwise inimical. Although the Olympic truce has been discussed by many scholars,[2] Raubitschek is unique in relating it to the political history of Panhellenism and to the disturbing presence of dedications of military spoils from inter-Greek rivalries in the very sanctuary at Olympia.

Whereas Raubitschek recalls how one kind of victory monument, war trophies, cluttered the older Olympic stadium and gave rise to denunciations by later Greeks, Raschke examines the use of athletic victor monuments at Olympia (and elsewhere) and the function of the sculptures on the Temple of Zeus as vehicles of the political messages of the age. The power of the sculpted figure, and the prestige of being commemorated at Olympia, not only enhanced the heroic image of successful athletes but enabled the Eleans to express political and agonistic themes. In the Temple of Zeus the pedimental and metope sculpture conveys, on various levels of interpretation, a mythic image, an image of athletic competition, and the democratic image of the age. This analysis of art historical evidence and political trends permits us to understand the complex response of the ancient visitor to the site in a way in which treatments of the sculpture in the currently standard works on Olympia fail to do.[3]

The modern Olympics purport to reflect the ancient ideals of Panhellenism and the Sacred Truce in their attempts to stage peaceful international competitions, and to resemble the ancient Games in their ability to heroize victors and to make political capital out of visual symbolism. Young, however, provides a much needed corrective to the modern myth that our Olympic movement was modeled on the ancient Greek ideal of amateurism. Through a careful rehearsal of the chain of events begun by Mahaffy in the nineteenth century, Young argues cogently that contemporary notions of amateurism arose from Victorian aristocratic class consciousness, anachronistically transferred to the ancient Greeks. Young has elsewhere expounded the reality of the pervasive professionalism in ancient athletics, and others have reviewed the attempts by the Greeks before Coubertin to establish Olympic Games, but Young's present treatment closely links modern Olympic amateurism to the blatant errors of academic historians during the past century.[4] This exposé is a sign of the progress made toward social equality in sports and other spheres in our own time, just as the erroneous scholarship of the past is a grim reminder of the elitism and segregation of classes in former times.

Even as Renfrew and Puhvel have explored and explained the difficult problems associated with the Olympics before the traditional date of their "refounding" in 776, so Mallwitz and Lee offer solutions to the much disputed questions of location, chronology, and format of the early festival. Mallwitz's years of first-hand experience with the Olympia excavations lend strong authority to his hypotheses concerning the interrelation of cult and competition locations. Proper skepticism toward the legendary theories of Pelopeian or Heraklean origins unites his views with those of Renfrew; both scholars also reject the notion of any continuity of cult for either Pelops or Zeus at the site. Mallwitz sees the introduction of Zeus as the contribution of the Achaeans through the Pisatans, and that of Pelops as coming from the Argolid, both perhaps occurring in the tenth or ninth centuries B.C. The athletic component is a later strand, added not in 776, but probably in 704, as Mallwitz boldly argues, in defiance of traditional scholarship but in accordance with the archaeological evidence of stadium wells, which date from the late eighth to the early seventh centuries B.C. Pelops then emerges not as a shadow of a pre-eighth-century founding father, but as the folk hero of the Pisatans, who in the seventh century use the figure to assert their prior claim to sponsorship of the festival.

Lee addresses the dilemma posed by Pausanias' chronology for the Olympics (beginning with the simple foot race in 776) and by archaeological and literary evidence, which suggests that the Games began considerably earlier, perhaps in 884. He proposes a comprehensive solution which admits that the Olympics may simply have been unimportant in those early times and thus were not recorded. Some of the eighth-century tripod dedications at Olympia may have been for those earliest contests or even for other athletic contests held elsewhere in Greece. Lee's study, like Young's, is an important reminder that one should not impose later values on earlier situations; in this case one should not project the later importance and elaborateness of the Olympics onto their early form. Lee differs from Mallwitz on the dating of the first Olympics to 704 B.C., suggesting that this date merely marks the increased popularity of the festival. His hypothesis has the advantage of economy, incorporating recent archaeological and literary interpretations of dating and program. Yet the controversy over those earliest Games is likely to continue on account of the ambiguous and contradictory nature of the evidence. The studies of both Lee and Mallwitz in any case demonstrate the necessity of calling into question the traditional explanations of chronology and program development listed neatly in most handbooks.[5]

The rise of the Olympics from humble Peloponnesian origins to true Panhellenic status by the sixth century B.C. gave impetus to the parallel formation of the other three major Panhellenic games, the Pythia, the Isthmia, and the Nemea. The existence of four "circuit" or "crown" games allowed athletes to compete in at least one and sometimes two of the Panhellenic games each year. As Fontenrose and Miller amply demonstrate, each festival had its unique program and sacred character but the Olympics stood apart as the archetype for the structure of the others. Surprisingly few general, reliable accounts of the circuit games, apart from the Olympics, exist in the scholarly literature.[6] Part of the reason for this is the ongoing excavation of the sites of Delphi, Nemea, and Isthmia. Thus, the accounts of the Pythia and Nemea included in the present collection not only fill a great need for up-to-date reports of those games, but also allow direct comparison and contrast with the Olympic festival itself.

Fontenrose provides a full survey of the religious and athletic history of the site of Delphi with reference to the latest archaeological reports and to his own authoritative analysis of the working of the cult at this most important center. The Pythian festival may have adopted the Olympic program and organization in large part, but its primary character as a musical festival in honor of Apollo is clearly seen in the presence of competitions in the kithara, lyre, flute, and dramatic readings, which were totally absent from the Olympics. Fontenrose's carefully documented observations on the chronological and archaeological problems surrounding the Pythian Games distinguish what we know of the history and monuments of Delphi from what must remain unknown, barring the discovery of new evidence. For example, Fontenrose proposes some possible competition sites in the sanctuary before the fifth century: these present a good alternative to traditional theories that the games were held on the plain of Krisa, far from Apollo's temple.

Miller's participation in the decade of excavations at Nemea lends special authority to her exposition of the present state of knowledge of the site and her directions for future study. Again Olympic parallels abound in both cult and competitive practice, including Nemea's polygonal heroön, its stadium rebuilt in the fourth century, its bathing and hostel facilities, and the direct connection of the temple with the stadium by way of a ceremonial entrance tunnel. Future excavations, Miller suggests, can hope to uncover the earlier stadium, the hippodrome, and the gymnasium. Like Raubitschek, she reminds us of how the Panhellenic games were subject to the vicissitudes of contemporary politics; modern analogies are all too familiar to observers of the twentieth-century Olympics.

The regimen of training and diet was certainly as great a concern to the ancients as it is to the modern athletic profession. In the spirit of Socratic nescience, Glass presents all the relevant evidence for gymnasia and palaestrae in Archaic and Classical Greece. Whereas other studies on this topic take many leaps of faith in positing a definition for these buildings of the sixth and fifth centuries, Glass points out that we have no physical remains of training facilities from this period, but can learn much indirectly from the literary testimonies. "Gymnasium," apparently a comprehensive term often incorporating a palaestra or palaestrae, reflects in its literal meaning of "the place where one goes naked" the pervasive Greek ideal of physical beauty. Although this ideal has its counterpart in the aerobics studios in America in this decade, the Greek phenomenon is noteworthy not only for having encouraged and nourished the growth of the Panhellenic festivals, but also for fostering the intellectual atmosphere which resulted in the schools of Plato and Aristotle.

The spread of gymnasia in the Classical period accompanied the institutionalization of trainers, and with them, dietary regulations for athletes. All of these phenomena not only led to increased sophistication in athletic skills, but also allowed greater participation by non-nobles—that is, the democratization of sports—as a result of the greater availability of local training programs.[7] J. Renfrew provides a very useful and thorough survey of the literary sources pertaining to athletic diets and their transformations in the sixth century. The inquiry is extended to the use of food in sacrifices, victory banquets, and provisions for spectators. It might well be urged that the meager fare of common visitors is to be contrasted with the rich feasts of the priests, victors, and the wealthy spectators. Food in all its varieties, in the training period, during the games, and at the end of the festival, distinguishes participants from spectators, the poor from the wealthy, the sacred from the secular. Although this study is not primarily archaeological, it adds an important, living dimension to a much ignored aspect of the ancient Olympics.

A proper perspective for understanding the ancient Olympics cannot be achieved without an explanation of some of the many contemporary athletic programs in Greece and Rome.[8] The sampling of certain of these local athletic activities in the essays by Scanlon, Gallis, and Harmon shows how greatly the particular forms of local athletics differ from the Panhellenic festivals. Yet each of these local programs shares some general similarities, if not close identity, with the Olympics in the political, social, and religious roles which the athletic festival played in the community. Scanlon's discussion of women's athletics in Sparta touches on the general topic of women's participation in sports elsewhere in Greece, and suggests that female contests were much more widespread than our sources reveal. The tantalizing evidence for women's games at Sparta, Olympia, and Brauron is a result of chance preservation in a few sources. Whereas Glass mentions the great importance of physical beauty in the institution of men's gymnasia, Scanlon notes that a prime motive for the physical education of Spartan females was eugenic: the insurance of beauty in the mother in order that she may bear beautiful and healthy children for the state. The Spartan social program thus gave rise to quasi-communistic, initiatory groups of boys and girls who literally trained for adulthood. As often in Greek athletics, a religious element was present in the girls' competitions, and this may have been carried over to similar games at Olympia and Brauron. Scanlon has also gathered the useful archaeological evidence of bronze figurines portraying Spartan girl athletes in the form of mirror handles, a further reminder of the healthfully narcissistic body culture of the Greeks.

The games of ancient Larisa, as described by Gallis, are in many ways typical of the numerous local festivals held especially in Hellenistic and Roman times. These games display some characteristics of the Panhellenic contests but mostly reflect local interests and traditions. The one major Panthessalian contest at Larisa, the Eleutheria, was a quadrennial festival including many of the hippic and athletic events of the Olympics. But owing to the fame of Thessaly as a horse-breeding region, the highlights of the games were the spectacular acrobatic horse races, some with torches, which were represented on Larisaean coins. Bull-wrestling by men on horseback was also a popular feature and one which may have indirectly found its way to Spain, and later to the rodeos of the western

United States. Minor local games held annually and catering more to local competitors probably offered value prizes which helped finance the training for successful athletes. Such games, which abounded in the Greek cities, no doubt also afforded athletes the funds to travel to and compete in the prestigious circuit games. It is significant that the Eleutheria was begun as a celebration of the Roman "liberation" of Greece from Macedon in 196 B.C.; this festival and the later Caesareia in honor of the Roman emperor are testimonies to the fact that under Roman domination the Greeks paid tribute to their political and economic overlords through competitive festivals. Although there were no such Romanized games at Olympia, the cult of the emperor was present in the Olympic sanctuary from the time of Augustus.

The Romans' own athletic festivals, as Harmon relates, reflect yet another aspect of the Olympic Games.[9] The historical resemblances of the Roman games to the Greek are restricted, certainly, to such contests as chariot racing, which may have been inherited from Greece through the Etruscans. The essential similarities between major Greek and Roman festivals are seen in their social and religious significance: periodic games signal a time of renewal for the community and an opportunity for the individual to transcend mortality through a share in heroic fame. Death is omnipresent in the symbolism of the Roman games, as is the renewal of life, according to Harmon. The association of Roman festivals with Mars, the dealer of death, is balanced by their ties to earth gods such as Dis, who promise renewal and life. The role of the emperor as a divine savior and as patron of the greatest Roman games gave hope to the Roman people, just as the omnipresence of Zeus during the Olympic Games reassured the Greeks of their salvation.

Certain general themes have emerged in the foregoing discussion which urge a re-evaluation of the received view of Olympia and the Olympic Games. The religious and athletic elements of the developed Olympics may have their roots in Minoan-Mycenaean times. During the eighth and seventh centuries, not only were games linked to cult at Olympia, but the idea of peaceful Panhellenic cooperation was first fostered. The sixth century saw the diffusion of Olympic practices and ideals to other religious sanctuaries, most notably the Panhellenic sites, where the crown prize marked a victor's fame. The fourth-century revival of Panhellenism culminated in a new unity imposed by Macedonian dominance and allowed reconstruction of stadia and temples at the major Panhellenic sanctuaries. The proliferation of minor local athletic festivals evidenced remarkable variety according to local custom, but still showed the influence of the Olympic model in cult and contests.

Athletics in general, and the Olympic Games in particular, are a far more instructive medium for the understanding of Greek culture than are their modern counterparts for contemporary Western society, because in antiquity athletics arose from and fostered so many aspects of social, political, and religious life. Competition in sports was paralleled closely by the contests in the courtroom, in the theater, and on the battlefield. Greek poetry, sculpture, and painting found inspiration in the athletics of the Archaic and Classical periods, just as those same arts were inspired by the Christian religion in the Middle Ages. For the Greeks the Olympics in their ideal form represented harmony among states and a joint celebration of religious and cultural values. The reality of the Games, as these essays have shown, may have often fallen short of those ideals. Yet in all its successes and failures, Olympia remains one of the few crucial cultural experiences of Greece, like the Homeric epics. And like those works it has continued to exercise its influence on each successive age, however incorrectly it has been understood or reinterpreted in support of a people's vision of the truth.

To understand the Olympics properly demands a gradual process of reinterpretation through exacting use of the evidence and the critical application of the methodology of each generation. And so it is the task of this work not merely to preserve the Olympic past, but to come closer to the truth of it through new elucidations of its archaeology.

Notes

1. Ch. Ulf and I. Weiler, "Der Ursprung der antiken Olympischen Spiele in der Forschung," *Stadion* 6 (1981) 1–38. Brief discussions and bibliography on the origins of the Olympics can also be found in I. Weiler, *Der Sport bei den Völker der alten Welt* (Darmstadt, 1981) 105–107, and in T. Scanlon, *Greek and Roman Athletics: A Bibliography* (Chicago, 1984) 20–21 and 62–63.

2. See M. Lämmer, "The Nature and Function of the Olympic Truce in Ancient Greece," *History of Physical Education and Sport,* vol. 3, (Tokyo, 1977) 38–49; H. A. Harris, *Greek Athletes and Athletics* (Bloomington, Ind., 1966) 155–156; J. Ebert et al., *Olympia von den Anfängen bis zu Coubertin* (Leipzig, 1980) 14–18.

3. See, for example, the comprehensive, recent treatment of the sculpture on the Temple of Zeus in: H.-V. Herrmann, *Olympia: Heiligtum und Wettkampfstätte* (Munich, 1972) 132–46.

4. D. C. Young, *The Olympic Myth of Greek Amateur Athletics* (Chicago, 1984), gives an accurate picture of ancient professionalism. R. Mandell, *The First Modern Olympics* (Berkeley and Los Angeles, 1976), and X. L. Messinesi, *A Branch of Wild Olives: The Olympic Movement and the Ancient and Modern Olympic Games* (New York, 1973), trace the various attempts to revive the Games on a (distorted) image of the ancient model.

5. See, for example, the recent listings of the Olympic program in S. G. Miller, *Arete* (Chicago, 1979) 102, and J. Swaddling, *The Ancient Olympic Games* (London, 1980; Austin, Tex., 1984) 38, to name only the most recent and generally reliable handbooks in English.

6. Compare the 60 items listed for the Pythia, Isthmia, and Nemea with the 186 for the Olympics in Scanlon (supra n. 1) 55–69. Most noteworthy regarding the non-Olympic Panhellenic festival studies (other than works cited by Fontenrose and Miller) are the following: J. H. Krause, *Die Pythien, Nemeen, und Isthmien* (Leipzig, 1841); R. Knab, *Die Periodoniken* (Giessen, 1934; repr. Chicago, 1980); S. G. Miller, "The Date of the First Pythiad," *CSCA* 11 (1979) 127–58; O. Broneer, "Isthmiaca," *Klio* 39 (1961) 249–70; idem, "The Isthmian Games and the Sanctuary of Poseidon," *Greek Heritage* 1 (1964) 42–49; S. G. Miller, "Tunnel Vision: The Nemean Games," *Archaeology* 33 (1980) 54–56.

7. See Weiler (supra n. 1) 92–95, with further bibliography on 100–101.

8. For bibliography on local Greek festivals, see Scanlon (supra n. 1) 70–73.

9. For a survey of the literature on the Roman games and a discussion of their importance, see Weiler (supra n. 1) 215–76.

Glossary   Indices

acontist: an athlete who throws the javelin.

adyton: the innermost sanctuary or holy of holies; used specifically of an inner room reached from the *cella* of a temple.

aegis: a shield or breastplate made of goatskin, used by Zeus or Athena, and bestowing magical powers of protection.

agon (pl: *agones*): an assembly convened to watch the games; hence the singular *agon* is used of a contest in the games or the games per se; the plural *agones* also is used as "the games."

agon stephanites: see *agon* and *stephanitic.*

agonothete (Gk: *agonothetes, -ai*): like the *Hellanodikai* of the Olympic Games, the *agonothetes* served as judges in the Pythian Games. Elsewhere they were directors, presidents and often sponsors of the games.

agora: often translated as "market-place," though this was only one function of this open area in the center of the Greek city, the focus of political, social and law court activity.

alabastron (pl: *alabastra*): a small flask with elongated body, round at the base and narrow at the neck, to contain perfume.

amphora: a high two-handled pot with a neck considerably narrower than the body. *Amphorae* were standard containers for liquids.

antefix: clay ornament on the ends of the covering tiles of a roof, concealing the joints of the tiles.

arete: a complex concept in Greek for which we have no simple English equivalent. It involved prowess and valour, nobility and excellence, moral virtue and goodness.

aryballos (pl: *aryballoi*): a small vase to contain oil used by athletes to lubricate their skin and cleanse it after exercise. *Aryballoi* were usually globular in shape with either a flat or hemispherical mouth. This type of vase had one or two small handles for attaching a thong to hang it on the wall or from the wrist.

aulos: usually a flute, though literally refers to any woodwind instrument. Also used to provide rhythm for some athletic activities.

bothros (pl: *bothroi*): a pit.

caduceus (Gk: *kerykeion*): herald's wand on which serpents are entwined, carried chiefly by Hermes (Mercury).

calyx krater: see *krater.*

cella: the enclosed main chamber of a temple.

chiton: a tunic, long or short, worn by men or women and made of light-weight fabric, often linen.

chlamys: short cloak of wool or similar heavy fabric fastened on the right shoulder and used by men and women for travelling.

cista: a box or chest; used specifically for a box, often of clay, for holding sacred objects used in religious celebrations.

diaulos: a footrace twice the length of a *stadion*, which involved sprinting down the track and back, a distance of some 400 yards; also, a double flute.

diazoma: a horizontal walkway or passage separating the several ranges of seats in a Graeco-Roman theatre or stadium.

dolichos: the long-distance foot race which at Olympia, at least, was almost 5,000 metres or 24 lengths of the stadium.

euthynteria: top course of a foundation or the levelling course of a building.

gymnasiarch: superintendent of athletic training at Athens and elsewhere, sometimes more specifically an honorary magistrate who supervised and funded gymnasia and the activities therein.

Hellanodikai: literally "judges of the Greeks," the judges who presided over the games at Olympia; their members fluctuated between one and twelve at various points in the history of the games.

hoplite and *hoplites:* a *hoplite* was a foot soldier equipped with helmet, shield and greaves. The *hoplites* was a race in armour for athletes so dressed. At a later stage the greaves were abandoned.

hydria: the hydria or "water jar" is a broad-shouldered, wide-bellied pot with two horizontal belly handles for lifting and one vertical shoulder handle at the back of the vase which was held while pouring. Such vases were used to collect water from the local fountain-house.

isolympian, (*isopythian*): literally "equal to the Olympia," "equal to the Pythia"—epithets of local games modelled respectively on the Olympic or Pythian Games.

kalos kagathos: a Greek phrase literally meaning "beautiful and good" and so indicating both physical and moral worth, but also specifically used to describe the aristocratic elite (cf. our "beautiful people"!).

keles: a race horse; also the horse race.

kerykeion: see *caduceus.*

kithara: a lyre or harp; used for musical contests at some games.

kore (pl: *korai*): literally a maiden (maidens); used specifically for free-standing archaic statues of maidens.

kouros (pl: *kouroi*): literally youth (youths); used specifically to indicate archaic freestanding statues of youths, frontal in attitude with one foot advanced and hands often held stiffly by the sides.

krater: a large vase used as a bowl for mixing water and wine.

A *calyx krater,* so called because it resembles the calyx of a flower, has a concave profile tapering in towards the base.

A *volute krater* is named from the shape of its handles which extend in a scroll form up to and over the lip of the vase.

kylix: a broad, open, shallow cup for wine, usually with a high stem and two horizontal handles on its exterior surface.

lekythos (pl: *lekythoi*): a small flask with tall narrow neck and flat lip, used for oil or perfume. The body is usually slender, but a squat version appears in the early fifth century and is popular in the late fifth and early fourth centuries. A large white-ground variant is used in Attica in funerary ritual.

metope: rectangular space between the triglyphs of a frieze in the Doric architectural order; frequently the location of sculptural decoration.

naïskos: diminutive of *naos* (temple), means "shrine"; used specifically of a small temple generally without columns.

obverse: side of a coin bearing the principal design (opposite of reverse).

oikos: literally "house"; used specifically of a small, one-room temple without columns.

oinochoe: a jug or pitcher for pouring liquids, its name literally means "wine-pourer."

opisthodomos: porch at the rear of a temple.

orgia (pl: orgiai): secret rites, used particularly of the worship of Dionysus and of Demeter at Eleusis, but also employed more generally of rites or sacrifice.

orthostate: bottom course of the walls of a *cella,* usually placed vertically.

palaestra (pl: *palaestrae*) (Gk: *palaistra, -ai*): specific training area for wrestling and boxing. Cf. S.L. Glass, passim.

pankration: a no-holds-barred event consisting of a mixture of wrestling and boxing in which only biting and gouging were prohibited.

paradromis: an open-air practice track.

patera: a broad, shallow bowl or dish, especially used in libations.

pediment: the triangular space which forms the gable of a ridged roof and is usually on the short sides of a Greek temple above the columnar porch. In buildings of the Doric order, relief or virtually freestanding sculpture is used to decorate this area.

pentathlon: a contest of five events: *stadion,* discus, long jump, javelin and wrestling, not necessarily in this order. Exactly how the winner was determined is unclear.

penteteris: a term or space of five years; hence a festival celebrated every four years, such as the Olympic Games or the Greater Panathenaea at Athens, since the Greeks counted inclusively.

peplos: a woollen garment worn by Greek women consisting of two panels of fabric joined on one or both sides and fastened with pins at the shoulders. The Doric type had an overfold at the front, and left the arms exposed; the Ionic version was so pinned as to form "sleeves."

peripteral: having a row of columns on all sides.

petasos: a hat with a broad rim, especially when travelling.

pithos: a large clay jar used for storing liquid or dry goods. *Pithoi* were often so large that they were sunk into the ground. Most were covered with lids to preserve the contents.

polis (pl: *poleis*): the Greek "city-state," that is, the city and its surrounding territory as a self-governing unit.

protome: the upper part of a human figure or the forepart of an animal.

quadriga: a four-horse chariot or race of four-horse chariots.

rhyton: a vessel, used primarily for libations, in the form of a horn or of an animal's head.

sphendone: literally a sling, or anything like a sling in shape; particularly used of the semicircular end characteristic of the later form of the stadium.

stade: see *stadion.*

stadion (race): sometimes called the stade race, it was a sprint of roughly 200 yards distance down one length of the track. The name referred originally to a unit of measure of 600 ancient feet (the exact length of a foot varied somewhat from place to place but was a little under a third of a metre).

stele (pl: *stelae*) (Gk: *stele, stelai*): an upright stone slab, often used for a gravestone or for public inscriptions.

stephanitic (games): an adjective applied to the four Panhellenic games at Olympia, Delphi, Isthmia and Nemea, where the only prizes were crowns of olive, laurel, pine or celery, and celery respectively. Hence these are sometimes called "Crown Games." The term is derived from the Greek *stephanos*—a crown.

stylobate: platform on which the columns of a building stood.

synoris: = Latin *biga*: a pair of horses or two-horse chariot; also used of the race for two-horse chariots.

temenos: a sacred precinct.

tethrippos: a team of four horses, a four-horse chariot or the race for four-horse chariots.

trittys: a sacrifice of three animals: a bull, a billy-goat and a boar or ram. Cf. the Roman *suovetaurilia.*

tutulus: a conical top-knot or woollen cap worn in religious ritual by women and priests.

volute krater: see *krater.*

xenon: a guest house.

xystos: a covered practice track one *stadion* in length.

Index of Personal Names

Acanthus, the Lacedaemonian, 158, 189
Acca Larentia, 247
Achilles, 16, 26, 28, 29, 30, 246
Aelian, 179
Aelius Aristides, 156
Aeneas, 249
Aeschines, 139*n13,* 160, 169*n20*
Aeschylus, 148*n12*
Agamemnon, 19, 124
Agariste, 161, 163
Agelaos, 131, 132, 134
Agias, 131, 132, 134
Agis (king of Sparta), 36
Ajax, 28
Akrisios, 168*n13,* 226
Alcibiades, 47, 178
Alcman, 187, 190, 191, 201, 207*n11,* 209*n29*
Alkamenes, 46, 53*n56*
Alkinoos, 17
Amykos, 168*n13*
Anchises, 249
Andersen-Schiess, G., 75*n34*
Andokides Painter, 43, 44, 51*n35*
Antenor, 54
Aphrodite, 91, 192
Apollo, 5, 6, 8, 18, 29, 39, 42, 43, 45, 48*n2,*
    50*nn23-24,26,* 51-52*nn33,42,* 91, 116*n13,*
    121-40 *passim,* 155, 190, 197*n16,* 226-27,
    260
Appian, 160
Apuleius, 229
Archidamos II, 209
Ares, 91, 247
Aristodemos of Elis, 117*n19*

Aristogeiton, 39
Aristokleia, 225
Aristomenes of Aegina, 134
Aristophanes, 35, 69, 157, 160, 187, 190, 192,
    197, 198, 201, 214*nn60-61*
Aristotle, 137, 160, 188, 260
Arkesilas of Kyrene, 134
Arrichion, 39
Artemis, 8, 113, 186, 190, 194, 212*n48*
Astarte, 210*n40*
Asteropaios, 28
Astylos of Croton, 41, 49*n18*
Atalanta, 168*n13,* 193, 196, 210*n39*
Athena, 43, 168*n13,* 179, 212*n48,* 226, 237,
    246
Athenaeus, 191
Atlas, 46
Augeias, king of Elis, 111, 112, 114
Augustus, 236, 237, 249, 262
Autolykos, 130

Bartoccini, R., 241
Bloch, R., 242
Bourdon, G., 65
Brasidas, 36
Brookes, W. P., 65
Brundage, A., 56, 71-72, 75*nn34-35*
Burkert, W., 239-40
Buschor, E., 81

Caesar, C. Julius, 225
Calame, C., 201
Calhoun, L., 72
Callimachus, 117, 187

273

Index of Subjects

Index Locorum

Index of Modern Authors

TEXT DESIGNED BY DAVID CORONA DESIGN ASSOCIATES
COMPOSED BY CONNELL TYPESETTING COMPANY,
KANSAS CITY, MISSOURI
MANUFACTURED BY BRAUN-BRUMFIELD, INC.
ANN ARBOR, MICHIGAN
TEXT IS SET IN BASKERVILLE
DISPLAY LINES ARE SET IN BASKERVILLE AND HELVETICA

Library of Congress Cataloging-in-Publication Data
The Archaeology of the Olympics.
Includes indices.
1. Greece—Antiquities. 2. Games, Greek and Roman.
I. Raschke, Wendy J.
DF78.A65   1987   938   87-40150
ISBN 0-299-11330-2
ISBN 0-299-11334-5 (pbk.)